FOREWORD
CARMELO EZPELETA

The 2013 MotoGP™ season proved to be nothing short of breathtaking from start to finish. Record books were rewritten and world champions were pushed beyond their limits, as season-long battles in all classes kept racing fans on the edge of their seats.

This was in no small part due to the emergence of Marc Marquez as one of the greatest talents the motorcycle racing world championship has ever seen, but also because his competitors stepped it up to the next level to counter the fight. Marquez's win in only his second premier-class race and a return to the top step for Valentino Rossi were just some of the truly memorable points of the year, while Jorge Lorenzo's ride in Assen with a double collarbone break was yet more proof of what fierce competitors this championship breeds.

It was the second year of the 1,000cc machines, as well as for the CRT class, with the latter upping the pace over the year and showing that innovation and determination can help even the newcomers scrap it out with the best. The intermediate Moto2™ class and the lightweight Moto3™ class once again produced some stunning displays of skill and extremely close racing, showing just how secure the future of MotoGP™ is, with great talent coming up through the ranks.

And now I'm pleased once again to introduce this latest edition of the *MotoGP Season Review* from Haynes Publishing, which will take you on a journey through a season that has offered so much to the motorcycle-racing enthusiast. Look back to a thrilling season that saw would-be World Champion Marquez and last year's victor Lorenzo fight tooth and nail for the much-coveted crown, and riders' spirit and desire to win tested on more than one occasion.

Cal Crutchlow became a regular podium contender, with some outstanding performances that led to him being offered a Ducati factory seat for 2014, while Dani Pedrosa was once again hindered by bad luck in what was a potential championship-winning year for him, with some dominant wins and numerous podiums.

The same can be said for Moto2™, which was filled with drama, emotion and some of the closest battles seen on track. Scott Redding gave Pol Espargaro one of the toughest seasons of his life as the Spaniard claimed the Moto2 crown, with the pair holding off charges from the likes of Tito Rabat, Dominique Aegerter and Mika Kallio.

In Moto3™ it was a battle of the KTMs and the trio of Maverick Viñales, Alex Rins and Luis Salom kept us guessing until the final race in Valencia – with Viñales triumphing in spectacular fashion. But the class also brought some fantastic new talents to the forefront such as Jack Miller, Philipp Oettl and Niccolò Antonelli, with great performances across the board. The stars of years to come are already well on their way, and I can safely say that the future of MotoGP looks bright.

So enjoy reading about the 2013 season, and I look forward to welcoming you all next year.

CARMELO EZPELETA

DORNA SPORTS CEO
NOVEMBER 2013

Published in February 2014

A catalogue record for this book is available from the British Library

ISBN 978 0 85733 408 4

Library of Congress catalog card no 2013944256

Haynes Publishing, Sparkford, Yeovil, Somerset BA22 7JJ, UK
Tel: +44 (0) 1963 442030
Fax: +44 (0) 1963 440001
E-mail: sales@haynes.co.uk
Website: www.haynes.co.uk

Haynes North America, Inc.,
861 Lawrence Drive, Newbury Park,
California 91320, USA

Printed and bound in the USA

This product is officially licensed by Dorna SL, owners of the MotoGP trademark (© Dorna 2012)

Managing Editor Steve Rendle
Design Richard Parsons
Sub-editor Kay Edge
Special Sales & Advertising Manager
David Dew (david@motocom.co.uk)
Photography Front cover, race action and portraits by Andrew Northcott/AJRN Sports Photography; technical images pp13-17 by Neil Spalding

Author's acknowledgements

This book wouldn't have happened without the help of Toby Moody, Neil Spalding, Martin Raines, Peter Clifford, Nereo Balanzin, Venancio Luis Nieto, Dean Adams and of course the photography of Andrew Northcott

www.motogpbook.com

CONTENTS
MotoGP™ 2013

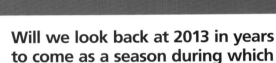

TOWARDS A NEW ERA

Will we look back at 2013 in years to come as a season during which everything changed? Mat Oxley

Older fans of motorcycle racing observed that 2013 brought back memories of 1978, when Californian Kenny Roberts turned up on Europe's Grand Prix scene and blew the status quo to smithereens. Marc Marquez certainly shook things up in MotoGP, changing the game with his wild riding technique and signalling an end to the follow-my-leader style of racing that had recently transformed MotoGP into something of a two-wheeled Formula 1, much to the chagrin of millions of fans. The Repsol Honda rider's talent is wondrous to behold, even to sublime genius Freddie Spencer, the man who had been bike racing's youngest premier-class World Champion until Marquez arrived in MotoGP, barely out of his teens.

'Marc is able to feel the edge of the limit even where there's a lot of movement from the bike and he can control that,' says the 1983 and 1985 500cc champ. 'He has incredible feel and is able to anticipate what's going to happen next. He is extremely intuitive. He is able to feel things when he's on the edge of control and that allows him to be more aggressive and still to be in control. That gives him a real advantage.'

Always at the limit and often a little beyond it, Marquez made MotoGP unpredictable and enthralling once again. His win-by-any-means-necessary approach showed Jorge Lorenzo (Yamaha Factory Racing) and Dani Pedrosa (Repsol Honda) that they would have to fight every inch of the way rather than playing their games of high-speed chess.

In the end, the title fight was a straight duel between Marquez, who won the crown, and Lorenzo, who won

ABOVE LEFT The relationship between the Repsol Honda riders was examined in microscopic detail; they stayed civil to each other – just

ABOVE RIGHT Cal Crutchlow left Yamaha with a season of two halves; the first brilliant, the second beset by injury and confusion

more races. Who was the better rider? Hard to tell, but there was little doubt about who was the more popular, just as there was little doubt a couple of decades ago when 'Revvin' Kevin Schwantz fought with 'Steady' Eddie Lawson. Most fans like to see a spectacle, so they tend to prefer racers who ride the ragged edge, who don't make it look easy.

Last season will be era-defining if it turns out to be the moment when MotoGP ceased to be a large-capacity four-stroke '250' class, ruled by former 250 riders who took over from the ex-superbike and dirt-track men who had ruled the 1980s and 1990s.

Marquez's riding technique is different because he has a different riding background from that of fellow Spaniards Lorenzo and Dani Pedrosa, his only real rivals during 2013. Not only did Marc ride a lot of dirt track when he was (even) younger, he came to MotoGP via Moto2, not 250s. That combination of inputs explains why he feels perfectly happy with the bike running amok, why he gets so physical with the machine and why he's able to ride around problems and turn negatives into positives. His two years in Moto2 also go some way to explaining his controversial ruthlessness – the new intermediate class is so tightly fought that at no stage in a race can a rider afford to lose a tenth or give an inch. Other former Moto2 riders like Scott Redding – who graduates to MotoGP in 2014 – believe this will become the norm in the premier class, once the category is full of ex-Moto2 firebrands.

Lorenzo and Pedrosa ride MotoGP bikes as they rode 250s: inch-perfect, beautifully smooth, rarely a wheel out of line. They are both devastatingly fast and use astonishing lean angles, their smoothness belying their speed, perhaps even making it all look easy to the average fan who doesn't fully appreciate the skills involved.

Marquez is the opposite. He is scary to behold: the rear tyre three inches in the air on the brakes, the bike snapping back in protest, the rear end stepping out and the front tyre squashing flat and starting to tuck under as he tips into the corner. Then, holding the handlebars like a motocross rider and hanging off the inside of the bike as far as he can go, he wrenches the bars and digs his elbow scraper into the track to stop the front from fully folding under. Finally, there's a bit of a wobble as he sorts things out, the bike is wrenched upright, the throttle is generously applied, there's a scrabble of wheelspin and he's gone.

The extreme hang-off comes from Moto2 – trying to bend a 150kg GP bike to his will with no rider aids.

'Leaning off the bike as much as I do comes from Moto2, because in Moto2 you really need to use all the power of your body to push the bike to turn, so this also makes the bike turn better in MotoGP,' he says.

The sideways corner entries come from both dirt track and Moto2, the latter through transforming the negative of too much engine braking into a positive, by deliberately kicking out the rear into corners. 'I try to create that because in Moto2 every corner is like that – you try to be smoother but it's impossible,' Marquez explains. 'So now I create that because it takes some weight off the front which makes me feel more comfortable.'

Although Marquez hasn't done much actual dirt-track racing, he has spent so long going round in anti-clockwise circles that he now prefers left-handers to right-handers, just like former dirt tracker and 500cc World Champion Wayne Rainey.

Kenny Roberts, the last rookie to win the title and another man who learned his skills on dirt ovals, watched Marquez at MotoGP's US rounds and understood immediately that a childhood spent going sideways has given the youngster the advantage of being able to steer the bike with the throttle. 'If you can let the bike drift, spin and go sideways, then point it where you want it, it's much easier than trying to do it by using lean angle and depending on the front tyre,' says Roberts.

Marquez was great fun to watch as he served his apprenticeship aboard the world's fastest racing motorcycles. But his willingness to flirt with disaster at every corner had inevitable consequences: he crashed at more than half of the 18 rounds, and only one rider (FTR Kawasaki rider Yonny Hernandez) fell more often than he did. Marquez tumbled 15 times during the season and yet he still won the title; another unique feat. And he found it all highly amusing. 'We won the championship, also we are near the top of the crashing rankings, ha ha ha!' beamed the 20-year-old new World Champion after the Valencia finale.

So how come someone who crashed so much could still amass more points than anyone else? It was because Marquez made sure he got his crashes out of the way *before* the racing started. He only fell once in a race, at Mugello. 'I crash more in practice because if you want to try something or find the limit, you need to find it then, because in the race you need to finish,' he says, stating an obvious fact that is nevertheless often overlooked. Marquez's 17 finishes from 18 races produced 16 podiums (his team was disqualified at Phillip Island for a rule infringement), an extraordinary achievement for a novice and another record broken.

Marc was undeniably brilliant and also lucky. Well, either lucky or he bounces well. Although he was battered and beaten in all those accidents – including his 337km/h (209.9mph) get-off at Mugello (yes, another record), he was never once unable to ride. Unlike Lorenzo, who crashed just three times during the season and yet managed to break a collarbone twice. Although Lorenzo's ride at Assen – 34 hours after he suffered his first injury – was undoubtedly the superhuman feat of the year, Marquez's bravery at Silverstone should not be overlooked. Just three hours after dislocating a shoulder, he battled the 2012 champ all the way, only losing the win at the penultimate corner.

Marquez would surely have crashed even more frequently if he hadn't perfected the new rescue technique of the elbow save. Way back in the early 1980s, Eddie Lawson learned to save front-wheel slides with his knees by riding his hulking great Kawasaki superbike around a wet go-kart track, soaked for the purpose. Thus the knee became an outrigger, and two outriggers are always going to be better than one. In fact, the elbow save became less important to Marquez as the year went on and he became better at locating the limit and staying on it, rather than too often tipping over the other side. During the last few races he was having 'only' one or two elbow saves per weekend.

If his ability to ride a motorcycle on the ragged edge drew gasps of awe the world over, his occasionally manic riding didn't sit well with everyone. He ended the season having accrued more penalty points than anyone else,

even though he went unpunished for two of his three most famous moves of the year.

First, there was Jerez, where he came charging past Lorenzo into the final turn, triggering a collision that became the moment of the year. Race Direction judged the move to be a normal racing incident and Lorenzo did later admit that he had left his young assassin too much room on the way into the hairpin.

His real *faux pas* happened during morning warm-up at Silverstone, where he was riding past yellow flags at the limit when he crashed. His careering Repsol Honda RC213V almost took out a group of marshals attending an already fallen bike. Quite rightly, he received two penalty points for that one. Four weeks later, at Aragon, where he accidentally disabled Pedrosa's traction-control system, he was only saved further censure by Honda taking the blame.

Whenever he was punished, Marquez accepted the punishment, and then blithely announced that he wouldn't be changing the way he rode any time soon. No surprises there, because (assuming the rest of the season had gone unchanged) he wouldn't have won the title if he hadn't passed Lorenzo at Jerez.

Lorenzo and Yamaha were always the new champion's most outspoken critics. At Jerez, Yamaha didn't merely complain to Race Direction about the last corner, they also grumbled that Marquez had spent much of the race getting too close to their rider on the brakes, most especially into the Dry Sack hairpin. Team director Massimo Meregalli declined to suggest what might be a sensible exclusion zone if riders were to be barred from getting too close.

BELOW Over at Yamaha, Jorge Lorenzo was always worth watching. No other Yamaha rider could make the M1 do what he could make it do

ABOVE LEFT Marquez came, saw and conquered. He also repainted the stands from yellow to red

ABOVE RIGHT Ducati lost its Americans. First Ben Spies retired after repeated shoulder trouble and then the factory decided that after five years they could afford to dispense with the services of Nicky Hayden

Lorenzo also prophesied that if MotoGP became a kind of *Rollerball* contest about who can be the most aggressive rider, then bad accidents will happen. He may be right. But riders have been tangling handlebars pretty much since they first started racing motorcycles. It's nothing new. Only in the last few years have such antics been frowned upon in the premier class.

Top satellite rider of the year Cal Crutchlow insisted that Lorenzo's constant criticism of his nemesis had nothing to do with riding tactics. 'Yeah, Marc rides very hot,' said the Briton. 'But some riders make controversy for no other reason than because they're annoyed they're getting beaten; simple as that.'

Lorenzo's riding was sublime all year long, but only at the last race did he finally succumb to the Marquez style – bumping and barging with his rivals. We will have to wait and see if he carries that style into 2014. Valencia was Lorenzo's last stand, the first time in seven years that the title duel had gone down to the final race. He could therefore be excused a little Marquez-style thuggery. Other than that, Lorenzo didn't change the way he rode. He mostly kept it super smooth to win eight races to Marquez's six.

Lorenzo had hideous luck in breaking his collarbone at Assen and then again at the next race in Germany. Technology wasn't on his side either. For the first time since MotoGP's 990cc days the Honda was clearly the better bike at pretty much every racetrack. Most importantly, Yamaha fell behind in braking performance as Honda found new ways of getting its RC213V into corners later than ever. Riders can get away with a lot

of minor machine disadvantages in MotoGP but the one thing they can't afford is to be outbraked.

At Phillip Island, Marquez could have wrapped up the title; instead someone in his team made an almighty mistake, Marc was disqualified and suddenly Lorenzo was back in the game. He deserved that break because his riding was heroic throughout the season – he used Casey Stoner's devastating bolt-from-the-start strategy to superb effect, leading each and every lap of six of the eight races he won. At Misano he was more metronomic than ever, his lap times varying by no more than 0.553s. As Valentino Rossi's former crew chief Jeremy Burgess said: 'Jorge is a machine.'

If Lorenzo was unlucky, Pedrosa of course had more than his share of ill fortune. For the umpteenth year in a row, his title challenge was derailed by injury, this time after a crash at Sachsenring's 70km/h (45mph) Turn 1 left him with a broken collarbone. With his luck, at least it wasn't he who crashed at the end of Mugello's start–finish straight. True, Pedrosa only made it to the top step of the podium at three races, but it's worth remembering that he was leading the World Championship when he was injured.

And what of the non-Spaniards? There were glimmers of hope for Valentino Rossi. Back on a competitive motorcycle, his storming ride to second place at the season-opening Qatar GP promised great things. But the promise went largely unfulfilled, and he spent much of the season locked in fourth place. He did win at Assen and he climbed the podium at Sachsenring, Laguna Seca, Aragon and Phillip Island, but at all these races one or more of *el trio Espagnol* hit trouble.

Burgess explained that things had moved on at the front, and new riding techniques had been learned while Rossi had been struggling on the Ducati. JB wasn't rewarded for his frankness. After 12 years together, Rossi sacked the Australian at Valencia. Only time will tell if a new face in his pit will return the seven-times MotoGP champion to the top once more. If it doesn't, 2014 could well be Vale's last year in MotoGP.

And what then? Not so much for Rossi, but for MotoGP as a whole. In recent years there had been suggestions that the sport would flat-line following the inevitable retirement of the world's all-time favourite bike racer. But the world always moves on and finds new heroes: Marquez is already slipping into Valentino's shoes very comfortably.

Rossi spent much of the year brawling with satellite riders Crutchlow (Monster Tech 3 Yamaha) and Alvaro Bautista (Go & Fun Honda Gresini). Crutchlow took four podiums, impressing especially in the first half of the season. His ride to second at the Sachsenring was his greatest, the Briton closing relentlessly on race-winner Marquez, despite some nasty injuries from a big tumble in practice. Bautista, by contrast, never made the top three, although his consistency later in the year, when he came close to the podium on several occasions, made up for consecutive blunders at Mugello and Catalunya where he didn't even survive the first laps.

Crutchlow's reward for his efforts was a lucrative two-year Ducati contract. At least, it will be a reward if Ducati can fix its Desmosedici. The Italian factory's continued struggles have removed an important dimension from MotoGP. Hopes for 2014 and beyond are pinned on the company's second management reshuffle in less than 12 months, in which former Aprilia brains Gigi Dall'Igna replaced former BMW engineer Bernhard Gobmeier who had taken over from the Desmosedici's creator Filippo Preziosi at the end of 2012.

Ducati's lack of success may rob the championship of some colour, but a bigger worry is its increasing domination by Spanish riders, despite Dorna's efforts to make the podium more multinational. If Rossi doesn't have a turnaround during 2014, and if Ducati don't build a winning bike, it's quite likely that all 19 races (a new record, thanks to the sport's return to Latin America) will be won by Spaniards.

Perhaps Dorna's efforts to improve MotoGP need a little more time to bear fruit. While Marquez showed the world a new way to ride a MotoGP bike, away from the limelight another kind of MotoGP machine was under development – another signal for the future. No-one knows exactly how competitive Honda's production RCV1000R and Yamaha's privateer YZR-M1 will be, but initial outings in the second half of 2013 suggested they will be very fast.

More importantly, this kind of machine – lower cost and running standard software – may well populate the entire grid from 2017, when the rules are up for a wholesale rewrite. Slowly but surely, Dorna are working towards levelling the playing field, aiming for a situation in which any moderately well-financed team will be able to run at the front, or at least close to the front. This is also a vital part of the process of helping non-Spaniards back to the sharp end of MotoGP, because it tends to be non-Latin teams who have less funding due to the sport's lower profile in their countries. Along with Marquez's super-physical style, these new machines could make

MotoGP as spectacular as it was during the thrilling early days of the four-stroke era, because fewer electronics mean more sideways thrills.

At least that's what 2011 champ Casey Stoner discovered when he tried out the RCV1000R – with lower-tech standard software – in his new role as HRC test rider. 'I enjoyed it because the electronics package wasn't the same as the factory bike and it allowed me to ride a little more loose,' said Stoner, who has often called for a reduction in rider-aid technology. 'The back end was stepping out into corners and out of corners which got the blood rushing again and reminded me what I love about racing.'

That's also what most fans love about motorcycle racing. These may be tough times, but there are signs that MotoGP's longer-term future looks bright.

ABOVE After 14 years and seven world championships together, Valentino Rossi sacked his race engineer Jerry Burgess before the last race of the year. It was an undignified end to a stellar relationship

BELOW Aleix Espargaro and the Aprilia ART dominated the second and final year of CRT just as they had dominated the first

RIDERS' RIDER
OF THE YEAR 2013

In each of its ten years of publication, the *Official Season Review* has asked every rider who raced more than one MotoGP to vote for their six top men of the year. As we've come to expect, there were some interesting differences from the real World Championship

At the end of the season Marc Marquez was World Champion by just four points. Not surprisingly, Marc was also the winner of our poll, but the margin of his victory was definitely a shock. Nearly four times as many of the 29 riders polled voted for Marquez as said Lorenzo was the best. They were the only riders who received first-place nominations. Third to fifth places also followed the real world, with the votes of Pedrosa, Rossi and Crutchlow (again top satellite man) pretty evenly spaced. We allocated six points for a first place, five for a second and so on, to get our result. Confidence in the result is nicely backed up by the observation that the men in first to fifth places all received most nominations for that position: Marquez had 19 nominations for first, Lorenzo 17 for second, Pedrosa 15 for third, Rossi and Crutchlow ten each for fourth and fifth, respectively. Then our voters veered off at a tangent.

The riders decided to promote Aleix Espargaro from his 11th place in the championship to sixth-placed in their estimation. The actual sixth-place man, Alvaro Bautista, was demoted two places to eighth, with Stefan Bradl seventh by both measures.

Espargaro was definitely boosted by the votes of his fellow CRT riders, some of whom all but ignored the factory and satellite men.

However, over three-quarters of the voters put Aleix somewhere in their top six, including both factory and satellite team riders. The other CRT man for whom there was a lot of love was Colin Edwards. He ended up joint ninth with exactly the same number of votes as Bradley Smith. That mirrors Bradley's tenth in the championship but is a serious improvement for the veteran Texan, who was 14th, and shows the regard in which he is still held by his fellow riders.

You might have thought there would be some sympathy for the men who fought the good fight with the Ducatis, but no. Both Hayden and Dovizioso did get a couple of votes, but not enough to make the top ten despite the fact they were eighth and ninth in the championship. Despite Valentino Rossi's fourth places, it was also easy to discern that the Ducati years continue to damage his once invulnerable reputation. He received just two third-place votes, the same as Cal Crutchlow.

Frankly, as this vote took place at the end of a season in which Jorge Lorenzo had rounded the year off with a hat-trick of wins, we expected the top two to be much closer. Instead, there was a massively impressive endorsement of the remarkable rookie's championship from the people who really know, the men who saw it close up.

PREVIOUS WINNERS

VALENTINO ROSSI	2004, 2005, 2008, 2009
LORIS CAPIROSSI	2006
CASEY STONER	2007
JORGE LORENZO	2010, 2012

HONDA
The Power of Dreams

EVOLUTION OF A
LEGEND

For 21 years Honda has evolved the Fireblade, focussing on exceptional performance and handling for everyone. As a testament to this central concept, 'Total Control', the CBR1000RR has become legendary with its victories in the World Super Bike championship and domination at the Isle of Man TT.

Now, for the very first time, performance enthusiasts can own a track-focused, fully road-legal special edition Fireblade that not only looks special – it is special.

Special edition features:

Factory-matched pistons and con-rods ensure optimum internal engine balance.

Fully adjustable Öhlins inverted fork and rear shock specifically developed for the Fireblade SP.

Brembo mono block four-piston calipers with specially designed pistons and pads give consistent and linear feel when braking hard from high speed.

HONDA

CBR1000RR Fireblade SP

Call 0845 200 8000 or
visit honda.co.uk/motorcycles to find out more

CBR
Fireblade

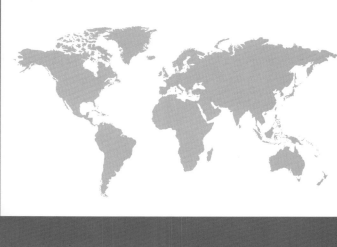

TECHNICAL REVIEW

CRT – Did it do what it was supposed to do? That, of course, depends on what you thought it was there to do…

CLAIMING RULES TEAMS

Back in 2008, as the financial world tottered on the brink, it rapidly became apparent that MotoGP racing was optional for many factories. The size of the grid was shrinking week by week. Team Roberts had already gone, sunk by a combination of the slowest 800 engine and the least grippy race tyres on the grid. Kawasaki quickly followed, and Suzuki reinterpreted their GP contract to mean the supply of a single bike. Something had to be done…

CLAIMING RULES BIKES

The solution was to allow machines with cheaper engines fitted into prototype chassis on to the grid. No-one actually said 'street-bike engines', but that was the only place where such engines were going to be found easily. Bikes so equipped were to be allowed up to 12 engines a year and could have 24 litres of fuel for a race. To make sure the bikes weren't 'back door' full factory race engines, any member of the MSMA (the manufacturers' racing association) could claim one engine each every year for just €20,000.

The chassis were to be open, anything a team wanted to build, but using the Bridgestone control tyres was a prerequisite, and that did rather limit the options. More than any other tyre in recent years, the Bridgestone control tyres have a very specific requirement for chassis behaviour in order to give of their best on track. The balance of weight, flexibility and load on the tyre has to be as near right as possible at all times. Get it right and they reward with amazing levels of grip; get it wrong and it's quite possibly very damaging indeed. These regulations attracted several different constructors and a variety of power plants: FTR built Kawasakis and a Honda Fireblade for Gresini; Aprilia built their ART; and Eskil Suter built a chassis for the BMW.

Michael Laverty sets off on his Paul Bird Aprilia-powered PBM CRT bike at Qatar.

ABOVE Hector Barbera used this pneumatic valve-spring Kawasaki engine from Akira in his FTR from Misano onwards; it only arrived after the claiming rule was dispensed with for Dorna ECU-equipped bikes.

Electronics, however, proved to be very costly. Most teams built their own ride-by-wire systems to suit their chosen bikes which meant there were a lot of systems under development, all desperately trying to catch up in a technology race where the main MotoGP manufacturers had had a decade-long head start. Aprilia brought their own well-proven Superbike electronics and masked off some areas of adjustment to try to keep their factory secrets. The FTRs used proven Motec equipment, Gresini used tried and tested World Superbike-spec Cosworth parts, but Bosch had a torrid time trying to find a set-up on the Suter BMW.

The first year of the CRTs saw a lot of work going into chassis and electronics, but most engines were simply World Superbike spec. For the second year Dorna offered a 'control' ECU free to those who would use it and help develop the strategies inside. This took most of the first half of the year to get to the point where it provided both good 'rider feel' and enough control strategies to make the bike work properly.

CLAIMING RULES POLITICS

The most obvious role for the Claiming Rules bikes was to fill the grid at a time of crisis. There was clearly a second agenda, however. Dorna were fully aware of their position as organisers of the one title the major factories prize above all others, while the MSMA had simply always believed that MotoGP would have rules that specified pure prototypes. Any subsidiary class would never be in a position to take over from the MSMA-built prototype bikes. Dorna, though, had other ideas. The biggest threat to Dorna's long-term profitability, success and value as an investment was the chance that the factories would one day go home.

Over the last few years there have been several occasions where it would have been quite easy, in fact arguably quite sensible, for the Japanese majors to have stopped racing altogether. First there was the financial crisis, which had repercussions for most major industries but which in the

motorcycle world seriously hurt Yamaha in particular. Then, in 2011, came the catastrophic Japanese earthquake and the subsequent tsunami and nuclear meltdown. Given the massive damage this caused to the Japanese people and their country's infrastructure, many countries would have simply cancelled all other commitments and focused on sorting out their problems. Not the Japanese. To their absolute credit their reaction was to say that Japan was open for business, because they wanted it to appear to the outside world that everything in Japan was normal, regardless of the cost of that effort. That meant the racing continued, and the sport let itself breathe again.

Nevertheless, two shocks, each capable of causing massive harm to their business, meant that Dorna needed, at the very least, to have a viable Plan B: what would they do if their most powerful group of supporters was unable or unwilling to continue? In the short term there was a requirement to populate the grid, and in the long term there was the need to make sure Dorna always had the ability to make and run bikes should industry support disappear. In its perfect world, Dorna would have the major manufacturers fighting a racing war with the best motorcycles in the world, and because those manufacturers wanted the series to remain 'full prototype' they would be prepared to produce the bikes for it at reasonable cost. Those same manufacturers, however, had only recently failed to fill the grid and had been leasing bikes at ruinous prices, so they were going to need some encouragement to produce good customer bikes and not charge too much for them.

The CRT bikes had many jobs to fulfil. They had to be bikes that would support the grid, look good, be fast and make the right noises, and be good enough to convince the factories that they were an acceptable substitute for their pure prototypes. One bike that made a lot of impact very quickly was Aprilia's ART. Based on their successful RSV4 Superbike, this bike was right on the cusp of the CRT/pure-prototype split.

GOING ROUND IN CIRCLES

The Aprilia RSV4 was a landmark bike for the Piaggio group, their first full sports bike and certainly the first with its engine designed in-house. They knew from the start that the bike would be raced in Superbike, so Aprilia's formidable race department had a hand in the initial design.

Most of the top men at Aprilia racing had spent some time on the educational but ultimately unsuccessful Aprilia Cube three-cylinder MotoGP bike. It had, however, taught them the benefits of a very compact power unit, one that would allow some choice in the positioning of the engine in the chassis, which was something they couldn't do when they raced the Cube. The V-angle on Claudio Lombardi's design is a noticeably narrow 65 degrees, very much the lower limit for good inlet port layout, and it does not require the inlet system to sit very high in the bike. Being a narrow-angle V, the engine's inertia torque is not fully cancelled out – a 90-degree V is needed for that – but vibration is cancelled out by the addition of a very small balancer.

Race-team input suggested the idea of adjustable position engine mounts and an airbox design that would still work with the engine raised in the chassis. A simple extruded beam chassis was also specified, with a fully adjustable swingarm pivot position and a massive plus-or-minus 9mm adjustable headstock position. In chassis terms the level of adjustment was greater than for most GP bikes, but it was exactly what was needed to turn a street-legal type-approved design into a full-blown racer.

In street trim the engine uses conventional bucket-and-shim valve actuators and production-friendly identical cylinder-head castings. With the cylinder heads placed on the engine as mirror images in an 'intakes in the middle' design, this requires cam drives on both sides of the engine for the front and rear cylinder banks. The cam drives are slightly different, with a chain driving the inlet cam via a sprocket, and a short gear train then driving the exhaust cam. The engine has a conservative 78mm bore, although the block was designed to be able to work at up to 82mm, and a stroke of 52.3mm.

The project leader was Gigi Dall'Igna, then Aprilia Racing's technical director, and the chassis chief was Marco Bertolatti, both veterans of the abortive but educational Cube project. Experience counts, and from the start Aprilia used the best they had. As the 125 and 250 GP teams shut down at the end of 2008, Aprilia had access to an entire

unit of GP team talent which they transferred to World Superbike. They then signed Max Biaggi as their number-one rider and reunited him with his old championship-winning crew chief, Giovanni Sandi.

In World Superbike trim the engine was capable of revving to over 15,000rpm and making 230bhp. Aprilia had their own in-house electronics, a development of the package they developed on the Cube MotoGP bike, the first 'ride-by-wire' racer.

After years of Dunlop tyres in 125 and 250 GPs, getting used to the World Superbike championship's control Pirellis also took some doing. These are based on road tyres, so their main characteristic of a fairly weak carcass is no surprise. Racing on them in Superbike means being very careful not to apply too much load on the brakes or under acceleration, requiring very prudent selection of springs and rear linkages. Aprilia took things much further, tuning the standard chassis to try to exert the correct pressure on to the tyres from full lean to fully upright. In the first year Biaggi had three different swingarm designs. At the front, the top triple clamp was weakened so the 42mm Ohlins were allowed to flex about the lower triple clamp more easily – again, though, only while the bike was at full lean. Aprilia took the 2010 and 2012 World Superbike titles with this machine.

In mid-2011, however, along came CRT. Although the CRT rules went out of their way to stop official factory

ABOVE Czech team Cardion AB used a pair of 2013 ART bikes. Both bikes used the 2013 version of the chassis.

BELOW LEFT The Aspar Power Electronics squad used the most up-to-date versions of the ART, and saw the best results.

BELOW RIGHT Espargaro had the use of a special version of the 'EVO3' engine with magnesium crankcases and a revised primary gear cover to reduce weight and allow more accurate ratio selection.

bikes, it was obvious that Aprilia had a race organisation capable of building a competitive bike, and with the RSV4 the basis of a good mid-level MotoGP bike. The only thing missing under the CRT rules was a prototype frame. The fundamental difference with which Aprilia had to contend at this first stage was the tyres – and they were going to need a different chassis anyway.

As Aprilia are a factory and not a small, specialist race constructor the Aprilia name could not be used, so the bikes were to be built and entered as ARTs. The first prototypes were seen at a combined Superbike and CRT test in Spain with Randy de Puniet and Alex Hofmann as the riders. It was clear the bike had a new fairing and a main frame using extruded aluminium beams; the rest, though, looked very familiar and Superbike-like. During the first tests Gigi Dall'Igna refused to be drawn on future design direction: 'We have to see what these tyres want before we make changes.'

The timescale was tight: Aprilia's tiny race department had to build and deliver eight bikes in just a few months. Unsurprisingly, they looked almost identical to the first test bike. All were the specification with chain-driven cams. The engines were detuned from their normal Superbike spec, as 12 engines had to last the whole 18-race season. In Superbike competition engines would be pulled out and at least the top end serviced every race meeting. The chassis were the same first-guess designs seen previously and looked to have a very close familial resemblance to the last of the Aprilia 250 GP bikes. One of each pair of bikes had different swingarms, as Aprilia simply ran out of time to make enough, so one bike in each pair had a new, slightly differently reinforced swingarm, while the other used a Superbike swingarm. The difference was a small change in the axle slot position, the newer design giving more room for adjustment.

The ART debuted just as Bridgestone were introducing their new, softer construction but quicker to warm up tyres. These made for quite radical changes in chassis set-up. Where the previous-generation tyres were extremely stiff and needed very short swingarms to keep the loads high, these new tyres were comparatively soft and wheelbase settings were not far from the ones used with the Pirellis. The tyre changes at least made Aprilia's job somewhat easier.

Once the racing was under way it took a while for new parts to start arriving. First there was a process of building enough spares; then it was a question of finding out what would make the most difference. The bikes were sold 'as is' and came with a support package. Further support from ART came at a price. It was soon clear that the Aspar Martinez squad, long-term customers of Aprilia Racing, wanted something a little quicker than the others. Initially they got reinforced swingarms; nothing special – just plates of aluminium welded on to the inside of the swingarm – but effective nevertheless. Not long after that there were updated engines. These motors were lightened with material removed from the sides of the heads and then the back of the crankcases. They were also fitted with a gear train to drive the camshafts. This last modification was previously used in Superbike racing where it caused, shall we say, a bit of a furore before it was banned. The additional strength this brought to the cam drive system allowed peak revs to be increased to 15,500.

For the last few races of the year Team Aspar also had two modified main frames, shorter in the headstock (so much so that cutaways were required to clear the clip-on brackets at full lock) and reinforced to assist braking stability. Each had a slightly different rigidity. For the last race at Valencia a completely new chassis was ready, with the whole area around the headstock redesigned. The beams were reshaped to brace the headstock more efficiently and the positioning was very similar, if not identical, to the two special frames made available earlier.

RIGHT Late 2011 version of the ART main frame. Note the way the air intake fits through the main beam.

FAR RIGHT The 2013 ART main frame has the main beams running to the steering head at a different angle and requiring a differing air intake to make up for it.

As the 2013 season started there were new swingarms and another two chassis designs. These were shorter in the headstock, and stiffer in that area too, to manage braking forces. Initially Aspar gave one each to Randy de Puniet and to Aleix Espargaro, but by mid-season it seemed that Aleix had both. Ohlins 48mm forks also arrived, on 'permanent loan' from Aprilia's World Superbike effort. These made a big difference, especially for Espargaro, giving him a lot more control into the corners.

There were also improvements on the engine side. The first year started with a simple, detuned Superbike engine with cam chains and a maximum of 15,000rpm. The first goal was to work out just how reliable the engine was. In Superbike, engines were being changed every race meeting, and that would have to improve for MotoGP. After a while Aspar's team wanted more power; the fastest way to deliver that was with more radical cam timing, and to deliver that accurately the old gear-driven cam drive sets were employed, originally designed for and used by Max Biaggi in World Superbike. The first Evo2 engines with gear-driven cams arrived in mid-2012 and revved to 15,500rpm.

For 2013 a new Evo3 tune was developed. It had a new clutch side cover that allowed a greater selection of primary gears, permitting the wheelbase to remain the same while the gearbox ratios were changed. The Evo3 engines made more power still, but maximum rpm did not increase. The external castings remained the same, with the exception of a special magnesium crankcase for Espargaro to cut the six kilos or so by which the ART exceeded the maximum weight limit.

For the final race of the 2013 season Aprilia brought the 2014 chassis, featuring a radical cutaway along the bottom of the main beam to encourage lateral flex while trying to retain torsional rigidity. It is unclear whether the finished 2014 chassis will look like this or whether this was simply an experiment.

THE FUTURE – STILLBORN?

The rules for 2014 do away with the CRT concept. There will be a 'sub-class' but in a somewhat Orwellian exercise the factory bikes have been renamed 'Factory MotoGP' and the rest, the ones that shouldn't be quite as quick, are called 'Open MotoGP'. The only restrictions on 'Open' bikes, over and above the normal maximum capacity of 1,000cc with an 81mm bore limit, is that they can only have 24 litres of fuel for the race and 12 engines for the

year. Both types must use the championship-supplied Marelli ECU, but 'Open' bikes are restricted to the series' own software.

All this could have worked quite well for Aprilia. The basic bike was proven, so all that would have been necessary was pneumatic valve springs, a seamless-shift gearbox, and a reworking of the chassis to cope with the 20 or so extra horsepower. Now, however, with orders falling away, there has to be a chance that this bike will never be built.

Gigi Dall'Igna's defection to Ducati Corse means that the whole MotoGP project has lost its main customers. Honda have stepped in with their production RCV and taken their best customers, Team Aspar and Cardion, so all that is left is the PBM operation. It is also likely that Dall'Igna will recruit several top members of his Aprilia race operation for Ducati, leaving Aprilia without some of the skills they will need. Just as the CRT category disappears, quite possibly so does one of its best bikes.

All is not lost, however. Piaggio group CEO Roberto Colaninno said at the season's end EICMA show that 'in 2016, Aprilia will return to MotoGP with the goal of winning and discovering the same success we have enjoyed in World Superbikes'. So maybe there will yet be a Son of ART?

ABOVE LEFT The 2012 swingarm had an axle adjustment range suited to the Pirellis in World Superbike.

ABOVE RIGHT Espargaro used this swingarm a lot with a different rigidity ratio and an axle adjustment range more suited to the Bridgestones supplied for CRT use.

BELOW The prototype 2014 ART chassis is a radical experiment in rigidity. Note the cutaway beams and the lighter section swingarm.

MotoGP 2013 WORLD CHAMPION

93 MARC MARQUEZ
Repsol Honda Team

The only one

Bridgestone for MotoGP™ 2013

THE BIKES

HONDA
RC213V

In 2013 the Honda came of age. Last year, development of the first of the 1,000cc V4s took a while; this year's bike didn't have any such problems.

The 1,000 machine is a direct development of the 800, a bike that took three years of painstaking development to get right. Honda have maintained the same centre of gravity position on the new, long-stroke 1,000 by opening up the V-angle to 90 degrees from the 800's 76. This caused some issues with exhaust-pipe routing for the rear cylinders but it was a cost Honda were happy to pay to retain their hard-won optimum weight distribution.

Honda's decision to develop a seamless gearbox was vindicated when Yamaha finally got one of their own and the resulting improvement in performance was easy to measure. Honda's gearbox has full seamless-shift capability in all gears, but to achieve this it has an N123456 pattern. The box was modified this year with a handlebar-mounted lever being used to apply a 'neutral gate' to prevent neutral accidentally being selected while the bike was on track.

It was also clear that Honda have made a massive advance with their electronics. Marc Marquez showed amazing skills on the bike, immediately leaning it over further than had ever been seen before, his ability to do so greatly helped, however, by a bike that was very easy to use. Honda have used technologies perfected on their Asimo robot to increase the accuracy of their lean sensor, and that in turn makes it easier to modify throttle operation at extreme lean angles.

The Honda is set up to be higher and shorter than the Yamaha, which means it wheelies too easily and gets very near to stoppies under hard braking, but it also means it is very manoeuvrable in corners, easily out-turning the Yamaha. Coupled with a power advantage and a very effective seamless shift, this made the bike both confidence-inspiring for the rider and extremely effective.

1 Marquez used a top triple clamp with a lot of the reinforcing machined away to help the bike flex a little more at full lean.

2 Pedrosa was slow to try out the various versions of the Honda rear swingarms but finally did so at the end of the year.

3 Marquez managed to accidentally cut the rear wheel sensor lead on Pedrosa's bike during the Aragon race which caused Dani to crash immediately.

4 Bautista's bike was chosen to develop the new Showa suspension. This is the second design to be tried during the year.

YAMAHA
YZR M1 2013

Yamaha simply don't have the race budget enjoyed by Honda. Their 1,000 is a very close relative of their 800, and to make up for a slight power disadvantage Yamaha have concentrated on maintaining high corner speeds. Their bike is long and low compared to the Honda, so it normally doesn't turn as quickly. It is a design concept that fits perfectly with their number-one rider's skills, but it didn't seem to work for the returning Valentino Rossi.

To make sure that the bikes had the best opportunity to use their performance throughout a race, Yamaha continually modified and improved the balance of the machine. The basic bike had a new 'web' design, where the side beams were CNC machinings from solid. All the struts and welds that reinforced the older chassis were gone, replaced by just one simple piece. Yamaha tried many different versions through the year, all with slight changes in rigidity. They started with a revised fuel-tank position, slightly lower and further back under the seat, then continued with a new swingarm and a different arrangement for holding the rear axle in place and spreading the clamping load.

For the first half of the year Yamaha maintained their stance that the seamless-shift gearbox enjoyed by the Honda riders didn't make that much difference. That position changed to 'we are developing one but it isn't ready yet' in late spring. A private test at Brno in August was all the riders needed to persuade themselves that the box was vital, not because of improved lap times but because it kept the tyre in much better condition right to the end of the race. This was critical, as Yamaha's high-corner-speed strategy had them relying on the tyre's edge grip far more than the quick-turning Hondas.

Once the gearbox was in place, Lorenzo put together an amazing end-of-year performance, with notable wins in Motegi and Valencia, but it still wasn't enough to stop Marquez. One does wonder what the result would have been if that gearbox had been ready at the start of the year.

1 By mid-season Yamaha had modified their pneumatic valve system so that the pressure lines were 'broken' after every session.

2 Cal Crutchlow had a lot of works parts by mid-season; and found the bike's revised weight distribution made it harder for him to ride. Yamaha now use a new 'web chassis' concept for their preferred mix of flexibilities.

3 Rossi tried out 340mm diameter discs at the Misano test for duty at Motegi, they still weren't enough.

4 Honda's project leader Takeo Yokoyama kept a very close watch on the works Yamahas all year.

DUCATI
DESMOSEDICI GP13

Ducati's misery continues. Once lauded as the masters of sweet-handling race bikes, they seem to have completely lost their touch. The year started with a motorcycle that could not hold a line through a corner and, depressingly, finished in much the same way.

There were a few moments of hope. A very experimental 'lab bike' was rolled out at the second Sepang test, featuring main beams with a replaceable outer skin to adjust flex. By Catalunya production versions of the chassis were available for testing by the works riders. Unfortunately, neither liked it. Dovizioso was prevailed upon to use the new design and to try to develop it; Hayden went back to the Rossi-era design he was used to as it was stiffer. New, less rigid swingarms also arrived, but still in carbon fibre.

As the season went on it was apparent that both riders were severely disillusioned, and few additional technical changes were made. There was a 'high inertia' engine design, to help riders apply the throttle smoothly mid-corner, and new exhaust pipes to go with it, plus another new fairing. Partway through the year the man who could be considered Audi's motorcycle expert, head of Audi Research & Development (and, in his youth, head of BMW Motorrad R&D) was relieved of his post. From that time onwards it seemed that the project slowed down, with little that was new arriving at the track.

At the end of the year there was another change of personnel. Ex-BMW designer Bernhard Gobmeier left his position as head of Ducati Corse to work in VW Group's racing department, and he was replaced by the very experienced Gigi Dall'Igna, previously head of all of Piaggio Group's racing activities and the mastermind behind the World Superbike-winning RSV4 and the very cost-effective ART MotoGP project. We now have to wait and see what magic he can bring to bear on the Desmosedici.

1 Ducati developed a new chassis based on their 'lab bike' but it didn't get complete support. Dovizioso rode several versions during the year but Hayden preferred the stiffer Rossi-era design.

2 By the end of the year Dovizioso had a new frame, a new engine 'tune', a new swingarm and a new fairing.

3 A lot of effort went into making the Ducati engines a lot more friendly in nature. The test team tried several different weight flywheels to slow the throttle response to more acceptable areas.

4 Ducati finally fitted a 'flexy' top triple clamp, very similar in concept to the one Yamaha have used since 2007.

APRILIA
ART GP13

Based on the successful RSV4 Aprilia road bike and their World Superbike-winning derivative, the ART had a prototype chassis and detuned engines. Over the course of the year new chassis were developed, shorter and stiffer at the front, and engines in a higher state of tune were introduced. These still had the gear cam drive and boasted more mid-range than the previous versions.

The bike was unusual among the CRT entries in continuing to use its own ECU and software, Aprilia's APX2 system. This gave anyone using the bike a head start over the teams that had opted for the still-developing control Marelli ECU. One of the reasons for Aprilia's decision to stay with their own system was the lack of a channel to operate the automated exhaust butterfly that seems to be an important part of the engine-braking control system.

Aleix Espargaro also had special engines with magnesium crankcases and revised primary gear housings to reduce weight and allow more adventurous gearing options. With that bike he was in a position seriously to embarrass Ducati at several of the more technical tracks. At the last race of the year an experimental chassis debuted that was cut away in the centre section to allow more lateral flex.

PAUL BIRD MOTORSPORT APRILIA

The standard Aprilia ART chassis had a hurried three-month development where the prime target was an acceptable prototype chassis to use on Bridgestone's notoriously fickle tyres. From its inception it suffered badly from chatter and was clearly capable of being further developed. Paul Bird decided that he would rather build his own chassis. He also decided to use the control ECU rather than the standard Aprilia APX2 system.

The combination of a relatively untried ECU and a completely new rolling chassis was a little unfortunate as there were several functions in the Aprilia ECU that would have helped the bike going into corners. The bike seemed very resistant to chatter and worked well, but it displayed a decided lack of enthusiasm for corner entry. The arrival of many more options in the 2014 Dorna software should vastly improve the situation.

1 Gigi Dall'Igna, the man responsible for the ART CRT bike, developed it to the point where it was capable of giving works Ducatis a hard time.

2 Aprilia had access to the works Aprilia ECU. That meant access to years of World Superbike experience and the team didn't have to suffer the development travails of the standard ECU-equipped bikes.

FTR HONDA
FTR MGP13

The FTRs had a good year, with four Kawasaki-powered versions and one Honda on track. The swingarms for all five bikes were identical, but the main frames differed slightly. All the Kawasakis used the control ECU and were held back by its slow development.

Several of the bikes were seen to use significant amounts of ballast high up, to work against an engine position that seemed a bit low; this was most probably because the Kawasaki engine is noticeably big, and because the only way to get air into the intakes was to bring it over the top of the cylinder head. The major departure was the Akira pneumatic-valve cylinder head that was used by Barbera for the second half of the season. This allowed a 1,000rpm higher rev limit and as much as 20 additional horsepower, but it was clearly difficult to ride and was rarely the fastest of the FTRs.

The Gresini Honda was better packaged in this regard but, despite retaining a full Ten Kate superbike engine and Cosworth ride-by-wire package, it was a disappointment and never showed any form.

1 FTR made several chassis for Kawasaki engines.

2 Hector Barbera had the use of a Kawasaki engine with pneumatic valves for the last races of the year. Here you can see the reserve gas reservoir.

3 It isn't easy to get a bike to work well when the engine is as big as the Kawasaki street engine. It is particularly difficult to get the air in over the top of the engine and also get the weight high enough.

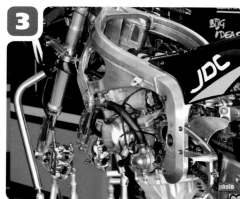

SUTER
SUTER CRT

The Suter BMW was the first of the CRTs and it has had a chequered development history. Last year the Bosch ECU proved extremely difficult to set up; this year the decision to use the control ECU must have seemed a blessed release. Chassis-wise, Suter made some big changes, with the engine moving forward and the seat unit moving up and back. The overall aim was for a roomier bike, enabling riders to move around more easily to better weight the bike on track.

The attempt to create a lower front engine mount was abandoned and the new chassis used the standard BMW pick-up points, including the one on the side of the cylinder head. This is a significant hindrance, as it virtually guarantees the bike will be too stiff for good grip while leaned right over.

1 The Suter chassis reverts to using the original engine mounting points in the 2013 version of the chassis. The engine, however, is further forward, and the seat unit has moved back and up.

2 The seat position change came from a simple extension to the back of the main beam.

3 The difficult-to-set-up Bosch electronics were replaced by the Marelli-based Dorna control equipment.

**BT Sport
The new home
of MotoGP™**

BT Sport is the only place to go for MotoGP™ for the next five years. Catch our exclusive live coverage of all 19 MotoGP™ races, Moto2 and Moto3 races. With all the warm-ups, practice and qualifying live. Plus exciting interactive digital features and extra programming.

£12 a month, or free with BT Broadband
Call 0800 678 1955   btsport.com

BT Sport

GREAT SPORT HAPPENS HERE

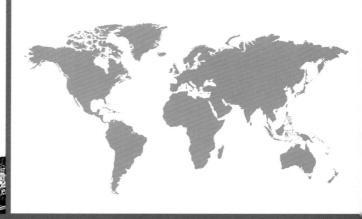

THE SEASON IN FOCUS

From the factory men to the wild cards, every MotoGP rider's season analysed

CHAMPIONSHIP

	Rider	Nation	Team	Points
1	Marquez	SPA	Repsol Honda Team	334
2	Lorenzo	SPA	Yamaha Factory Racing	330
3	Pedrosa	SPA	Repsol Honda Team	300
4	Rossi	ITA	Yamaha Factory Racing	237
5	Crutchlow	GBR	Monster Yamaha Tech 3	188
6	Bautista	SPA	GO&FUN Honda Gresini	171
7	Bradl	GER	LCR Honda MotoGP	156
8	Dovizioso	ITA	Ducati Team	140
9	Hayden	USA	Ducati Team	126
10	Smith	GBR	Monster Yamaha Tech 3	116
11	Espargaro	SPA	Power Electronics Aspar	93
12	Iannone	ITA	Energy T.I. Pramac Racing	57
13	Pirro	ITA	Ignite Pramac Racing	56
14	Edwards	USA	NGM Mobile Forward Racing	41
15	De Puniet	FRA	Power Electronics Aspar	36
16	Barbera	SPA	Avintia Blusens	35
17	Petrucci	ITA	Came IodaRacing Project	26
18	Hernandez	COL	Paul Bird Motorsport	21
19	Corti	ITA	NGM Mobile Forward Racing	14
20	Aoyama	JPN	Avintia Blusens	13
21	Spies	USA	Ignite Pramac Racing	9
22	Nakasuga	JPN	Yamaha YSP Racing Team	5
23	De Angelis	RSM	Ignite Pramac Racing	5
24	Abraham	CZE	Cardion AB Motoracing	5
25	Laverty	GBR	Paul Bird Motorsport	3
26	Staring	AUS	GO&FUN Honda Gresini	2
27	Del Amor	SPA	Avintia Blusens	1

Marc Marquez. World Moto GP Champion, 2013.

The Edge...

We all know it exists but not all of us know how to get there - and fewer still, how to go beyond it.

So this is for the explorers, the rebels, the 'crazies' who continue to push at those boundaries, not only for themselves but for all of us. Because when those boundaries, that edge is pushed - we all move forward together just a little bit more.

So this is our thank you to these rebels, these fearless explorers - the ones for whom rules are for other people and opinions for gossip columns - for who each new day is just another part of the journey - but a journey that is always forward.

So may we all 'see a little further by standing on the shoulders of these giants'...

www.shoeiassured.co.uk

shoeihelmetsuk 🐦 f

SHOEI®

PREMIUM HELMETS

1 MARC MARQUEZ
REPSOL HONDA TEAM

NATIONALITY Spanish
DATE OF BIRTH 17 February 1993
2013 SEASON 6 wins, 16 rostrums,
9 pole positions, 11 fastest laps
TOTAL POINTS 334

Marquez became the youngest-ever World Champion in the top class and the first rookie champion since Kenny Roberts Snr in 1978. He broke records all the way, setting the fastest lap at the first race, then getting the full set – pole, win and fastest lap – at the second, and he never slowed down. As soon as Marc turned a wheel on a MotoGP bike any thoughts of the absent Casey Stoner vanished. The rookie rode fast, loose and aggressively, always teetering on the edge of a crash. And he did crash – frequently – but only in practice, with the sole exception of Mugello. If he had any luck it was that he avoided serious injury while his rivals both hurt themselves in the middle of the season. Marquez had no fear of the bike and certainly no fear of his rivals:

Lorenzo was sideswiped at Jerez, Rossi handed a large dose of his own medicine at Laguna Seca.

Marc's relationship with authority was as strained as it had been in Moto2. His tendency to run up close to the opposition in the braking area drew criticism from Lorenzo as early as Jerez and would eventually earn him a penalty at Aragon. That decision might have been harsh, but getting away with two points for crashing under yellows at Silverstone and nearly collecting marshals dealing with an earlier incident was not. The win-at-all-costs approach of the first part of the season was modified from around two-thirds' distance as he protected the points lead built up when Pedrosa and Lorenzo were injured. He may only be 20, but he's fast and clever.

2 JORGE LORENZO
YAMAHA FACTORY TEAM

NATIONALITY Spanish
DATE OF BIRTH 4 May 1987
2013 SEASON 8 wins, 14 rostrums,
4 pole positions, 2 fastest laps
TOTAL POINTS 330

Eight wins, two more than Marquez and the most in any class this year, on a motorcycle that was no longer the best package out there tell us all we need to know about Jorge's year. Coming out of Cataluyna he was only 7 points behind Pedrosa and 23 in front of Marquez. Next time out, at Assen, he was massively faster than the rest in the wet when he touched a white line, launched himself over the bars and broke his collarbone. The mistake was a function of over-confidence, but astonishingly Jorge had the break pinned and rode anyway, limiting the damage to his chances. When he crashed in Germany two weeks later and re-broke the bone there was no way he could ride. He rode at Laguna Seca the following week, but a haul

of 21 points from three races in which Marquez scored 70 and went from third, 23 points behind title leader Pedrosa, to leading Dani by 16 points, dropped Jorge from a close second to third with a deficit of more than a race win's worth of points.

From then on a pattern emerged. Jorge would get the holeshot, build up an early lead and try to hold off the Repsol Hondas. After the summer break it either worked or it didn't. He won five races and came third in three. The only second place was at Aragon after Pedrosa crashed out. Beating the Hondas required extracting the absolute maximum of the Yamaha's potential. The precision of his riding on the limit was astonishing. No-one rode better than Jorge Lorenzo in 2013.

3 DANI PEDROSA
REPSOL HONDA TEAM

NATIONALITY Spanish
DATE OF BIRTH 29 September 1985
2013 SEASON 3 wins, 13 rostrums,
2 pole positions, 4 fastest laps
TOTAL POINTS 300

Still the third alien but still the nearly man, Dani started the season fit but again it was the first corner at the Sachsenring that ended his championship chances. An old-fashioned 500cc-style highside in practice put him out of the race and lost him the lead in the World Championship. He was still hurting a week later in the USA, where he finished fifth. He had, in fact, broken his collarbone again but hadn't displaced the break so surgery was not necessary.

In the second half of the year he was never off the rostrum until the freak incident at Aragon which effectively ended his chances of the title. His win in Malaysia reminded the rest of what Dani could do, always assuming he could get the grip he wanted. His physical stature still seemed to make it difficult for him to search for grip by moving on the bike.

Perhaps the most significant aspect of his year was the split with Svengali-like mentor Alberto Puig, who spotted Dani back in the late 1990s in a domestic one-make series and has been at his side ever since. Puig will be in charge of a similar talent search sponsored by Honda and Shell in Asia. Currently, there is no more important subject for the Japanese factories than the Asian markets so it's no surprise that Puig has been sent there, but equally it's a sign that Pedrosa is not the priority. This season was (yet another) last chance at the championship for Dani. Will he have another?

4 VALENTINO ROSSI
YAMAHA FACTORY TEAM

NATIONALITY Italian
DATE OF BIRTH 16 February 1979
2013 SEASON 1 win, 6 rostrums,
1 fastest lap
TOTAL POINTS 237

Rossi was back with Yamaha for a chance at redemption after two fallow years with Ducati. Frankly, it didn't happen. Valentino flattered to deceive, with a brilliant second behind his team-mate at the opening round, but then things rapidly worsened. Average or poor qualifying performances condemned him to hard work early in races when he also had problems with the front of the bike. On worn tyres he was as fast as anybody but always too far back to do anything about the top three. After the break he settled into regular fourth-place finishes, usually after a fight with all or any of Bautista, Bradl and Crutchlow.

There was the glorious exception of Assen, scene of so many of his triumphs. True, Lorenzo was nursing a very recently repaired collarbone, but Rossi rolled back the years with a great win and the crowd lapped it up. He backed up the victory with third places in Germany and the USA, one of which pleased him and one didn't due to the very different gaps to the winner. Two more third places consolidated his fourth place overall but they depended on one of the top three not finishing, just as the two earlier thirds came when Lorenzo and Pedrosa were hurt. The uncomfortable truth is that he never beat his team-mate on a level playing field, which pushed Valentino into making the decision to split with race engineer Jerry Burgess. It was an undignified end to a 14-year partnership and, outside Italy, sympathy was very much with Burgess.

5 CAL CRUTCHLOW
MONSTER YAMAHA TECH 3

NATIONALITY British
DATE OF BIRTH 29 October 1985
2013 SEASON 4 rostrums, 2 pole positions
TOTAL POINTS 188

A game of two halves. For the first half of the year Cal managed the almost impossible by improving on his 2012 season. By the summer break he had notched up four rostrums and a pole position and looked odds-on to break the domination of the top three. He had also beaten Rossi's factory bike in fair fights in France and Germany. Then he got what he'd wanted, the tank and seat unit from the factory bikes. Cal was convinced it would help him at the start of races where he was having problems stopping the bike on a full tank. The other side of the coin was that his pace in the closing laps was awesome. He got the equipment at Indianapolis but it didn't turn out to be the magic ingredient he'd been searching for. He did get pole next time out but crashed, and then came Silverstone where three crashes left him needing an operation at the end of the year. The nearest he got to another rostrum was Australia where he was fourth, right on Rossi's tail. Despite a disappointing second half, Cal achieved his objective of being the top non-works rider.

As well as the seat unit and the injury there was the matter of Ducati. Cal announced in the summer that he'd be a factory Ducati rider for the next two years. What he saw as the lack of support from Yamaha, his insistence that only factory riders could hope to win, and the imminent arrival of Pol Espargaro with a much-coveted factory Yamaha contract, all drove Cal into the arms of the Bologna factory.

6 ALVARO BAUTISTA
GO&FUN HONDA GRESINI

NATIONALITY Spanish
DATE OF BIRTH 21 November 1984
TOTAL POINTS 171

Many considered Alvaro lucky to hang on to his ride for 2013, but a couple of rostrum finishes towards the end of the 2012 season kept him at Gresini – and then the same questions were asked again this year. There were no rostrums this year, however, and only two front-row starts. Also, the season did not begin well, then first-lap crashes in Italy and Catalunya dropped him to ninth place in the championship after six races. His crash in Mugello took out Rossi – he was lucky to avoid a lynching – and in Barcelona he only just missed repeating the offence, where Valentino saw fit to deliver some stinging public criticism of Bautista's riding. Things did not look good.

All credit to Alvaro, then, for a second half of the year in which he raced with Rossi, Bradl and Crutchlow, usually for fourth place. He ended the season with a run of five races in which he finished either fourth or fifth. If the man to whom Alvaro should be compared is the other satellite Honda rider, Stefan Bradl, then overall there was very little between them over the season. And as Alvaro was again the only Honda rider working with Nissin brakes and Showa suspension it is doubly difficult to evaluate his year. However, there is no doubt that the consistency he displayed from Germany onwards was impressive. He will have a third season on Fausto Gresini's Honda in 2014, with fast rookie Scott Redding alongside him on a customer bike. Bautista's first job will be to stop his new team-mate from usurping his status as the team's lead rider.

7 STEFAN BRADL
LCR HONDA MotoGP

NATIONALITY
German

DATE OF BIRTH
29 November 1989

2013 SEASON
1 rostrum,
1 pole position

TOTAL POINTS
156

That difficult second year … and he did not pick up where he left off, making it three crashes in the first four races – but switching to Brembo brakes changed things enough for Stefan to get his first front row, at Assen. He led his home race, took his first pole and rostrum at Laguna Seca, but then appeared to lose his way a little. Just as he was finding consistency again he broke his ankle in freak circumstances in Malaysia. However, the majority of Stefan's season was a model of consistency, with only one finish lower than sixth place after Le Mans. He was re-signed for 2014.

8 ANDREA DOVIZIOSO
DUCATI TEAM

NATIONALITY
Italian

DATE OF BIRTH
23 March 1989

TOTAL POINTS
140

Early on there were signs of hope, with front-row starts in France and Italy. He led the race for eight laps at Le Mans, only losing a rostrum position two laps from the flag. The problems were obvious, but the factory Ducati riders found some reason for optimism in the first half a dozen races. Then came the post-Catalunya test and the terrible realisation that nothing was going to improve. Any enthusiasm Dovi had seemed to evaporate quickly and he and team-mate Hayden spent most of the rest of the season racing each other. Occasionally they alleviated the boredom by trying to put each other into the stands on the last corner.

9 NICKY HAYDEN
DUCATI TEAM

NATIONALITY
American

DATE OF BIRTH
30 July 1981

TOTAL POINTS
126

A fifth and final year at Ducati saw few bright moments to lighten the darkness. Like his team-mate Dovizioso, he had his best result in France on a track that started out wet and then dried. And like Dovi he had difficulty hiding his disappointment with the Desmosedici after the let-down of the Barcelona test. As he couldn't discern any improvement in the modified bike, Nicky stuck with the original. He was also displeased not to be offered new parts late on in the season after the factory had announced they wouldn't require his services in 2014. Nicky takes his grudges to Aspar's team and a customer Honda for 2014.

10 BRADLEY SMITH
MONSTER YAMAHA TECH 3

NATIONALITY
British

DATE OF BIRTH
28 November 1990

TOTAL POINTS
116

The best ever points total by a British rookie in MotoGP in a model first season. Smith's progress can be charted by his position relative to the Ducatis. He started by following them, then racing them, and finally being well ahead of them. By the end of the year he was also capable of leading his team-mate early on and staying with him when he went past. Even a nasty hand injury sustained at Mugello and the operation to repair it after the Barcelona test didn't interrupt the progress. Bradley rounded off the year by being second fastest at the Valencia test, but now he has to translate that into progress against the other satellite bikes.

11 ALEIX ESPARGARO
POWER ELECTRONICS ASPAR

NATIONALITY
Spanish

DATE OF BIRTH
30 July 1989

TOTAL POINTS
93

Dominated the second season of CRT just as he did the first, being top CRT finisher 13 times in 18 races, including the first eight in succession. Not only did he dominate his class, he was able to harass the slower satellite bikes and the factory Ducatis on slower tracks. Granted he benefited from a very special Aprilia, but Aleix's riding was quite brilliant. There was a definite feeling that the progress of his younger brother Pol would block his way to a factory bike, but the Forward team will field him on their Open Class bike in 2014, based on a Yamaha M1 engine and frame.

12 ANDREA IANNONE
ENERGY T.I. PRAMAC RACING

NATIONALITY
Italian

DATE OF BIRTH
9 August 1989

TOTAL POINTS
57

A tough rookie year on the recalcitrant satellite Ducati. 'Manic Joe' spent much of the year suffering from injury, the worst being the dislocated shoulder he sustained in practice for the German GP, the effects of which lasted through the second half of the year. His best finish was eighth in the strange bike-change Australian race, and there were ninth places at Qatar and the Czech Republic. Andrea's chances of adding to his 12 victories in 125 and Moto2 depend on the bike being improved over winter. He will be back for a second season with the Pramac team.

13 MICHELE PIRRO
IGNITE PRAMAC RACING

NATIONALITY
Italian

DATE OF BIRTH
5 July 1986

TOTAL POINTS
56

Ducati's test rider was scheduled to do three wild-card rides but ended up doing ten, mainly as a replacement for the absent Ben Spies. He rode both the satellite bike and the 'lab bike', making no secret of his preference for the latter. Not surprisingly, he usually found himself racing with the other Ducatis. His best results, a seventh and an eighth, came at Mugello and Le Mans – not surprising, given the number of testing laps Pirro must have done at the Italian track and the Ducati's preference for wet conditions. The similarity in the abilities of the two bikes unfortunately showed just what a big job the factory has on its hands.

14 COLIN EDWARDS
IGNITE PRAMAC RACING

NATIONALITY
American

DATE OF BIRTH
27 February 1974

TOTAL POINTS
41

By the time the Forward team had got their FTR Kawasaki's electronics raceworthy there was absolutely no chance of the Texan winning the CRT class. The fact that a rider as experienced as Colin pulled out of the first two races and only scored three points in the next three races shows how badly development was needed. But from Germany, round eight, onwards he finished every race and was only out of the points once, twice finishing as top CRT. Colin will be 40 years old when the 2014 season starts, but he will be back with the Forward team and leading development of their Yamaha M1-based Open Class bike.

15 RANDY DE PUNIET
POWER ELECTRONICS ASPAR

NATIONALITY
French

DATE OF BIRTH
14 February 1981

TOTAL POINTS
36

Randy stayed with Aspar's team for a second year but was never in contention for top CRT honours. He didn't get the same level of machinery as his team-mate and struggled for much of the year with lack of confidence in the front end. Things did come good towards the end of the year, though, and Randy was top CRT at the tricky Australian race. However, he was dividing his time between Aspar's Aprilia and the re-formed Suzuki Grand Prix team for which he was test rider. It seems likely that this will be his future in MotoGP and with luck he will be seen not just as a test rider but as a wild-card entry before Suzuki return full-time.

16 HECTOR BARBERA
AVINTIA BLUSENS

NATIONALITY
Spanish

DATE OF BIRTH
2 November 1986

TOTAL POINTS
35

Hector's first year in CRT on the Avintia team's FTR Kawasaki resulted in one class victory, at Laguna. Midway through the year the team gave him a new motor with pneumatic valves, but he found the power delivery abrupt and, combined with Hector's preference for using lots of traction control, there was no visible advantage. He had expected to be at least third overall in the CRT class (beating Edwards or Espargaro would have been a seriously good result) but he ended up just one point behind de Puniet. Hector will be back in MotoGP in 2014 with the Avintia team.

17 DANILO PETRUCCI
CAME IODARACING PROJECT

NATIONALITY
Italian

DATE OF BIRTH
24 October 1990

TOTAL POINTS
26

Even Danilo's good humour was tested at times this year. Lack of development of the Ioda team's Suter BMW was the main reason for his frustration. He is also the biggest bloke on the grid at 76kg, so 11 points-scoring rides has to be some sort of achievement. The fact that his team-mate, an experienced Grand Prix rider with two wins and nine rostrum finishes on his CV, didn't score a point also suggests that Danilo got the maximum out of his machinery. Next year, 'Petrux' will stay with the Ioda team but their swap to Aprilia ART machinery should allow him to be more competitive.

18 YONNY HERNANDEZ
PAUL BIRD MOTORSPORT

NATIONALITY
Colombian

DATE OF BIRTH
25 July 1988

TOTAL POINTS
21

The only South American in MotoGP started his rookie year in the top class with Paul Bird's team, riding an Aprilia ART, and ended it on a satellite Ducati. There appeared to be no change from his old Moto2 riding style: the throttle was either fully open or fully closed, and the result was a lot of crashes. It says something about the problems of making the Aprilia competitive that Yonny found the Ducati easier to ride; he was the only guy all year who actually looked happy to be on one. His best result, tenth, came on the Ducati in Malaysia. He stays with Pramac for 2014 to ride the factory's experimental Open Class bike.

19 CLAUDIO CORTI
NGM MOBILE FORWARD RACING

NATIONALITY
Italian

DATE OF BIRTH
25 June 1987

TOTAL POINTS
14

Another cheerful Italian who grinned his way through a bunch of problems with an under-developed CRT bike. It took him until Catalunya to score a point with an impressive 12th place, after which there were five more top-15 finishes, although none of them was better than 13th. With the Forward team retaining Colin Edwards and recruiting double CRT champion Aleix Espargaro to ride their Yamaha, 'Shorts' (the Italian word for 'short' is 'cort') was surplus to requirements for 2014. He is off to the Yakhnich MV Agusta team in the World Superbike Championship in the paddock where he was three times a European Superstock runner-up.

20 HIROSHI AOYAMA
AVINTIA BLUSENS

NATIONALITY
Japanese

DATE OF BIRTH
25 October 1981

TOTAL POINTS
13

In truth, the last 250cc champion hasn't been the same since his Silverstone crash in 2010 when he broke a vertebra. His confidence was further knocked by two nasty injuries early in the year: knee ligaments and a mangled finger. As usual, it was the injury to the joint that took longer to get over, but towards the end of the year Hiro was able to put in three consecutive points-scoring rides and out-perform team-mate Barbera as often as not. After years of bad luck maybe it's justice that he'll be on one of the new Honda customer V4s in 2014.

21 BEN SPIES
IGNITE PRAMAC RACING

NATIONALITY
American

DATE OF BIRTH
11 July 1984

TOTAL POINTS
9

The move from Yamaha to Ducati didn't improve Ben's luck. He wasn't fully recovered from a winter shoulder operation and did more damage at the second race trying to compensate. There was an ill-advised attempt to come back at Mugello and when he did return fit, at Indianapolis, he injured the other shoulder. He had operations on both shoulders but it was soon clear he was out for the season. Then came the shock announcement that he had decided to retire from racing. It could and should have been different – he's one of only a handful of racers outside of the aliens to have won a MotoGP race in recent years.

22 KATSUYUKI NAKASUGA
YAMAHA YSP RACING TEAM

NATIONALITY
Japanese

DATE OF BIRTH
9 August 1981

TOTAL POINTS
5

Yamaha's veteran test rider, reigning Japanese Superbike Champion and Suzuka Eight-Hour pole-man raced at his home GP at Motegi as a wild card. Unlike Valencia in 2012, when he replaced Spies and scored a fairytale rostrum, this year his race was about the day job. That meant testing parts destined for the 2014 Yamaha M1, which he did by staying on the bike and coming home in 11th. He wasn't exactly overcome with excitement by his finishing position, but dutifully said that he was confident he'd done a good job for the team.

23 ALEX DE ANGELIS
IGNITE PRAMAC RACING

NATIONALITY
Sammarinese

DATE OF BIRTH
26 February 1984

TOTAL POINTS
5

Alex spent most of the year riding a Moto2 bike with a Speed Up chassis for the Forward team, but that meant he wasn't riding at Laguna Seca because only the MotoGP class goes to the US GP. So when the Pramac team couldn't use regular replacement Michele Pirro in place of Ben Spies (Ducati's test rider had a scheduled test session at Mugello), then de Angelis was an obvious choice. One of the few men available with MotoGP experience, Alex's first GP was in 1999 and he has scored 40 rostrum finishes in all classes; he repaid the team's faith with a solid 11th place.

24 KAREL ABRAHAM
CARDION AB MOTORACING

NATIONALITY
Czech

DATE OF BIRTH
2 January 1990

TOTAL POINTS
5

Another rider who suffered in the year of the shoulder. A fall in Qatar started the season badly, then a broken collarbone (his fault) in practice for the second round meant he missed two races. Karel struggled with the Aprilia, managing a best finish of 14th in the first half of the year. At Indianapolis he sustained a nasty shoulder injury and although he tried a comeback at his home race in Brno next time out, he needed an operation. He had the sense to admit immediately that a proper recovery demanded he miss the rest of the season, but he returns for 2014 with a customer Honda V4.

25 MICHAEL LAVERTY
PAUL BIRD MOTORSPORT

NATIONALITY
British

DATE OF BIRTH
7 June 1981

TOTAL POINTS
3

Made his GP debut at the tender age of 31 with the daunting prospect of developing the PBM team's own bike using an Aprilia ART engine and a home-built chassis. His sole points-scoring ride of the year came in Jerez, after which the limitations of the bike and the effects of zero testing time became apparent. When his team-mate, Hernandez, was seconded to the Pramac team to replace Spies, Michael moved across the garage to the Aprilia ART. That was at Aragon and resulted in more confusion and crashes in that and the next race. There was never a lack of effort, though, and Laverty retains his ride for 2014.

26 BRYAN STARING
GO&FUN HONDA GRESINI

NATIONALITY
Australian

DATE OF BIRTH
1 June 1987

TOTAL POINTS
2

There had to be an Australian in the paddock, and so triple domestic champion Bryan Staring got the call. With race-winning form in the European Superstock 1,000 Championship but no Grand Prix experience, he was drafted into the Gresini Honda team to ride their Fireblade-engined FTR, the only bike of its type on the grid. Not surprisingly, he struggled. The highlight was 14th at Catalunya, Bryan's only points-scoring race of the year; the low point was being disqualified from his home race (albeit for the same reason as Marquez). A far from happy season, and it probably wasn't all his own fault.

27 JAVIER DEL AMOR
AVINTIA BLUSENS

NATIONALITY Spanish
DATE OF BIRTH 8 June 1976
TOTAL POINTS 1

The feel-good story of the year: Javier turned up at Catalunya to give pit-box tours, but when Aoyama was injured he was sent home to pick up his leathers. He raced and scored a point in his first Grand Prix.

LUKAS PESEK
CAME IODARACING PROJECT

NATIONALITY Czech
DATE OF BIRTH 22 November 1985

A truly dreadful year, especially given his record in the smaller classes. How can a double GP winner score no points in a whole season? The answer is when he never develops any confidence in his bike.

BLAKE YOUNG
ATTACK PERFORMANCE RACING

NATIONALITY American
DATE OF BIRTH 20 September 1987

Entered all three American GPs on the Attack Performance Kawasaki CRT machine, finishing out of the points in Texas, failing to qualify in California and crashing out in Indianapolis.

LUCA SCASSA
CARDION AB MOTORACING

NATIONALITY Italian
DATE OF BIRTH 23 August 1983

Replaced the injured Karel Abraham on the Cardion team's ART Aprilia for the last five races of the year. Frustratingly, he just missed out on points. He will ride a Kawasaki in the World Superbike Championship next season.

IVÁN SILVA
AVINTIA BLUSENS

NATIONALITY Spanish
DATE OF BIRTH 12 June 1982

Recalled by the Avintia team, for whom he rode in the 2012 MotoGP Championship, to replace Hiroshi Aoyama at Assen. Ivan brought the bike home and then went back to his day job in the Spanish Championship.

DAMIAN CUDLIN
PAUL BIRD MOTORSPORT

NATIONALITY Australian
DATE OF BIRTH 19 October 1982

Rode the Paul Bird team's PBM machine when Hernandez went to Pramac and Laverty moved across to the stock Aprilia. Even the experienced Aussie couldn't make up for the lack of saddle time, finishing just two races out of five.

MARTIN BAUER
REMUS RACING TEAM

NATIONALITY Austrian
DATE OF BIRTH 30 December 1975

After a compulsory test at Brno to prove he had the pace, the veteran ex-German Superbike Champion entered the Czech Republic and Valencian GPs on a Suter BMW and finished both races.

MIKE BARNES
GP TECH

NATIONALITY American
DATE OF BIRTH 21 October 1968

Rode the test at Circuit of the Americas and entered the GP but failed to qualify the Suzuki-engined CRT for the race. Mike's plans to enter the other two GPs on American tracks came to naught.

2014

HERTZ BRITISH GRAND PRIX (MotoGP™)

29–31 AUG

Tickets from £12.50*
*Terms and conditions apply

After a fantastic event in 2013, which saw one of the best race finishes we have seen here at Silverstone, don't miss your chance to witness some of the world's top riders battle it out once again as the pinnacle of two wheeled motorsport returns for another unmissable year!

Off track there is always plenty of entertainment for the whole family inc. displays, competitions and much more!

Why not make the most of your weekend and book camping at Silverstone's official campsite, Woodlands. Prices are just £60 per adult and £15 per child.

For information on all of Silverstone's events or to book

Call 0844 3750 740
Visit silverstone.co.uk

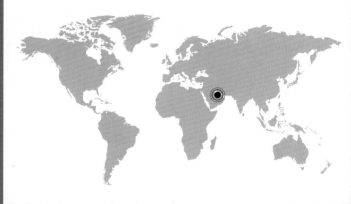

COMMERCIAL BANK GRAND PRIX OF QATAR

DANCING IN THE DARK

Lorenzo started his title defence in immaculate style, Marquez announced his arrival and Rossi returned to the rostrum

It could easily have been an anti-climax, but the opening round of 2013 lived up to the somewhat fevered pre-season hype. All of the established stars, save Dani Pedrosa, had weekends that were more or less encouraging, and all of the manufacturers, even Ducati, could point to positives. Even the much-maligned CRT bikes took a major step forward.

Losail was buzzing with talk of the new young contender, Marc Marquez, and his radical riding style; of Valentino Rossi's fabulous ride to the rostrum after two years in the wilderness; and of the grit of Cal Crutchlow. It was all too easy to overlook the near-perfect race run by the winner, Jorge Lorenzo. He took pole position off Crutchlow with his last flying lap, knowing that come race day he couldn't afford to get tangled up with the Hondas. The interlinked high-speed corners that comprise most of the Losail International Circuit were a happy hunting ground for the Yamahas, provided they didn't encounter a Honda in the middle of the corner. Rossi demonstrated this perfectly in the race. He spent six laps searching for a way past Stefan Bradl's Honda, then took eight laps to cross a gap of three-and-a-half seconds to Crutchlow. Lorenzo knew the score and knew he had to get the holeshot and open a gap. Again, he did it perfectly with a stunning opening lap, and then increased his lead every lap until the very last one. He said that in taking a couple of tenths out of the pursuers each time over the opening half-dozen laps he was truly at the limit. When he saw he had opened a gap of over two seconds, things came easier. Behind

ABOVE Marc Marquez started his first MotoGP race from sixth on the grid, set the fastest lap and finished on the rostrum

RIGHT The lights of the Losail Circuit shine on the first lap of 2013; the timing tower is showing qualifying positions

OPPOSITE Alvaro Bautista finished sixth despite being one of only two riders on the soft rear tyre

Jorge, there were heroics from Rossi, Marquez and Crutchlow but none of them so much as laid a glove on the World Champion.

Before the race, Rossi said that his 'target to be happy' was to win a race, but afterwards he admitted that in November he had set himself the goal of a rostrum finish on his return to Yamaha. He was as excited and voluble about this second place as about most of his victories, talking about seeing his rostrum going away when he couldn't get past Bradl and then how he could see it coming back to him as he closed in on Crutchlow and the two Repsol Hondas, who were fighting over the remaining rostrum positions. Cal's challenge ended when he ran on as Rossi arrived. He was of the opinion that Marc Marquez, in his first race for the factory Honda team, had been toying with Pedrosa and could have gone past half a dozen times before he did, five laps from the flag. Rossi was up to third two laps later and then had a short, sharp dice with Marquez. It was hard to avoid the feeling that one was watching the new order sizing up the outgoing regime.

Marc said all the right things before and after the race – trying to improve in every session, learning from following Dani and Valentino – but everything he did – fastest in free practice, fastest lap in the race – suggested a young man in a hurry to win races, and more.

Dani Pedrosa bore it all with stoicism at a circuit where he has never won. In the race he'd held on to second place until three-quarter distance, a much better performance than practice had predicted.

Everyone suffered from lack of grip due to even more dust than usual on track, thanks to massive construction projects nearby, but Dani could hardly touch the throttle without spinning the tyre. He was eighth in free practice and just got on the front row, both times 0.4s slower than Lorenzo. The man who was nearly on the front row instead of Dani was Andrea Dovizioso on his Ducati debut. Although his race followed the Rossi pattern of the last two years, Andrea was only one-thousandth of a second behind Valentino in the third free practice session and handily outqualified him. Dovi also ran at the front early on,

the sight of the red bike ahead of him causing Rossi to go deep at the end of the first lap and lose a place. The old problems of understeer and tyre wear reared their heads in the race but Andrea was calm and analytical; it was, he said, exactly what he expected.

There was also cautious optimism in the CRT teams. Their big change in regulation, the ability to use a softer tyre than the prototypes, wasn't an issue here because of track conditions, yet the gap closed considerably. Twelve months previously the top CRT rider, Colin Edwards, qualified 3.01s behind pole and finished 58s behind the winner. This year

Aleix Espargaro was 2.35s down on pole and finished 49s behind Lorenzo. The elder Espargaro brother was riding brilliantly, but Aprilia had certainly made use of a season's experience with Bridgestone tyres. Non-Aprilia CRT teams took advantage of the spec electronics from Magneti Marelli and were a little taken aback at the basic nature of the software. However, regular upgrades were promised and most teams were sure it was a better option than trying to develop their own systems.

The main topics of debate over the close season had been how long it would take Rossi and Marquez to get on the pace of the two Spaniards everybody expected to be fighting for the title, and how much the championship would miss Casey Stoner. The answers turned out to be no time at all and not a lot, for despite their protestations it was obvious that the nine-times World Champion and the rookie weren't just going to be contenders for the occasional race win but also for the title. Maybe that shouldn't have been a surprise.

'PEDROSA DIDN'T WANT TO LET ME GET AWAY, BUT AFTER A FEW LAPS I OPENED A GAP'
JORGE LORENZO

PRACTICE TWO-STEP

The major change in sporting regulations for 2013 was a total revamp of the qualifying session for the MotoGP class only. Out went the old hour-long session to decide grid positions, in came a three-stage procedure. The Saturday afternoon (Friday at Assen) schedule now consists of a half-hour untimed session known as Free Practice 4 followed by a 10-minute interval. Qualifying 1 follows for the riders who finished from 11th downwards on combined times from the first three free practices. This lasts 15 minutes and decides starting positions for the back half of the grid, but the fastest two men in Q1 are seeded through to the final session to decide the top 12 places on the grid.

After another 10-minute break Qualifying 2 takes place and again lasts 15 minutes. On a long track like Qatar, the tactics were obvious: two runs consisting of an out-lap, two flying laps and an in-lap. A rider promoted from Qualifying 1, though, might have concerns about the number of tyres used and not be able to take advantage. Aleix Espargaro, for instance, only did four laps in Q1 and the same number again in Q2. Bradley Smith did not pit for a new tyre in Q2 having used his resources in FP3 to ensure he didn't have to try to get through Q1.

Despite the small number of bikes and the long lap, the Repsol Hondas nearly had a coming-together and Valentino Rossi said he'd been held up by traffic. Nevertheless, rider reaction was positive and there was surprisingly little controversy over the new system.

COMMERCIAL BANK GRAND PRIX OF QATAR
LOSAIL INTERNATIONAL CIRCUIT

ROUND 1
APRIL 7

S SPEED TRAP
1 CORNER NUMBER
1 GEAR SELECTION/SPEED
SECTOR 1
SECTOR 2
SECTOR 3

RACE RESULTS

CIRCUIT LENGTH 3.343 miles
NO. OF LAPS 22
RACE DISTANCE 73.546 miles
WEATHER Dry, 21°C
TRACK TEMPERATURE 23°C
WINNER Jorge Lorenzo
FASTEST LAP 1m 55.445s, 104.204mph, Marc Marquez
LAP RECORD 1m 55.135s, 104.452mph, Casey Stoner, 2008

QUALIFYING

	Rider	Nation	Motorcycle	Team	Time	Pole +
1	Lorenzo	SPA	Yamaha	Yamaha Factory Racing	1m 54.714s	
2	Crutchlow	GBR	Yamaha	Monster Yamaha Tech 3	1m 54.916s	0.202s
3	Pedrosa	SPA	Honda	Repsol Honda Team	1m 55.151s	0.437s
4	Dovizioso	ITA	Ducati	Ducati Team	1m 55.160s	0.446s
5	Bradl	GER	Honda	LCR Honda MotoGP	1m 55.477s	0.763s
6	Marquez	SPA	Honda	Repsol Honda Team	1m 55.645s	0.931s
7	Rossi	ITA	Yamaha	Yamaha Factory Racing	1m 55.711s	0.997s
8	Bautista	SPA	Honda	GO&FUN Honda Gresini	1m 55.870s	1.156s
9	Smith	GBR	Yamaha	Monster Yamaha Tech 3	1m 56.315s	1.601s
10	Iannone	ITA	Ducati	Energy T.I. Pramac Racing	1m 56.523s	1.809s
11	Hayden	USA	Ducati	Ducati Team	1m 56.667s	1.953s
12	Espargaro	SPA	ART	Power Electronics Aspar	1m 57.064s	2.350s
13	Spies	USA	Ducati	Ignite Pramac Racing	1m 57.440s	Q1
14	De Puniet	FRA	ART	Power Electronics Aspar	1m 57.551s	Q1
15	Pesek	CZE	Ioda-Suter	Came IodaRacing Project	1m 57.926s	Q1
16	Hernandez	COL	ART	Paul Bird Motorsport	1m 58.058s	Q1
17	Aoyama	JPN	FTR	Avintia Blusens	1m 58.263s	Q1
18	Abraham	CZE	ART	Cardion AB Motoracing	1m 58.271s	Q1
19	Edwards	USA	FTR Kawasaki	NGM Mobile Forward Racing	1m 58.361s	Q1
20	Petrucci	ITA	Ioda-Suter	Came IodaRacing Project	1m 58.486s	Q1
21	Corti	ITA	FTR Kawasaki	NGM Mobile Forward Racing	1m 58.755s	Q1
22	Barbera	SPA	FTR	Avintia Blusens	1m 58.806s	Q1
23	Staring	AUS	FTR Honda	GO&FUN Honda Gresini	1m 58.912s	Q1
24	Laverty	GBR	PBM	Paul Bird Motorsport	1m 59.572s	Q1

FINISHERS

1 JORGE LORENZO The perfect start to his title defence. Pole position against a strong challenge from Crutchlow and never headed in the race, pressing hard over the opening laps to open up a gap, then in control.

2 VALENTINO ROSSI A fabulous result after two years of purgatory, despite messing up qualifying and making a potentially disastrous early mistake. Passed the Hondas with ease, then had to fight hard to fend off Marquez. Broke Agostini's record of a podium finish in 13 successive seasons.

3 MARC MARQUEZ What a debut: fastest in FP3, nervous in qualifying, then scored fastest lap on the way to the rostrum via a wonderful dice with Rossi. Shadowed his team-mate for almost two-thirds of the race before passing and pulling away. The most impressive top-class debut since Biaggi's.

4 DANI PEDROSA As usual, when grip levels are low, Dani suffered all weekend. Never looked comfortable – it's a circuit where he has never won in any class – complaining of rear-grip problems in both practice and the race.

5 CAL CRUTCHLOW Brilliant in practice and qualifying, and able to run with the factory Hondas for most of the race. Made a mistake when Rossi came past which detached him from the group. Was also down on power as his team were worried about fuel consumption, so the engine management system was set accordingly.

6 ALVARO BAUTISTA His best finish at Qatar despite recently broken fingers and the decision to use the softer front tyre (which compromised stability) to cope with the same front-end problems he had last year. The hope is that this was down to track conditions.

7 ANDREA DOVIZIOSO After the promise of qualifying, the race was, as Andrea said, a return to reality. As usual, the Ducati was fine when it had grip in the early laps but the understeer problem returned as the tyres wore.

8 NICKY HAYDEN Not happy in practice, but a change for the race saw him do his best time of the weekend by two-tenths of a second and run his qualifying times in the early laps. Got across a gap to join the Dovizioso group but couldn't get past on the brakes so finished right behind his team-mate.

9 ANDREA IANNONE Suffered from arm pump for the first time in practice and again after just four laps of the race, despite painkilling injections. Also reported edge grip problems after six laps.

10 BEN SPIES Far from fit, with his repaired shoulder aggravated by a nasty fall in qualifying. Dug deep for what he called the best tenth place of his life.

11 ALEIX ESPARGARO Took up where he left off in 2012, as top CRT rider. Had to accept that the speed differential made it all but impossible to race with even the slower prototypes, but happy to have solved his chatter problem and finished only 49s behind the winner.

12 RANDY DE PUNIET Spent most of the race running with his team-mate, but eight laps from the flag he suffered a problem with an air intake coming loose and interfering with the steering.

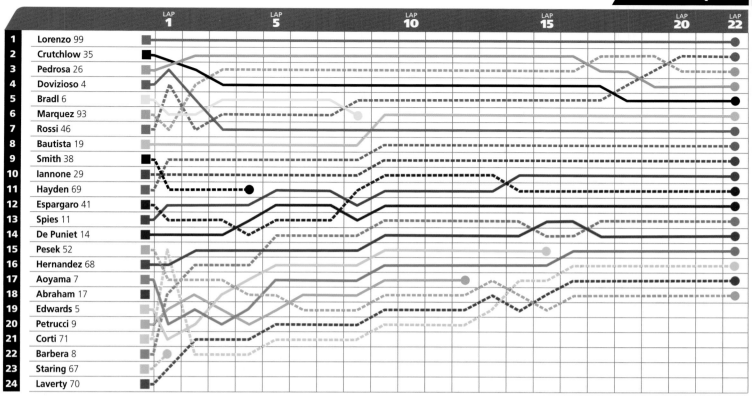

		LAP 1	LAP 5	LAP 10	LAP 15	LAP 20	LAP 22
1	Lorenzo 99						
2	Crutchlow 35						
3	Pedrosa 26						
4	Dovizioso 4						
5	Bradl 6						
6	Marquez 93						
7	Rossi 46						
8	Bautista 19						
9	Smith 38						
10	Iannone 29						
11	Hayden 69						
12	Espargaro 41						
13	Spies 11						
14	De Puniet 14						
15	Pesek 52						
16	Hernandez 68						
17	Aoyama 7						
18	Abraham 17						
19	Edwards 5						
20	Petrucci 9						
21	Corti 71						
22	Barbera 8						
23	Staring 67						
24	Laverty 70						

RACE

	Rider	Motorcycle	Race Time	Time +	Fastest Lap	Avg. Speed	B
1	Lorenzo	Yamaha	42m 39.802s		1m 55.569s	103.396mph	H/M
2	Rossi	Yamaha	42m 45.792s	5.990s	1m 55.756s	103.148mph	H/M
3	Marquez	Honda	42m 46.003s	6.201s	1m 55.445s	103.148mph	H/M
4	Pedrosa	Honda	42m 49.275s	9.473s	1m 55.953s	103.023mph	H/M
5	Crutchlow	Yamaha	42m 58.566s	18.764s	1m 55.804s	102.651mph	H/M
6	Bautista	Honda	43m 01.950s	22.148s	1m 56.122s	102.526mph	S/M
7	Dovizioso	Ducati	43m 04.157s	24.355s	1m 56.494s	102.402mph	H/M
8	Hayden	Ducati	43m 04.722s	24.920s	1m 56.437s	102.402mph	H/M
9	Iannone	Ducati	43m 16.926s	37.124s	1m 56.599s	101.905mph	H/M
10	Spies	Ducati	43m 24.710s	44.908s	1m 57.280s	101.594mph	H/M
11	Espargaro	ART	43m 29.611s	49.809s	1m 57.748s	101.408mph	H/M
12	De Puniet	ART	43m 36.297s	56.495s	1m 57.710s	101.159mph	H/M
13	Barbera	FTR	43m 49.401s	1m 09.599s	1m 57.989s	100.662mph	H/M
14	Hernandez	ART	43m 50.544s	1m 10.742s	1m 58.640s	100.600mph	H/M
15	Aoyama	FTR	43m 53.402s	1m 13.600s	1m 59.011s	100.538mph	H/M
16	Corti	FTR Kawasaki	44m 09.246s	1m 29.444s	1m 59.322s	99.916mph	H/M
17	Laverty	PBM	44m 14.143s	1m 34.341s	1m 59.713s	99.730mph	H/M
18	Pesek	Ioda-Suter	44m 14.485s	1m 34.683s	1m 59.405s	99.730mph	S/M
NF	Edwards	FTR Kawasaki	29m 53.645s	7 Laps	1m 58.383s	100.600mph	H/M
NF	Petrucci	Ioda-Suter	24m 07.698s	10 Laps	1m 59.512s	99.730mph	H/M
NF	Bradl	Honda	15m 39.731s	14 Laps	1m 56.233s	102.402mph	H/M
NF	Smith	Yamaha	7m 56.931s	18 Laps	1m 56.828s	100.911mph	H/M
NF	Staring	FTR Honda	2m 09.807s	21 Laps		92.709mph	H/M
NF	Abraham	ART					H/M

CHAMPIONSHIP

	Rider	Nation	Team	Points
1	Lorenzo	SPA	Yamaha Factory Racing	25
2	Rossi	ITA	Yamaha Factory Racing	20
3	Marquez	SPA	Repsol Honda Team	16
4	Pedrosa	SPA	Repsol Honda Team	13
5	Crutchlow	GBR	Monster Yamaha Tech 3	11
6	Bautista	SPA	GO&FUN Honda Gresini	10
7	Dovizioso	ITA	Ducati Team	9
8	Hayden	USA	Ducati Team	8
9	Iannone	ITA	Energy T.I. Pramac Racing	7
10	Spies	USA	Ignite Pramac Racing	6
11	Espargaro	SPA	Power Electronics Aspar	5
12	De Puniet	FRA	Power Electronics Aspar	4
13	Barbera	SPA	Avinitia Blusens	3
14	Hernandez	COL	Paul Bird Motorsport	2
15	Aoyama	JPN	Avinitia Blusens	1

13 HECTOR BARBERA Saved the day with a combative ride from a lowly 22nd on the grid after electrical problems on Saturday. Didn't know if he could have beaten the Aspar bikes but was sure he would have given them something to think about.

14 YONNY HERNANDEZ Got over a bad start and a couple of crashes in practice to fight with Barbera and bring home a couple of points for the Paul Bird team.

15 HIROSHI AOYAMA Hit chatter in the race for the first time during the weekend, but happy with his progress and managing to score a point.

16 CLAUDIO CORTI Ran off track early on after making up seven places and had a front-wheel vibration when he rejoined. Also reported that a problem from winter testing was unsolved.

17 MICHAEL LAVERTY An impressively professional debut in MotoGP on the team's own bike with an Aprilia engine. Hampered by rear suspension troubles in practice, and when they were sorted out problems were discovered elsewhere: just what you'd expect from a new design with very little testing.

18 LUKAS PESEK Qualified an impressive 15th but wasn't able to back it up in his first MotoGP race.

NON-FINISHERS

COLIN EDWARDS Clutch and gearbox problems led to a catastrophic failure of the rear sprocket.

DANILO PETRUCCI Ran off track while dicing with Barbera. Couldn't restart as the electronics had shut down.

STEFAN BRADL Crashed at Turn 7 when he lost the front. Echoes of problems that held him back last year, exacerbated by a failure to sort it out after it first appeared on Friday and a lack of explanation for the crash.

BRADLEY SMITH Like Bradl, crashed at Turn 7 when he lost the front, but very impressive right up to that moment. Unlike Bradl, he knew why he crashed. New-found rear grip encouraged him to get on the throttle early, which took weight off the front tyre with too much lean angle.

BRYAN STARING Crashed without injury on the second lap.

KAREL ABRAHAM Following de Puniet after a quick start when he lost the front, the result of trying to make up for a bad qualifying in the early laps.

BRIDGESTONE

FRONT SOFT (**S**) / HARD (**H**)

REAR MEDIUM (**M**) / HARD (**H**)

MILD ● ● ● ● ● SEVERE

RED BULL GRAND PRIX OF THE AMERICAS

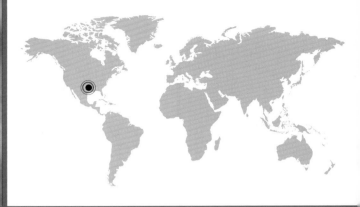

RECORD BREAKER

Marc Marquez won in his second MotoGP race as Honda dominated, but not by the margins expected

No-one can remember a race where the top three were regarded as such cast-iron certainties before anyone turned a wheel. As the highly impressive Circuit of the Americas was a new track for MotoGP there had been a test before the season in which the factory Hondas, the factory Yamahas and Stefan Bradl's LCR team got a couple of days of track time. All the evidence said that the Hondas would have a field day and, as experience didn't come into the equation and Marc Marquez was fastest in the test, the only question was in what order the two factory Hondas would finish.

It didn't seem strange to anybody to be seriously suggesting that 20-year-old Spaniard Marquez, in only his second MotoGP race, was going to win. In fact it seemed like a safe bet, especially to the locals who'd seen him in the test. And sure enough he was quickest in three out of four free practice sessions and then took pole position. This was despite the first session being so cold and the track so green that Bradley Smith reported it was like riding on ice. Conditions were so difficult that by the end of FP1 on Friday there were more than two seconds between fastest man Marquez and Nicky Hayden in fifth, and there were big gaps all down the field.

Practice and qualifying did nothing to dispel the idea that as long as the Hondas stayed on two wheels they would top the rostrum. Jorge Lorenzo, third on the grid, was over a second slower than Marquez. Cal Crutchlow, who'd never seen the circuit before and had his preparation disrupted by a fire in the Tech 3 pit, was a close fourth. The track's three or four first-gear corners, notably the one on to the

ABOVE Dani Pedrosa
won the steep uphill drag
race to the Circuit of the
Americas' first corner

RIGHT Cal Crutchlow
split the factory Yamahas
after passing fast-starting
Stefan Bradl

OPPOSITE It's Texas,
so it must be Stetsons.
Herve Poncharal and the
Tech 3 team go native

very long back straight and the drag out of the last
corner to the uphill hairpin of Turn 1, played to the
strength of the RC213V, with its ability to get the
power down smoothly. By contrast, the run from the
second corner down to the back straight consisted of a
succession of right–left–right corners much like several
of Silverstone's Maggotts–Becketts sections laid end
to end. The Yamahas could keep up with the Hondas
here, but passing was not easy.

As much as the first track of the year, Qatar,
played to the strengths of the Yamahas, this one
favoured the Hondas, so it was no surprise on race
day when the two Hondas were never headed;
indeed Lorenzo stayed in third all race long. What was
surprising was that Jorge finished the race only 3.38s
behind the winner. He had changed tactics for the
race, taking the slowest corners in second gear rather
than first, thus finding the feel and acceleration he
needed at least to keep the Repsol bikes in sight. It
was Jorge's hundredth rostrum, but he couldn't help
but think about what might have happened if he'd
found another tenth or two. He was also fulsome in
his praise of Cal Crutchlow who, in turn, kept Jorge
honest despite running off track while trying to find
a way past Bradl. Cal was pleased to finish only six
seconds behind the winner and well in front of Bradl
and Rossi, who had both tested at COTA. It was
probably a better ride than both his rostrum finishes
in MotoGP.

The mixed fortunes of the Yamaha men were
overshadowed by the achievements of Marc Marquez.
His pole position made him the youngest-ever rider to

'HE IS VERY FAST
AND IT WILL BE
VERY HARD TO
BEAT HIM'
VALENTINO ROSSI

start from pole in the top class, and in the race he put a clean pass on Pedrosa towards the end of the linked ess-bends. Despite Dani fighting back, and being clearly better on the brakes, a mistake three laps from the flag gifted Marc a gap of over a second and the win. Dani said the nature of the circuit meant his arms simply couldn't take the strain any more.

It wasn't just Marquez's riding that impressed, because we had already become accustomed to his elbow-scraping, on-the-edge style. What we hadn't seen before was the mental strength and sheer trust in his own judgement that enabled him to go against both Bridgestone's and his team's advice to use the harder rear tyre. Marc knew it would give him the ability to attack in the closing stages, which he considered his best chance of winning. So the youngster followed his own instincts, tailed Pedrosa for most of the 21 laps, passed him cleanly at a spot where no-one else had managed to overtake and won, setting the fastest lap on the way. The full set, then: pole, the win and that fastest lap, in only his second MotoGP, helped no doubt by the level playing field of a track on which no-one had raced. Any doubts anyone still entertained about Marquez's all-round abilities were well and truly dispelled.

We'd expected the two Hondas and Jorge Lorenzo's Yamaha to finish on the rostrum and that duly transpired, although no-one thought the top three, or Crutchlow, would be so close. What we didn't expect was to see three of Freddie Spencer's 30-year-old records to be beaten in one weekend by a MotoGP rookie.

ABOVE Two Texans not having a good time at home. Ben Spies tore pectoral muscles, Colin Edwards had to pull in

BELOW The race was a head-to-head between the factory Hondas of Dani Pedrosa and Marc Marquez

OPPOSITE Kentuckian Nicky Hayden didn't have a much better time than the Texans, finishing ninth

MARQUEZ REWRITES THE RECORD BOOK

Anyone whose racing memory goes back over 30 years can tell you about the impact the 20-year-old Freddie Spencer made when he arrived in GPs, with Honda's new triple, for the 1982 season. Records he set in his first season survived for 31 years – until Marquez arrived.

The first record went at Qatar, when Marc set the fastest lap in his first MotoGP race. He was 20 years and 49 days old, 112 days younger than Spencer when Freddie set the fastest lap at Misano in the fifth round of the 1982 championship.

Two records went in Texas, youngest pole-setter and youngest winner in the top class. At 20 years and 62 days, when Marc set pole, he beat Freddie by 99 days, and a day later he beat him by 133 days to become the youngest winner. Spencer's pole came at Jarama, Spain, the fourth race of the year, with the win at Spa, Belgium, the seventh race of the '82 season.

Another, even older, record that went to Marquez in Texas was the youngest rider to take back-to-back rostrums in the top class. This time the man he eclipsed was Randy Mamola, who was 134 days older when he finished second at the French GP of 1980, having finished third in Spain the previous week.

The win in Texas also moved Marc to the top of the points table, level with Jorge Lorenzo, which made him the youngest rider ever to lead the top category. The previous holder of that distinction was Lorenzo himself, who was 20 years and 345 days old when he won the 2008 Portuguese GP and led the championship for the first time. The bad news for Jorge, and others, is that Marquez still has plenty of time to break the records for back-to-back poles and race wins.

RED BULL GRAND PRIX OF THE AMERICAS
CIRCUIT OF THE AMERICAS

ROUND 2
April 21

RACE RESULTS

CIRCUIT LENGTH 3.427 miles
NO. OF LAPS 21
RACE DISTANCE 71.967 miles
WEATHER Dry, 23°C
TRACK TEMPERATURE 38°C
WINNER Marc Marquez
FASTEST LAP 2m 04.242s, 99.233mph, Marc Marquez (Record)
LAP RECORD 2m 04.242s, 99.233mph, Marc Marquez, 2013

- **S** SPEED TRAP
- **1** CORNER NUMBER
- **1** GEAR SELECTION/SPEED
- SECTOR 1
- SECTOR 2
- SECTOR 3

QUALIFYING

	Rider	Nation	Motorcycle	Team	Time	Pole +
1	Marquez	SPA	Honda	Repsol Honda Team	2m 03.021s	
2	Pedrosa	SPA	Honda	Repsol Honda Team	2m 03.275s	0.254s
3	Lorenzo	SPA	Yamaha	Yamaha Factory Racing	2m 04.100s	1.079s
4	Crutchlow	GBR	Yamaha	Monster Yamaha Tech 3	2m 04.267s	1.246s
5	Bradl	GER	Honda	LCR Honda MotoGP	2m 04.445s	1.424s
6	Dovizioso	ITA	Ducati	Ducati Team	2m 04.873s	1.852s
7	Bautista	SPA	Honda	GO&FUN Honda Gresini	2m 04.942s	1.921s
8	Rossi	ITA	Yamaha	Yamaha Factory Racing	2m 05.380s	2.359s
9	Espargaro	SPA	ART	Power Electronics Aspar	2m 05.389s	2.368s
10	Hayden	USA	Ducati	Ducati Team	2m 05.568s	2.547s
11	Smith	GBR	Yamaha	Monster Yamaha Tech 3	2m 06.740s	3.719s
12	Spies	USA	Ducati	Ignite Pramac Racing	2m 07.044s	4.023s
13	Iannone	ITA	Ducati	Energy T.I. Pramac Racing	2m 06.872s	Q1
14	De Puniet	FRA	ART	Power Electronics Aspar	2m 07.129s	Q1
15	Barbera	SPA	FTR	Avintia Blusens	2m 07.717s	Q1
16	Hernandez	COL	ART	Paul Bird Motorsport	2m 07.738s	Q1
17	Laverty	GBR	PBM	Paul Bird Motorsport	2m 08.259s	Q1
18	Edwards	USA	FTR Kawasaki	NGM Mobile Forward Racing	2m 08.475s	Q1
19	Corti	ITA	FTR Kawasaki	NGM Mobile Forward Racing	2m 08.792s	Q1
20	Petrucci	ITA	Ioda-Suter	Came IodaRacing Project	2m 08.825s	Q1
21	Aoyama	JPN	FTR	Avintia Blusens	2m 09.062s	Q1
22	Staring	AUS	FTR Honda	GO&FUN Honda Gresini	2m 10.098s	Q1
23	Pesek	CZE	Ioda-Suter	Came IodaRacing Project	2m 10.507s	Q1
24	Young	USA	APR	Attack Performance Racing	2m 10.606s	Q1
25	Abraham	CZE	ART	Cardion AB Motoracing	2m 23.317s	Q1

FINISHERS

1 MARC MARQUEZ Youngest-ever pole-sitter and winner of a 500cc/MotoGP race, breaking Freddie Spencer's 30-year-old records – and at only his second attempt. Insisted on using the harder rear tyre, against advice, and used it perfectly to stay with Pedrosa until nine laps from the end when he overtook at Turn 7.

2 DANI PEDROSA Led until Marquez came past at two-thirds distance and then stayed with his team-mate. Dani looked stronger on the brakes but a mistake lost him over 1.5 seconds, after which there was no way back.

3 JORGE LORENZO Much closer to the Hondas than anticipated, taking his 100th GP podium. Did everything that could be expected of him but couldn't find the tenth or two he needed. The big improvement came in warm-up when he started taking the first-gear corners in second and found much better drive on to the straights.

4 CAL CRUTCHLOW Probably his best race to date. No testing, the garage fire, running off track while dicing with Bradl which dropped him to seventh, yet still fourth and closing on Lorenzo in the final laps.

5 STEFAN BRADL Second after a great start but again a little wary of the front end with a full tank, so not as aggressive as some others in the early laps. Reckoned fifth was where he expected to finish, which sounded a little defeatist given the fact he did pre-season testing here.

6 VALENTINO ROSSI Doesn't seem to like new tracks, and he never looked comfortable in Texas. Reported vibration in the race from a brake problem, but on walking back into the garage he was miming tucking the front. Not happy.

7 ANDREA DOVIZIOSO Seventh again after a last-corner pass on Bautista, but as in Qatar there were signs of hope. Lap times did not drop off as expected and Dovi was much closer to the leaders for the whole race.

8 ALVARO BAUTISTA Expected to improve on his practice times but didn't. Lost ground after a good start as he again struggled for feeling, and confidence, from the front. Dropped back to the second group, then lost out to Dovizioso after a late charge made up two seconds.

9 NICKY HAYDEN A tough weekend. Lacked confidence in the front when changing direction – that old Ducati understeer problem – which really hurt through the long Esses section.

10 ANDREA IANNONE Faster at the start of the race than in qualifying, even heading Hayden for a while, then ran into arm-pump problems as he had in Qatar.

11 ALEIX ESPARGARO Top CRT again and in front of two prototypes, as well as 30 seconds in front of his team-mate. Another dominant performance.

12 BRADLEY SMITH Did exactly what was required after the team's difficult start to the weekend. Ran the harder front tyre on Bridgestone's advice and steadily increased his pace as he took time to understand it. Faster on the penultimate lap than in qualifying.

13 BEN SPIES Suffered acute pains in his chest in warm-up, probably due to a trapped nerve and related to his still-recuperating shoulder. Raced after treatment but was exhausted eight laps from the flag.

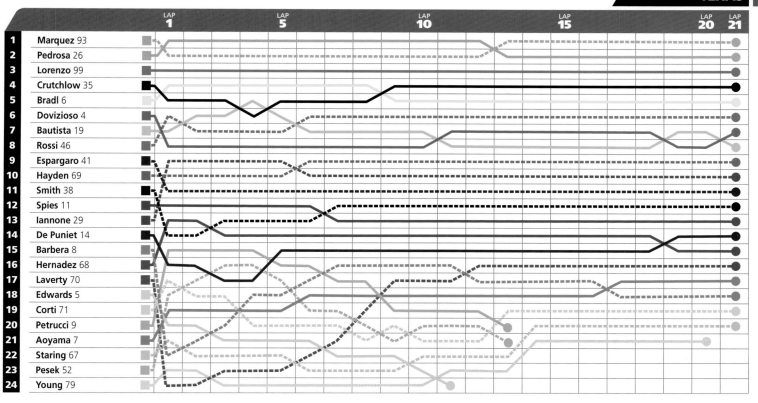

		LAP 1	LAP 5	LAP 10	LAP 15	LAP 20	LAP 21
1	Marquez 93						
2	Pedrosa 26						
3	Lorenzo 99						
4	Crutchlow 35						
5	Bradl 6						
6	Dovizioso 4						
7	Bautista 19						
8	Rossi 46						
9	Espargaro 41						
10	Hayden 69						
11	Smith 38						
12	Spies 11						
13	Iannone 29						
14	De Puniet 14						
15	Barbera 8						
16	Hernandez 68						
17	Laverty 70						
18	Edwards 5						
19	Corti 71						
20	Petrucci 9						
21	Aoyama 7						
22	Staring 67						
23	Pesek 52						
24	Young 79						

RACE

	Rider	Motorcycle	Race Time	Time +	Fastest Lap	Avg. Speed	B
1	Marquez	Honda	43m 42.123s		2m 04.242s	98.736mph	M/H
2	Pedrosa	Honda	43m 43.657s	1.534s	2m 04.303s	98.674mph	M/M
3	Lorenzo	Yamaha	43m 45.504s	3.381s	2m 04.470s	98.612mph	M/M
4	Crutchlow	Yamaha	43m 48.739s	6.616s	2m 04.615s	98.487mph	M/M
5	Bradl	Honda	43m 54.797s	12.674s	2m 04.725s	98.239mph	M/H
6	Rossi	Yamaha	43m 58.738s	16.615s	2m 04.797s	98.115mph	M/M
7	Dovizioso	Ducati	44m 04.497s	22.374s	2m 05.146s	97.928mph	M/M
8	Bautista	Honda	44m 04.977s	22.854s	2m 05.038s	97.866mph	M/M
9	Hayden	Ducati	44m 15.896s	33.773s	2m 05.787s	97.493mph	M/M
10	Iannone	Ducati	44m 24.235s	42.112s	2m 05.422s	97.182mph	M/M
11	Espargaro	ART	44m 30.960s	48.837s	2m 06.562s	96.934mph	M/S
12	Smith	Yamaha	44m 32.828s	50.705s	2m 06.415s	96.872mph	S/M
13	Spies	Ducati	44m 56.255s	1m 14.132s	2m 06.607s	96.002mph	S/M
14	De Puniet	ART	44m 57.774s	1m 15.651s	2m 07.211s	95.940mph	M/S
15	Hernandez	ART	45m 01.714s	1m 19.591s	2m 07.456s	95.815mph	M/S
16	Laverty	PBM	45m 16.514s	1m 34.391s	2m 08.044s	95.318mph	M/S
17	Aoyama	FTR	45m 21.946s	1m 39.823s	2m 08.426s	95.132mph	M/S
18	Barbera	FTR	45m 22.075s	1m 39.952s	2m 07.796s	95.132mph	M/S
19	Corti	FTR Kawasaki	45m 28.896s	1m 46.773s	2m 08.996s	94.883mph	S/S
20	Staring	FTR Honda	45m 30.207s	1m 48.084s	2m 09.112s	94.821mph	M/S
21	Young	APR	43m 46.367s	1 Lap	2m 09.953s	93.889mph	M/S
NF	Petrucci	Ioda-Suter	28m 11.943s	8 Laps	2m 09.420s	94.697mph	S/S
NF	Pesek	Ioda-Suter	28m 12.358s	8 Laps	2m 09.140s	94.697mph	S/S
NF	Edwards	FTR Kawasaki	24m 18.297s	10 Laps	2m 09.169s	93.019mph	M/S

CHAMPIONSHIP

	Rider	Nation	Team	Points
1	Marquez	SPA	Repsol Honda Team	41
2	Lorenzo	SPA	Yamaha Factory Racing	41
3	Pedrosa	SPA	Repsol Honda Team	33
4	Rossi	ITA	Yamaha Factory Racing	30
5	Crutchlow	GBR	Monster Yamaha Tech 3	24
6	Bautista	SPA	GO&FUN Honda Gresini	18
7	Dovizioso	ITA	Ducati Team	18
8	Hayden	USA	Ducati Team	15
9	Iannone	ITA	Energy T.I. Pramac Racing	13
10	Bradl	GER	LCR Honda MotoGP	11
11	Espargaro	SPA	Power Electronics Aspar	10
12	Spies	USA	Ignite Pramac Racing	9
13	De Puniet	FRA	Power Electronics Aspar	6
14	Smith	GBR	Monster Yamaha Tech 3	4
15	Barbera	SPA	Avintia Blusens	3
16	Hernandez	COL	Paul Bird Motorsport	3
17	Aoyama	JPN	Avintia Blusens	1

14 RANDY DE PUNIET Still not confident in the front and lost ground in the early laps when he braked almost to a standstill avoiding a collision. That put him in a five-bike group from which he escaped and caught Hernandez.

15 YONNY HERNANDEZ Impressively fast in the first half of the race when he mixed it up with Spies and Smith, after making up three places off the start, but later slowed with tyre wear.

16 MICHAEL LAVERTY Achieved his objective of beating the FTR Kawasakis, despite an off-track excursion. Impressive work from both the rider and the team's rapidly developing PBM machine.

17 HIROSHI AOYAMA Started well but ran into chatter. Hiro said the result didn't feel too bad after all the problems the team had suffered over the weekend.

18 HECTOR BARBERA Very disappointed. Suffered an array of problems, but specifically a slipping clutch and vicious chatter from the third lap onwards.

19 CLAUDIO CORTI Like his team-mate, Claudio suffered from set-up problems attributable to a total lack of testing time.

20 BRYAN STARING Happy to finish a MotoGP race for the first time and to get in much-needed track time. Improved on his qualifying time in the race.

21 BLAKE YOUNG Wild-card entry on the Attack Performance bike, a heavily modified Kawasaki motor in the team's own chassis. Qualified and finished with few dramas, as they did at Indianapolis in 2012 with rider Steve Rapp.

NON-FINISHERS

DANILO PETRUCCI Going well when the engine suddenly cut out and, to make matters worse, his team-mate hit him and fell.

LUKAS PESEK Fell when he tagged his team-mate's bike after its engine cut out. Not a lucky day for Ioda Racing.

COLIN EDWARDS Pulled in at half-distance with a catalogue of technical issues. The drive-train problem from Qatar reappeared and he also found chatter on Sunday morning. Not how Colin would have wanted to celebrate a GP in his home state.

NON-STARTERS

KAREL ABRAHAM Broke his right collarbone when he crashed with Staring after an ill-advised move in qualifying.

MIKE BARNES Wild-card entry on a Suzuki-engined BCL, but did not qualify.

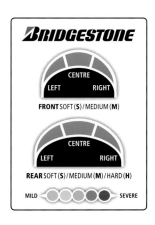

BRIDGESTONE

CENTRE
LEFT RIGHT
FRONT SOFT (**S**) / MEDIUM (**M**)

CENTRE
LEFT RIGHT
REAR SOFT (**S**) / MEDIUM (**M**) / HARD (**H**)

MILD — SEVERE

GRAN PREMIO bwin DE ESPAÑA

COLLISION COURSE

Pedrosa reminded everyone he was a contender, but the only topic of conversation was the last-corner pass Marquez made on Lorenzo

For a country that's supposed to be on its knees financially, Spain's motorcycle racing is in pretty rude health. All the front-row starters in MotoGP, plus the pole-men in Moto2 and Moto3, were Spanish, as were all the rostrum finishers in MotoGP and the winners of the two smaller classes. And for the first time in a few years the atmosphere at Jerez was back. By Saturday the grandstands and hillsides were well populated with noisy flag-waving fans, most of whom seemed to have come to see Marc Marquez.

The big question over Marc's race was whether the experience of the opposition on the upcoming run of European tracks would be enough to counter his blazing speed. And how would his still-loose riding style serve him on the interlinked corners of Jerez? Another question concerned Valentino Rossi, and was something he himself had mentioned in Qatar: how would he fare now that the series had returned to the circuits where he grew up? Historically, Jerez is one of his best tracks, with six top-class wins and three more podium finishes since 2000.

On Saturday Marquez was one of several notable crashers, although he nearly saved it – much to the admiration of Cal Crutchlow, who was following closely. Marquez's crash was a gentle spin-out, but Cal then had two enormous crashes, with Rossi and Pedrosa also suffering one each. Even Colin Edwards fell off. The Jerez tarmac changes character radically when it heats up and loses grip in the afternoon. Not ideal, especially if the team has just slapped on a new soft rear slick and the rider has his mind focused on the front row. Rossi's fifth place in qualifying started tongues wagging. His failure to make the front row could no longer be put down to a mere dislike of the new qualifying system.

ABOVE Aleix Espargaro listens to team owner Aspar Martinez before finishing inside the top ten and keeping his run of CRT wins going

BELOW Yonny Hernandez didn't make it three points-scoring rides in a row

OPPOSITE The last-corner incident. You could overlay the Rossi–Gibernau clash of 2005 and there would be practically no difference

Given Cal Crutchlow's form, could this have been his race? He was fastest in the third free practice session and closing in on a front-row start, but then it all went wrong. On the other hand, Stefan Bradl looked like he was in for humiliation when he had to go into first qualifying, from which he then escaped and nailed eighth place on the grid. It was a total turnaround in fortunes for the two.

Cal was well beaten up, with blood on a kidney, and like most of the rest of the riders was not enamoured of the tyres selected for this event. The harder front option was still too soft and it was impossible to use the harder rear, according to the dissidents, although Jorge Lorenzo continued to confound his opposition by using angles of lean that, if replicated by lesser beings, cause them to fall instantly. Saturday was his 26th birthday, so they named the last corner after him.

As in qualifying, track temperature played a major part in the race. The Hondas got the extra heat they needed for grip, and the Yamahas lost the edge grip they required. Dani Pedrosa won and won splendidly, dealing with an early charge from Lorenzo, then pulling away. However, no-one was talking about the win because Marc Marquez and Jorge Lorenzo re-enacted the infamous 2005 Rossi–Gibernau last-corner encounter, with Marc playing the part of Rossi.

It was a carbon copy of that incident. Lorenzo stayed wide on the last corner, inviting a charge up the inside. Marquez accepted the invitation and they touched mid-corner, although without consequences quite as dramatic as eight years previously. Jorge was relegated to a disgruntled third, however, and refused to shake hands with Marquez in parc fermé or to clink champagne bottles on the rostrum, each refusal being accompanied

'I THINK THAT THE END OF THE RACE WAS REALLY GOOD FOR THE FANS'
MARC MARQUEZ

by a magisterial wag of the forefinger. Marquez turned away and smirked at his crew. In truth, Jorge must have been annoyed at himself. Marquez had tried a charge at the corner at the end of the back straight on the last lap and run wide, Jorge had thought the challenge ended there and didn't try and close the door at the final corner – with the inevitable result.

It looked at first as if Lorenzo was waiting for the inevitable lunge and was going to let Marc go through and overshoot, but as soon as Marquez appeared instinct took over and he tried to block him. If Jorge had resisted the temptation he might very well have been able simply to drive underneath the Honda and take second. HRC team-manager Livio Suppo thought so too, and offered another interesting observation: Casey Stoner would never have made a move like that.

Jorge then refused to answer questions about the incident in the post-race press conference while Marc managed to portray himself as the soul of reason, saying it was natural to be 'warm' if you were on the wrong end of something like that and equally natural to be extremely happy about getting the other end of the stick. Nobody thought it was a good idea to remind Lorenzo that it all happened at the corner that had been named after him the previous day. Dramas aside, the result put all three Spaniards just four points apart at the top of the table, with Marquez top by three points.

A straw poll showed the vast majority of riders didn't think Marquez had a case to answer, and although Race Direction did look at the incident they too decided that no action should be taken, and everyone began to forget about it. Except Jorge Lorenzo.

ABOVE Danilo Petrucci opened his and the Ioda team's account with 14th place

BELOW Jorge Lorenzo makes his feelings very clear in parc fermé; no handshake, just finger wagging

OPPOSITE Bradley Smith on his way to the first top-ten finish of his MotoGP career

POINTS ON THE LICENCE

Race Direction has a new structure of penalty points at its disposal this season. Previously, any disciplinary action has been somewhat ad hoc, with no-one entirely sure why a penalty has been given. When Marc Marquez ran into Ratthapark Wilairot in practice at Phillip Island in 2011 he was sent to the back of the grid; when John Hopkins skittled the pack at Motegi's first corner in 2003 he was banned for a race, as was Jorge Lorenzo for knocking Alex de Angelis off in 2005. There was no transparency, no scale of penalties and no indication of whether a verdict had been reached by 'totting up', namely taking previous indiscretions into account.

The new system for 2013 gave Race Direction the power to dish out between one and ten penalty points, in addition to any other penalty. Points would be totted up throughout the season and when the four-, seven- and ten-point thresholds were reached automatic penalties would be applied. Four points meant starting the next race from the back of the grid, seven meant starting from pit lane, and ten would mean exclusion from the next race. Points will not be carried over to the following season, and the slate will be wiped clean after ten points are accumulated.

The Grand Prix Commission's announcement of the new system mentioned the need to deal with repeat offenders but so far, despite serious temptation, Race Direction has resisted the temptation to apply its new sanction. Given Nicky Hayden's observation that the guys in the top class shouldn't need this sort of treatment, an opinion shared by his fellow MotoGP men, who would get the first points on their licence? There would be very few complaints if efforts were made to stop some of the scary behaviour of riders in qualifying for Moto2 and Moto3, loitering on-line and looking for a tow.

GRAN PREMIO bwin DE ESPAÑA
CIRCUITO DE JEREZ

ROUND 3
May 5

Expo-92
60mph

165mph

Alex Criville
100mph

Ferrari
110mph

Peluqui
70mph

Jorge Martinez Aspar

Michelin
95mph

Angel Nieto
80mph

80mph

100mph

95mph

Ducados
45mph

Dry Sack
45mph

Sito Pons
80mph

170mph

- **S** SPEED TRAP
- **1** CORNER NUMBER
- **1** GEAR SELECTION/SPEED
- SECTOR 1
- SECTOR 2
- SECTOR 3

RACE RESULTS

CIRCUIT LENGTH 2.748miles

NO. OF LAPS 27

RACE DISTANCE 74.205 miles

WEATHER Dry, 27°C

TRACK TEMPERATURE 47°C

WINNER Dani Pedrosa

FASTEST LAP 1m 39.565s, 99.357mph, Jorge Lorenzo (Record)

PREVIOUS LAP RECORD 1m 39.731s, 99.171mph, Dani Pedrosa, 2010

QUALIFYING

	Rider	Nation	Motorcycle	Team	Time	Pole +
1	Lorenzo	SPA	Yamaha	Yamaha Factory Racing	1m 38.673s	
2	Pedrosa	SPA	Honda	Repsol Honda Team	1m 38.920s	0.247s
3	Marquez	SPA	Honda	Repsol Honda Team	1m 38.971s	0.298s
4	Crutchlow	GBR	Yamaha	Monster Yamaha Tech 3	1m 39.262s	0.589s
5	Rossi	ITA	Yamaha	Yamaha Factory Racing	1m 39.300s	0.627s
6	Bautista	SPA	Honda	GO&FUN Honda Gresini	1m 39.509s	0.836s
7	Hayden	USA	Ducati	Ducati Team	1m 39.654s	0.981s
8	Bradl	GER	Honda	LCR Honda MotoGP	1m 39.847s	1.174s
9	Dovizioso	ITA	Ducati	Ducati Team	1m 39.848s	1.175s
10	Barbera	SPA	FTR	Avintia Blusens	1m 39.980s	1.307s
11	Iannone	ITA	Ducati	Energy T.I. Pramac Racing	1m 40.087s	1.414s
12	Smith	GBR	Yamaha	Monster Yamaha Tech 3	1m 40.356s	1.683s
13	Espargaro	SPA	ART	Power Electronics Aspar	1m 40.085s	Q1
14	Pirro	ITA	Ducati	Ducati Test Team	1m 40.182s	Q1
15	De Puniet	FRA	ART	Power Electronics Aspar	1m 40.466s	Q1
16	Aoyama	JPN	FTR	Avintia Blusens	1m 40.654s	Q1
17	Petrucci	ITA	Ioda-Suter	Came IodaRacing Project	1m 40.852s	Q1
18	Staring	AUS	FTR Honda	GO&FUN Honda Gresini	1m 41.324s	Q1
19	Corti	ITA	FTR Kawasaki	NGM Mobile Forward Racing	1m 41.513s	Q1
20	Edwards	USA	FTR Kawasaki	NGM Mobile Forward Racing	1m 41.536s	Q1
21	Hernandez	COL	ART	Paul Bird Motorsport	1m 41.779s	Q1
22	Laverty	GBR	PBM	Paul Bird Motorsport	1m 41.935s	Q1
23	Pesek	CZE	Ioda-Suter	Came IodaRacing Project	1m 43.220s	Q1
24	Abraham	CZE	ART	Cardion AB Motoracing		Q1

FINISHERS

1 DANI PEDROSA Reminded everyone that he is not to be overlooked by taking a well-crafted victory. Had to push past Lorenzo early on, then built a lead despite describing the tyres as being on the limit and therefore having to ride carefully. Able to control the gap late on in what he called 'a beautiful race'.

2 MARC MARQUEZ Shadowed Lorenzo for most of the race, making the occasional lurid lunge on the brakes at the end of the back straight. Saved it for the last corner when he dived into a big gap and punted Jorge out of the way, just as

Rossi did to Gibernau in 2005. Apologised for the 'racing incident', but displayed no contrition whatsoever.

3 JORGE LORENZO Very upset by Marquez's last-corner move but in reality annoyed with himself for thinking the challenge was over before the last corner, so didn't cover the inside move. The heat on race day compromised the edge grip he needs to ride as he wants, with massive lean angles and corner speed.

4 VALENTINO ROSSI Fifth in qualifying was his best in two years, but worryingly just off the pace of the top three both in practice and the race, at a track he loves. The main problem was balance, which

meant he couldn't push early in the race, but was able to run the same pace as the leaders late on.

5 CAL CRUTCHLOW Lucky to be able to race after two heavy crashes on Saturday. Had looked a genuine rostrum candidate until then, and on Sunday fought off a spirited challenge from Bautista to claim a solid fifth place and again be the leading satellite team rider.

6 ALVARO BAUTISTA Once more rear-grip problems compromised his race, as did a bad start. Recovered to give Crutchlow a good fight for fifth until the bike started moving around on worn tyres.

7 NICKY HAYDEN Arrived with his right hand and wrist badly swollen, for unknown reasons. Put together a good race but lost touch with Crutchlow and Bautista when Bradl crashed, then gritted his teeth to come home top Ducati.

8 ANDREA DOVIZIOSO Knew it was going to be a tough weekend, but it was worse than he'd expected. The front tyre was the main problem, but Dovi said he didn't ride well, unlike his team-mate.

9 ALEIX ESPARGARO Made up for being outqualified by Barbera with another brilliant race to top CRT position. Got in front of Dovizioso a couple of times and finished sliding wildly on destroyed tyres.

10 BRADLEY SMITH Another learning experience, this time how to ride the M1 in low-grip conditions. Cautious in qualifying but rode across a gap in the race to join the dice for eighth place.

11 MICHELE PIRRO Rode as a wild card, not as a replacement for Spies, and therefore used his own engines, not those allocated to the American. Raced the 'lab bike' that Dovizioso rode on the last day of the pre-season test in Malaysia but with a very different frame from the team bikes plus engine-management upgrades.

12 HECTOR BARBERA Qualified superbly as top CRT but again suffered from lack of grip, this time on the brakes.

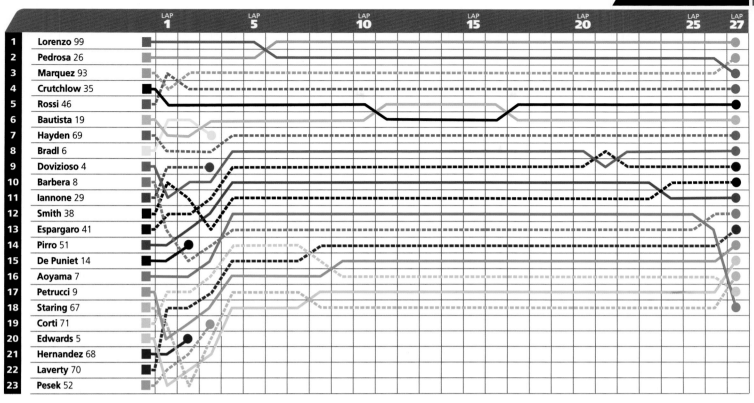

		LAP 1	LAP 5	LAP 10	LAP 15	LAP 20	LAP 25	LAP 27
1	Lorenzo 99							
2	Pedrosa 26							
3	Marquez 93							
4	Crutchlow 35							
5	Rossi 46							
6	Bautista 19							
7	Hayden 69							
8	Bradl 6							
9	Dovizioso 4							
10	Barbera 8							
11	Iannone 29							
12	Smith 38							
13	Espargaro 41							
14	Pirro 51							
15	De Puniet 14							
16	Aoyama 7							
17	Petrucci 9							
18	Staring 67							
19	Corti 71							
20	Edwards 5							
21	Hernandez 68							
22	Laverty 70							
23	Pesek 52							

RACE

	Rider	Motorcycle	Race Time	Time +	Fastest Lap	Avg. Speed	B
1	Pedrosa	Honda	45m 17.632s		1m 39.671s	98.239mph	M/S
2	Marquez	Honda	45m 20.119s	2.487s	1m 39.765s	98.177mph	M/S
3	Lorenzo	Yamaha	45m 22.721s	5.089s	1m 39.565s	98.052mph	M/S
4	Rossi	Yamaha	45m 26.546s	8.914s	1m 39.994s	97.928mph	M/S
5	Crutchlow	Yamaha	45m 30.295s	12.663s	1m 40.247s	97.804mph	M/S
6	Bautista	Honda	45m 32.726s	15.094s	1m 40.342s	97.742mph	M/S
7	Hayden	Ducati	45m 43.264s	25.632s	1m 40.484s	97.369mph	M/S
8	Dovizioso	Ducati	45m 59.513s	41.881s	1m 41.041s	96.747mph	M/S
9	Espargaro	ART	46m 01.444s	43.812s	1m 41.335s	96.685mph	M/XS
10	Smith	Yamaha	46m 02.093s	44.461s	1m 41.443s	96.685mph	M/S
11	Pirro	Ducati	46m 03.606s	45.974s	1m 41.165s	96.623mph	M/S
12	Barbera	FTR	46m 17.491s	59.859s	1m 41.593s	96.126mph	M/XS
13	Laverty	PBM	46m 27.375s	1m 09.743s	1m 42.293s	95.815mph	M/XS
14	Petrucci	Ioda-Suter	46m 35.445s	1m 17.813s	1m 42.522s	95.505mph	M/XS
15	Edwards	FTR Kawasaki	46m 35.809s	1m 18.177s	1m 42.072s	95.505mph	M/XS
16	Staring	FTR Honda	46m 36.560s	1m 18.928s	1m 42.260s	95.505mph	M/XS
17	Corti	FTR Kawasaki	46m 36.939s	1m 19.307s	1m 42.249s	95.505mph	M/XS
18	Aoyama	FTR	46m 37.089s	1m 19.457s	1m 41.439s	95.505mph	M/XS
NF	Bradl	Honda	5m 07.945s	24 Laps	1m 40.738s	96.375mph	M/S
NF	Iannone	Ducati	5m 09.445s	24 Laps	1m 40.642s	95.878mph	M/S
NF	Pesek	Ioda-Suter	5m 16.707s	24 Laps	1m 42.599s	93.703mph	M/XS
NF	De Puniet	ART	3m 30.575s	25 Laps	1m 41.575s	93.951mph	M/XS
NF	Hernandez	ART	3m 33.793s	25 Laps	1m 42.831s	92.522mph	M/XS

CHAMPIONSHIP

	Rider	Nation	Team	Points
1	Marquez	SPA	Repsol Honda Team	61
2	Pedrosa	SPA	Repsol Honda Team	58
3	Lorenzo	SPA	Yamaha Factory Racing	57
4	Rossi	ITA	Yamaha Factory Racing	43
5	Crutchlow	GBR	Monster Yamaha Tech 3	35
6	Bautista	SPA	GO&FUN Honda Gresini	28
7	Dovizioso	ITA	Ducati Team	26
8	Hayden	USA	Ducati Team	24
9	Espargaro	SPA	Power Electronics Aspar	17
10	Iannone	ITA	Energy T.I. Pramac Racing	13
11	Bradl	GER	LCR Honda MotoGP	11
12	Smith	GBR	Monster Yamaha Tech 3	10
13	Spies	USA	Ignite Pramac Racing	9
14	Barbera	SPA	Avintia Blusens	7
15	De Puniet	FRA	Power Electronics Aspar	6
16	Pirro	ITA	Ducati Test Team	5
17	Laverty	GBR	Paul Bird Motorsport	3
18	Hernandez	COL	Paul Bird Motorsport	3
19	Petrucci	ITA	Came IodaRacing Project	2
20	Edwards	USA	NGM Mobile Forward Racing	1
21	Aoyama	JPN	Avintia Blusens	1

13 MICHAEL LAVERTY The first points for both Laverty in the riders' championship and the Paul Bird team in the constructors' championship: impressive stuff from the tiny British team and its rookie rider.

14 DANILO PETRUCCI Delighted to score his and the Ioda team's first points of the season, not least because he could now shave (he had sworn to grow his beard until he finished in the top 15).

15 COLIN EDWARDS Overtook Corti, and benefited from Aoyama's problems on the last lap to score his first point of the season.

16 BRYAN STARING Only 0.7s away from his first World Championship point and part of an entertaining four-man dice for the latter part of the race, after making up for a slow start.

17 CLAUDIO CORTI Enjoyed fighting with Petrucci for most of the race, but not the way the rear tyre chattered after a few laps or the fact that the identical Avintia team bikes were a second a lap quicker.

18 HIROSHI AOYAMA A much better weekend than his finishing position suggests. Found the confidence in the front he'd been looking for and was right behind his team-mate on the last lap when he ran off track, losing six places.

NON-FINISHERS

STEFAN BRADL Crashed because he couldn't push the front, a recurrence of the problem that had been dogging him all season and a good deal of the last one as well.

ANDREA IANNONE Rode with staples in a knee wound after a nasty qualifying crash, then crashed again in the race. Went straight to hospital for an operation to relieve the arm pump that's been troubling him all season.

LUKAS PESEK One of three CRT riders who lost the front early in the race.

RANDY DE PUNIET Crashed at the Angel Nieto corner early on when he released the brake. Tried to smooth his riding out, but the heat made conditions for the front tyre very difficult.

YONNY HERNANDEZ Never happy with the front end and crashed out early.

NON-STARTERS

KAREL ABRAHAM Rode on Friday but had to cry off because of his collarbone injury from the previous round.

BEN SPIES Pulled out after America to give his shoulder more time to heal.

BRIDGESTONE

CENTRE
LEFT   RIGHT

FRONT EXTRA-SOFT (**XS**) / SOFT (**S**)

CENTRE
LEFT   RIGHT

REAR EXTRA-SOFT (**XS**) / SOFT (**S**) / MEDIUM (**M**)

MILD ───────── SEVERE

MONSTER ENERGY
GRAND PRIX DE FRANCE

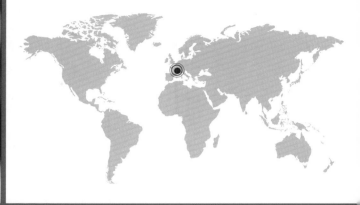

PEDROSA AT THE DOUBLE

Wet weather produced an entertaining race but didn't stop Dani Pedrosa making it two wins in a row

Le Mans certainly lived up to its reputation for drama. The winner had a couple of near-misses, the World Champion had a nightmare followed by an argument, the Brit with Grit had a career best, the wonder kid walked on water, and Ducati didn't know whether to laugh or cry.

Repsol Honda put two bikes on the rostrum for the third race in a row, with Dani Pedrosa making it two consecutive wins, against a background of dissent in the Yamaha camp. Andrea Dovizioso, who again cheered up Ducati folk by leading for much of the race as well as starting off the front row, was adamant: it was nothing to do with the Honda or the Ducati; it was all down to Pedrosa. The only reason he'd led so much, said Andrea, was that Dani ran on a couple of times. Dovi was delighted with the Ducati's traction and, for a man who was only deprived of a rostrum in the final laps, surprisingly upbeat. His team-mate Nicky Hayden wasn't overjoyed with his own best finish of the year so far, however, having lost touch with the podium group when Rossi crashed in front of him and he was forced to go wide taking avoiding action. As getting past Rossi is never an easy task, Nicky was waiting to make a clean pass rather than losing time with a lunge. Would he have been pleased with the team's fourth- and fifth-place finishes on Thursday? In the dry, of course he would, but Hayden remained resolutely unthrilled with them in the wet. But, as was becoming routine, there were now reasons to smile in Bologna.

It could have been worse for the factory Ducati men; they could have had a day like the factory Yamahas. Rossi really did look like he was on for the sort of result we might expect from him in wet conditions

ABOVE Cal Crutchlow got a grid visit from F1 ace Lewis Hamilton

RIGHT Yes, that is a Ducati at the front. Andrea Dovizioso took advantage of the conditions but just missed out on a rostrum finish

OPPOSITE The traditional we're-great-friends-really photo opportunity that always follows a controversial incident, in this case the last corner at Jerez

on this track, but a bump at Garage Vert put him on the ground. However, his problems with qualifying still remain and no-one in the team can explain them. Jorge Lorenzo had a horrible race, yet still managed to beat his team-mate. He pointed the finger at the rear tyre afterwards, which didn't amuse Bridgestone. They countered that his lap times at the end of the race were as fast as anyone's out there. Other riders mentioned Jorge's crash helmet: they reported that he was slapping it as early as lap three. It was left to Cal Crutchlow to fly the Yamaha flag, despite suffering his third big crash in two weeks on Saturday when he had the unpleasant experience of seeing blood on the inside of his visor. On Sunday, with a crack in the top of his shin bone, he posted his career-best MotoGP result – second place – making him top Yamaha and, again, top satellite bike rider by some distance. All that, and the visiting Lewis Hamilton invited him to an F1 race as well.

Cal's worst moment in the race, he said, was seeing the name Marquez appear on his pit board. Fortunately for him, pole-man Marquez made nearly as big a mess of the race start as he did of his first-ever wet-weather MotoGP warm-up, when he managed to spin the Honda through 180 degrees. In the front-row press conference he explained with a straight face that it 'takes time' to get up to speed with the RCV at new tracks. In Marc Marquez-land, two days is obviously a long time, although his qualifying did include a crash that meant he set pole on his second bike. At the start of the race Marc got it rolling OK, assumed he'd done the difficult bit and gassed it. The bike fishtailed spectacularly as he struggled to get both feet back on the pegs,

'AN IMPORTANT VICTORY, I'VE BEEN TRYING TO WIN AT THIS CIRCUIT FOR MANY YEARS IN MOTOGP'

DANI PEDROSA

which meant he spent the rest of the race catching up, although he did it in a spectacular fashion that included a high-speed run-on at the Dunlop chicane. He stayed upright, however, and continued his run of rostrum finishes. His wet-weather experience on the V4 before this race totalled an hour at Jerez on a tyre that was shot after three laps. Amazingly, the young man had the nous to settle for third, despite closing on second place. Cal was fast, Marc said, and he himself was on or over the limit. It looks like he really does have everything, doesn't it?

Amid the chaos and the crashes it was easy to overlook what Dani Pedrosa achieved this weekend. In the past he's always qualified well at Le Mans – four poles – but had problems on race day. This time he qualified badly – he crashed and had to use his second bike – but he raced perfectly, although as Dovizioso noted he was willing to take chances. Dani had now taken back-to-back race wins on tracks that were supposed to favour the Yamaha with a pair of almost perfect races, neither of which were the lone runaways in which he used to specialise.

Over at Yamaha there was a distinct lack of harmony. Lorenzo commented after qualifying that he did the best he could 'with the bike I have', Rossi was muttering about corner entry, and Crutchlow continued to make undiplomatic remarks about his future with or without Yamaha. Meanwhile, Honda's factory riders were still managing to be civil about each other. Marquez continued his jaw-dropping progress and Pedrosa did everything right. For a bloke who didn't like a fight and couldn't race in the wet, Dani was doing rather well.

JEAN-CLAUDE OLIVIER, 1945–2013

The factory Yamahas of Lorenzo and Rossi carried a discreet little tribute to one of the greats of French motorcycling. It said: 'In memory of JCO.'

Jean-Claude Olivier was the driving force behind Yamaha in France for over 40 years. He started sweeping warehouse floors for Sonauto, the French Porsche importer. When the company took on Yamaha he then criss-crossed the country in a van to show potential dealers the four-bike range. This was in 1965; he sold one hundred bikes. Three years later the figure was one thousand. When the AT-1 trail bike arrived he contrived to have Brigitte Bardot photographed on one. He'd recognised that these made-for-the-States trail bikes would suit the French market perfectly and he was right.

JCO wasn't just an intuitive business brain, however; he was also an accomplished rider. He raced in the Bol d'Or in 1969 on a 250 Yamaha and rode the Le Touquet enduro 25 times, finishing in the top 20 on 15 occasions. Most famously, he raced in the Paris–Dakar nine times, once on a four-cylinder FZ750-engined monster. In 1985 he finished second, behind Gaston Rahier.

JCO's relationship with Japan was such that in 1990, when Yamaha Motor France was formed, he continued as managing director. Under his guidance Yamaha was present in both on- and off-road racing for he believed passionately in competition, 'the engine of progress', with YMF taking Patrick Pons, Christian Sarron, Stéphane Peterhansel and others to the top. Olivier left Yamaha in 2010, after working for them for 45 years.

OPPOSITE TOP Dovizioso lost out when the track dried and the old Ducati problems resurfaced

OPPOSITE BOTTOM Rossi crashed and remounted, finishing 12th on a track where he had been on the rostrum for the last two years

BELOW Differing fortunes for the Aspar Aprilias; de Puniet led the class but crashed, Espargaro won again

MONSTER ENERGY GRAND PRIX DE FRANCE
LE MANS

ROUND 4
May 19

RACE RESULTS

CIRCUIT LENGTH 2.597 miles
NO. OF LAPS 28
RACE DISTANCE 72.812 miles
WEATHER Wet, 12°C
TRACK TEMPERATURE 18°C
WINNER Dani Pedrosa
FASTEST LAP 1m 43.597s, 90.347mph, Dani Pedrosa
LAP RECORD 1m 33.617s, 99.979mph, Dani Pedrosa, 2011

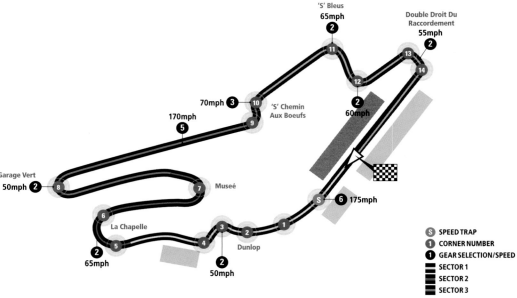

'S' Bleus 65mph

Double Droit Du Raccordement 55mph

'S' Chemin Aux Boeufs

70mph 60mph

170mph

Garage Vert 50mph

Museé

175mph

La Chapelle

Dunlop

65mph

50mph

S SPEED TRAP
1 CORNER NUMBER
1 GEAR SELECTION/SPEED
SECTOR 1
SECTOR 2
SECTOR 3

QUALIFYING

	Rider	Nation	Motorcycle	Team	Time	Pole +
1	Marquez	SPA	Honda	Repsol Honda Team	1m 33.187s	
2	Lorenzo	SPA	Yamaha	Yamaha Factory Racing	1m 33.217s	0.030s
3	Dovizioso	ITA	Ducati	Ducati Team	1m 33.603s	0.416s
4	Crutchlow	GBR	Yamaha	Monster Yamaha Tech 3	1m 33.609s	0.422s
5	Bradl	GER	Honda	LCR Honda MotoGP	1m 33.634s	0.447s
6	Pedrosa	SPA	Honda	Repsol Honda Team	1m 33.639s	0.452s
7	Bautista	SPA	Honda	GO&FUN Honda Gresini	1m 33.984s	0.797s
8	Rossi	ITA	Yamaha	Yamaha Factory Racing	1m 34.009s	0.822s
9	Smith	GBR	Yamaha	Monster Yamaha Tech 3	1m 34.222s	1.035s
10	Hayden	USA	Ducati	Ducati Team	1m 34.242s	1.055s
11	Espargaro	SPA	ART	Power Electronics Aspar	1m 34.754s	1.567s
12	De Puniet	FRA	ART	Power Electronics Aspar	1m 35.086s	1.899s
13	Iannone	ITA	Ducati	Energy T.I. Pramac Racing	1m 35.062s	Q1
14	Pirro	ITA	Ducati	Ignite Pramac Racing	1m 35.228s	Q1
15	Barbera	SPA	FTR	Avintia Blusens	1m 35.714s	Q1
16	Petrucci	ITA	Ioda-Suter	Came IodaRacing Project	1m 35.770s	Q1
17	Edwards	USA	FTR Kawasaki	NGM Mobile Forward Racing	1m 36.221s	Q1
18	Abraham	CZE	ART	Cardion AB Motoracing	1m 36.271s	Q1
19	Corti	ITA	FTR Kawasaki	NGM Mobile Forward Racing	1m 36.330s	Q1
20	Laverty	GBR	PBM	Paul Bird Motorsport	1m 36.596s	Q1
21	Staring	AUS	FTR Honda	GO&FUN Honda Gresini	1m 36.714s	Q1
22	Pesek	CZE	Ioda-Suter	Came IodaRacing Project	1m 36.768s	Q1
23	Hernandez	COL	ART	Paul Bird Motorsport	1m 36.961s	Q1
24	Aoyama	JPN	FTR	Avintia Blusens	1m 37.523s	Q1

FINISHERS

1 DANI PEDROSA Finally got the Le Mans win that had always eluded him, and under the most unpromising circumstances. Started from the end of the second row, made mistakes, but was twice able to repass Dovizioso and pull away.

2 CAL CRUTCHLOW Cracked his tibia on Saturday and then took a career-best second place on Sunday with a ride through from seventh place that included overtakes on Bradl, Rossi, Lorenzo, Dovizioso and Hayden in the trickiest of conditions. Yet to be beaten by another satellite team rider.

3 MARC MARQUEZ Started from pole for the second time this year but made a total mess of the start and had to come back from ninth place. Survived a high-speed run-on at Dunlop and decided to settle for third in the final laps, despite the chance of catching Crutchlow.

4 ANDREA DOVIZIOSO Delighted with the result, despite losing third place two laps from the flag. Led the race for a total of eight laps, including the first four of the race, but the drying track was his undoing. In the wet the Ducati worked superbly, the traction being particularly impressive, but the tyres wore rapidly after the rain stopped.

5 NICKY HAYDEN Not nearly as happy as his team-mate. Annoyed because he ran off track when Rossi fell right in front of him rather than holding his line. That mistake put him out of range of the leading group, and when Marquez came by it was a case of staying upright and getting to the flag.

6 ALVARO BAUTISTA Lost time at the start, then put in good lap times in the wet without making too much progress. Frustrated because the result could have been better, but almost happy with the outcome on a track he's never liked.

7 JORGE LORENZO Complained loudly about a total lack of edge grip from his rear tyre after the race, which drew a tart response from Bridgestone. Other riders reported Jorge fiddling with his crash helmet from as early as lap three. He agreed he'd had a minor issue, but still insisted the tyre was the major problem.

8 MICHELE PIRRO Took over Ben Spies's ride as a replacement, so this time rode the American's Desmosedici, not the factory's 'lab bike'. Like the other Ducati riders, enjoyed the first two-thirds of the race in really wet conditions but had to manage rapid tyre wear as the track dried.

9 BRADLEY SMITH Last into the first corner after nearly crashing. Passed all the CRTs by lap five, Iannone two laps later, and then crossed a 12-second gap to Pirro.

10 STEFAN BRADL Another victim of a misting visor. Fell at Dunlop while dicing with the leaders but managed to remount.

11 ANDREA IANNONE Still beaten up from his Jerez crashes and sporting stitches from an arm-pump operation, but it was his knee which gave him the biggest problem; he even considered pulling in.

12 VALENTINO ROSSI Just when it looked like he was on for a rostrum finish he fell at Garage Vert. Lying fourth, about a second behind Crutchlow, he lost the front on a bump on lap 18. Remounted to finish but was not happy to have lost the chance of a top-three place.

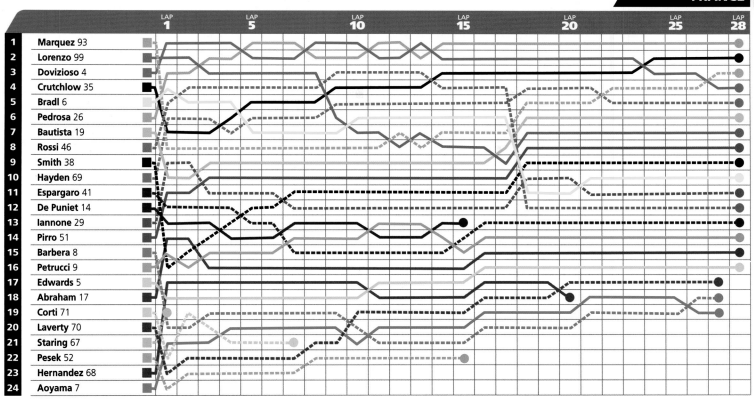

		LAP 1	LAP 5	LAP 10	LAP 15	LAP 20	LAP 25	LAP 28
1	Marquez 93							
2	Lorenzo 99							
3	Dovizioso 4							
4	Crutchlow 35							
5	Bradl 6							
6	Pedrosa 26							
7	Bautista 19							
8	Rossi 46							
9	Smith 38							
10	Hayden 69							
11	Espargaro 41							
12	De Puniet 14							
13	Iannone 29							
14	Pirro 51							
15	Barbera 8							
16	Petrucci 9							
17	Edwards 5							
18	Abraham 17							
19	Corti 71							
20	Laverty 70							
21	Staring 67							
22	Pesek 52							
23	Hernandez 68							
24	Aoyama 7							

RACE

	Rider	Motorcycle	Race Time	Time +	Fastest Lap	Avg. Speed	
1	Pedrosa	Honda	49m 17.707s		1m 43.597s	88.608mph	WS/WS
2	Crutchlow	Yamaha	49m 22.570s	4.863s	1m 44.161s	88.421mph	WS/WS
3	Marquez	Honda	49m 24.656s	6.949s	1m 44.267s	88.359mph	WS/WS
4	Dovizioso	Ducati	49m 27.794s	10.087s	1m 44.313s	88.297mph	WS/WS
5	Hayden	Ducati	49m 36.178s	18.471s	1m 44.255s	88.048mph	WS/WS
6	Bautista	Honda	49m 41.268s	23.561s	1m 44.721s	87.862mph	WS/WS
7	Lorenzo	Yamaha	49m 45.668s	27.961s	1m 45.261s	87.738mph	WS/WS
8	Pirro	Ducati	49m 58.482s	40.775s	1m 45.497s	87.365mph	WS/WS
9	Smith	Yamaha	49m 59.114s	41.407s	1m 45.404s	87.365mph	WS/WS
10	Bradl	Honda	50m 18.702s	1m 00.995s	1m 44.786s	86.806mph	WS/WS
11	Iannone	Ducati	50m 22.817s	1m 05.110s	1m 45.935s	86.681mph	WS/WS
12	Rossi	Yamaha	50m 34.075s	1m 16.368s	1m 44.061s	86.371mph	WS/WS
13	Espargaro	ART	50m 41.907s	1m 24.200s	1m 46.690s	86.122mph	WS/WS
14	Petrucci	Ioda-Suter	50m 43.433s	1m 25.726s	1m 47.288s	86.122mph	WS/WS
15	Abraham	ART	50m 49.818s	1m 32.111s	1m 47.365s	85.936mph	WS/WS
16	Edwards	FTR Kawasaki	50m 58.309s	1m 40.602s	1m 47.268s	85.687mph	WS/WS
17	Laverty	PBM	49m 30.391s	1 Lap	1m 46.968s	85.066mph	WS/WS
18	Barbera	FTR	49m 49.705s	1 Lap	1m 47.445s	84.506mph	WS/WS
19	Aoyama	FTR	49m 50.038s	1 Lap	1m 48.186s	84.506mph	WS/WS
NF	Hernandez	ART	36m 46.263s	8 Laps	1m 48.728s	84.817mph	WS/WS
NF	De Puniet	ART	27m 20.724s	13 Laps	1m 47.221s	85.563mph	WS/WS
NF	Pesek	Ioda-Suter	28m 16.315s	13 Laps	1m 50.101s	82.767mph	WS/WS
NF	Corti	FTR Kawasaki	13m 16.145s	21 Laps	1m 49.600s	82.270mph	WS/WS
NF	Staring	FTR Honda	2m 04.083s	27 Laps		75.434mph	WS/WS

CHAMPIONSHIP

	Rider	Nation	Team	Points
1	Pedrosa	SPA	Repsol Honda Team	83
2	Marquez	SPA	Repsol Honda Team	77
3	Lorenzo	SPA	Yamaha Factory Racing	66
4	Crutchlow	GBR	Monster Yamaha Tech 3	55
5	Rossi	ITA	Yamaha Factory Racing	47
6	Dovizioso	ITA	Ducati Team	39
7	Bautista	SPA	GO&FUN Honda Gresini	38
8	Hayden	USA	Ducati Team	35
9	Espargaro	SPA	Power Electronics Aspar	20
10	Iannone	ITA	Energy T.I. Pramac Racing	18
11	Bradl	GER	LCR Honda MotoGP	17
12	Smith	GBR	Monster Yamaha Tech 3	17
13	Pirro	ITA	Ignite Pramac Racing	13
14	Spies	USA	Ignite Pramac Racing	9
15	Barbera	SPA	Avintia Blusens	7
16	De Puniet	FRA	Power Electronics Aspar	6
17	Petrucci	ITA	Came IodaRacing Project	4
18	Laverty	GBR	Paul Bird Motorsport	3
19	Hernandez	COL	Paul Bird Motorsport	3
20	Abraham	CZE	Cardion AB Motoracing	1
21	Edwards	USA	NGM Mobile Forward Racing	1
22	Aoyama	JPN	Avintia Blusens	1

13 ALEIX ESPARGARO Top CRT again, despite a run-on that cost him two places. Had to battle with his team-mate and Petrucci before pulling away.

14 DANILO PETRUCCI Was in front of the Aspar Aprilias for a few laps before a moment lost him two places. Happy to score points for two races in a row and finish second CRT.

15 KAREL ABRAHAM Happy to finish and get his first point of the year. Disappointed to let Petrucci through, his front tyre was wrecked and a result mattered.

16 COLIN EDWARDS Rode with no traction control for most of the race.

Tyre wear meant the end of the race was a matter of survival, not racing.

17 MICHAEL LAVERTY Spent the first half of the race learning the Bridgestone wets, then on lap 19 set the second-fastest CRT time of the race, slower only than Espargaro.

18 HECTOR BARBERA Lack of experience with the bike in the wet and a broken finger from a practice crash conspired to make it a bad weekend.

19 HIROSHI AOYAMA Electrical problems that surfaced in FP3 meant the progress seen at Jerez was not continued. Not a good weekend.

NON-FINISHERS

YONNY HERNANDEZ Pulled in because the tyre was spinning so much he assumed there was a problem.

RANDY DE PUNIET Was top CRT in 13th place when he fell on lap 15, fortunately unhurt. Flew out to test the 2014 MotoGP Suzuki in Japan.

LUKAS PESEK Retired with a bike he hadn't been happy about all weekend.

CLAUDIO CORTI Engine decided to cut out after seven laps.

BRYAN STARING Crashed on the second lap, thus losing valuable track time and wet-weather experience. Said it was 'a rookie mistake'.

NON-STARTERS

BEN SPIES Withdrew to give his shoulder more recovery time. Replaced by Michele Pirro.

BRIDGESTONE

FRONT WET SOFT **(WS)** / WET HARD **(WH)**

CENTRE
LEFT   RIGHT

REAR WET SOFT **(WS)** / WET HARD **(WH)**

MILD ⸺ SEVERE

GRAN PREMIO D'ITALIA TIM

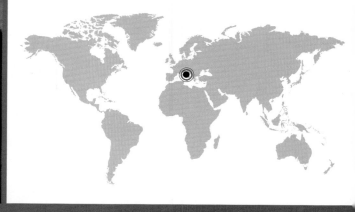

BLOOD AND GUTS

Big crashes, heated arguments – and another stealthy win for Jorge Lorenzo

The race itself hinged on a couple of first-lap incidents, but the fallout lingered a lot longer. In short, Jorge Lorenzo shoved Dani Pedrosa aside in the first corner, then put in his now expected succession of metronomic laps. Pedrosa hung on to him for 14 laps before dropping into the clutches of team-mate Marc Marquez. Dani's bike never looked settled and it seemed that Marquez was going to do some damage to his rival's championship lead. However, two laps after he took second place from Dani, Marquez had his fourth crash of the weekend. The final three paled into complete insignificance compared to the first one (see inset story).

Marc's first crash, on Friday afternoon, was the scariest and fastest since Shinya Nakano experienced tyre failure at almost the same place on Mugello's front straight in 2004, but the Spanish rider escaped with severe bruising, a cracked bone in his right shoulder and a swollen chin. Fellow rookie Bradley Smith followed suit with two highsides in practice, resulting in a little finger in need of a skin graft and a cracked scaphoid. Both men raced.

However, the race crash that received most attention happened on the first lap at Turn 3 when Alvaro Bautista and Valentino Rossi came together. Bautista came out of the Turn 2 left-hander on a tight line and was picking up his bike to go right; Rossi, meanwhile, had been wide in the left-hander and was moving to his left to get a quicker line into the right-hander. Nothing wrong with either of those choices, especially on the first lap, but unfortunately their lines intersected and both men hit the barriers hard. Not surprisingly, their opinions of who was at fault differed, but when tempers

'I WON FOR THE LAST THREE YEARS HERE SO THIS TRACK IS MAGIC FOR ME AND VERY POSITIVE FOR YAMAHAS'

JORGE LORENZO

had calmed a little Race Direction declared it a racing incident and, frankly, it is difficult to argue otherwise. Bautista's contention that he couldn't possibly see Rossi was accepted by all parties, but given his previous for this sort of thing the acceptance was grudging. Valentino reckoned he could have challenged for the rostrum, but he'd again probably given himself too much to do by qualifying on the third row. However, having the prospect of a top-three finish dashed so early in the race did not improve his temper.

Italian fans, back in numbers after the mass desertion of 2012, couldn't look to Ducati for much solace, despite Andrea Dovizioso's front-row start. As he feared and predicted, the best the Ducatis could do was fight among themselves at a respectful distance from the other factory bikes. The works Ducatis, plus factory tester and wild card Michele Pirro, spent the race fighting with Stefan Bradl, another rider with a bit of pressure building on his shoulders. When the German won the entertaining fight and equalled his best-ever finish with fourth place some of that pressure lifted. Ben Spies suffered another blow to his long-running recovery from shoulder surgery when he again attempted to come back too early. He tried to ride on Friday morning but realised he could be a danger to himself and other riders. Ducati talked about him being back for Laguna Seca, but Ben himself thought Indianapolis was the more likely target.

Cal Crutchlow's race followed the now familiar pattern of impressive qualifying then slightly hesitant opening laps, followed by stunning pace in the closing stages. Cal was two seconds behind Pedrosa and closing

OPPOSITE Bradley Smith crashed twice in practice, mangling a finger and cracking a bone in his wrist

LEFT Lorenzo led from start to finish. Marquez chased but crashed for the only time in a race this year

ABOVE Alvaro Bautista became the villain of the piece, at least as far as the home fans were concerned

ABOVE Barbera and de Puniet were second and third CRTs, but nearly ten seconds behind Espargaro

BELOW Crutchlow made it to the rostrum for the second race in a row

fast when Marquez went down, after which he decided that back-to-back rostrums were a better idea than crashing while trying to convert third place into second. Considering the last British rider to score back-to-back rostrums in the top class was Ron Haslam in 1987, it's easy to see Cal's point. Add in Scott Redding making it back-to-back wins in Moto2 and British fans realised they would have to come to terms with having genuine contenders for wins in two classes – something they hadn't had to deal with for a while.

Dani Pedrosa could also have been feeling a little pressure, as his championship lead was trimmed by five points. It could have been worse. Frankly, scoring 20 points on a bike that looked seriously unstable at times, at a track where Lorenzo had won for the previous two years, should have made him happy. However, when Catalan radio asked him in parc fermé about Marquez's pace Dani snapped that of course Marc was quick, he'd been able to use his – Pedrosa's – settings.

Dani never mentioned Jorge's first-corner pass. Nevertheless, Lorenzo felt the need to apologise for it, saying he didn't like to make moves that way. No apology was needed, but the World Champion's remarks were clearly aimed at Marquez with reference to his last-lap move at Jerez. Judging by his remarks before and after the race, Jorge was still bearing a serious grudge. As for the man himself, the only sign that Marc Marquez had had a tough, four-crash weekend was the graze on his chin. The race incident that cost him his 100 per cent rostrum finish record was familiar from many rookies' mistakes, simply riding off the side of the tyres, but also meant he did not become the first man ever to finish on the rostrum in his first five races in the top class. As usual, Marc found a positive in what looked like a totally disastrous weekend: the fact he'd set the fastest lap.

Yet again it was all too easy to overlook Lorenzo's superb race. He eclipsed Pedrosa's astonishing pole instantly, put the pressure on when the fuel load dropped and Dani just couldn't match the increase in pace. It was another master class. But again nobody was talking about it.

CRASH DAMAGE

Marc Marquez's Friday afternoon crash was truly terrifying. He locked the front wheel on Mugello's front straight, recovered, but then found himself heading for the wall, at which point he made the decision to jump off, sliding up against the concrete which is uncomfortably close to the tarmac at this point. Thanks to the data logged by the airbag electronics in his Alpinestars Air Tech suit we know exactly the speeds and forces involved in what was the fastest crash in MotoGP history. Back in 2004 Shinya Nakano had a crash at nearly the same spot when his rear tyre failed. The *Official Season Review* described the speed of that crash as between 190 and 200mph. The Air Tech's accelerometers detected that the onset of Marquez's crash happened while the bike was doing 209.9mph (337.9km/h). This is the point at which the airbag is deployed; it takes 0.05s to inflate fully. The first impact happened

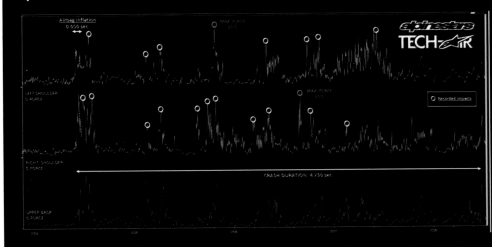

0.08s after the trigger point, so 0.03s after the bag inflated. Forces of 25g were recorded on both the left and right shoulder, with that first impact with the ground being suffered by Marc's right arm. Indeed, the only injury he thought might be a problem for the race was a seriously sore right elbow, although he also suffered a cracked bone in his shoulder and a blow to his chin that left it swollen and grazed.

It is a tribute to modern safety equipment, as well as to the rider himself, that a crash faster than 200mph had no serious consequences.

BELOW Rossi didn't get to show the home crowd his ironic helmet design after he was taken out on the first lap

GRAN PREMIO D'ITALIA TIM
MUGELLO

ROUND 5
June 2

RACE RESULTS

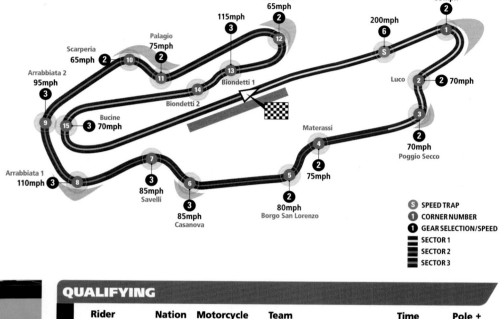

CIRCUIT LENGTH 3.259 miles
NO. OF LAPS 23
RACE DISTANCE 74.959 miles
WEATHER Dry, 21°C
TRACK TEMPERATURE 42°C
WINNER Jorge Lorenzo
FASTEST LAP 1m 47.639s, 108.989mph, Marc Marquez (Record)
PREVIOUS LAP RECORD 1m 47.705s, 108.934mph, Dani Pedrosa, 2012

Track map labels:
San Donato 55mph; Correntaio 65mph; 115mph; 200mph; Palagio 75mph; Scarperia 65mph; Arrabbiata 2 95mph; Biondetti 1; Biondetti 2; Luco 70mph; Poggio Secco 70mph; Bucine 70mph; Materassi; Arrabbiata 1 110mph; 85mph Savelli; 85mph Casanova; 80mph Borgo San Lorenzo; 75mph

S SPEED TRAP
1 CORNER NUMBER
1 GEAR SELECTION/SPEED
SECTOR 1
SECTOR 2
SECTOR 3

QUALIFYING

	Rider	Nation	Motorcycle	Team	Time	Pole +
1	Pedrosa	SPA	Honda	Repsol Honda Team	1m 47.157s	
2	Lorenzo	SPA	Yamaha	Yamaha Factory Racing	1m 47.226s	0.069s
3	Dovizioso	ITA	Ducati	Ducati Team	1m 47.628s	0.471s
4	Crutchlow	GBR	Yamaha	Monster Yamaha Tech 3	1m 47.632s	0.475s
5	Bradl	GER	Honda	LCR Honda MotoGP	1m 47.737s	0.580s
6	Marquez	SPA	Honda	Repsol Honda Team	1m 47.763s	0.606s
7	Rossi	ITA	Yamaha	Yamaha Factory Racing	1m 47.872s	0.715s
8	Hayden	USA	Ducati	Ducati Team	1m 48.006s	0.849s
9	Bautista	SPA	Honda	GO&FUN Honda Gresini	1m 48.355s	1.198s
10	Pirro	ITA	Ducati	Ducati Test Team	1m 48.564s	1.407s
11	Smith	GBR	Yamaha	Monster Yamaha Tech 3	1m 48.706s	1.549s
12	Espargaro	SPA	ART	Power Electronics Aspar	1m 48.765s	1.608s
13	Iannone	ITA	Ducati	Energy T.I. Pramac Racing	1m 49.265s	Q1
14	De Puniet	FRA	ART	Power Electronics Aspar	1m 49.266s	Q1
15	Barbera	SPA	FTR	Avintia Blusens	1m 49.847s	Q1
16	Petrucci	ITA	Ioda-Suter	Came IodaRacing Project	1m 50.518s	Q1
17	Edwards	USA	FTR Kawasaki	NGM Mobile Forward Racing	1m 50.701s	Q1
18	Corti	ITA	FTR Kawasaki	NGM Mobile Forward Racing	1m 50.729s	Q1
19	Laverty	GBR	PBM	Paul Bird Motorsport	1m 50.787s	Q1
20	Abraham	CZE	ART	Cardion AB Motoracing	1m 51.089s	Q1
21	Hernandez	COL	ART	Paul Bird Motorsport	1m 51.239s	Q1
22	Staring	AUS	FTR Honda	GO&FUN Honda Gresini	1m 51.981s	Q1
23	Aoyama	JPN	FTR	Avintia Blusens	1m 52.148s	Q1
24	Pesek	CZE	Ioda-Suter	Came IodaRacing Project	1m 52.345s	Q1

FINISHERS

1 JORGE LORENZO Rode a perfect race to make it three in a row here. Dived through a very small gap at the first corner to take the lead from Pedrosa, then put together a typically robotic run of very low 1m 48s laps. When Dani dropped into the 49s on lap 14, Jorge's lead was over 2s. As at Qatar, it would've been difficult to do that with a Honda in the way.

2 DANI PEDROSA Started from pole but the bike never looked right: unable to follow Lorenzo's pace and passed by Marquez. Short of rear grip, despite the increase in track temperature, and looked almost unstable at times. Very grateful to pick up 20 points and limit the damage to his title lead.

3 CAL CRUTCHLOW Back-to-back rostrums for the first time as Cal underlined his status as far and away the most outstanding satellite team rider. Had problems with hayfever and a big crash in qualifying, but again rode superbly and was closing on the Hondas at the end.

4 STEFAN BRADL Equalled his career-best finish, which was at Mugello the previous season, after a race-long struggle with Dovizioso and Hayden. After a trying start to the season the LCR team welcomed him back to the pit as if he'd won.

5 ANDREA DOVIZIOSO A second front-row start in two races, but the gap to the leaders in the race was as expected. Spent most of the race in a fight with Bradl and Hayden, swapping places with the German four times in the final stages.

6 NICKY HAYDEN Not exactly enamoured with the finishing position but happy to have found some grip for the race and able to fight with his team-mate and Bradl. Still handicapped by his swollen right wrist.

7 MICHELE PIRRO His second, scheduled wild-card ride on Ducati's 'lab bike'. Again made a bad start, lost his seat pad on the second lap, and then swapped places with Iannone three times.

8 ALEIX ESPARGARO Equalled the best-ever finish by a CRT bike (Aleix himself, in Sepang 2012), despite having to race his second bike because the number-one machine wouldn't start for the sighting lap. Amazingly, was able to put in 1m 49s laps in the first half of the race.

9 BRADLEY SMITH Made mincemeat, all too literally, of his left little finger in practice, then crashed heavily in warm-up. Raced in pain from finger and wrist injuries, but nearly caught Espargaro on the final lap.

10 HECTOR BARBERA Second CRT and best result of the season so far. Satisfied that he'd got all that was possible out of the bike.

11 RANDY DE PUNIET His confidence in the front end was severely dented by a crash in Sunday morning warm-up. Started the race cautiously and found it hard to get the ART to turn into corners. Under the circumstances, the points were a pleasant surprise.

12 DANILO PETRUCCI Very happy with the pace he could run right to the flag – he used the word 'amazed' – and with finishing in front of Iannone's prototype. Couldn't race with Barbera and de Puniet but felt optimistic, especially about the Magneti Marelli electronics.

13 ANDREA IANNONE Hit problems with rear grip in the race, which led to

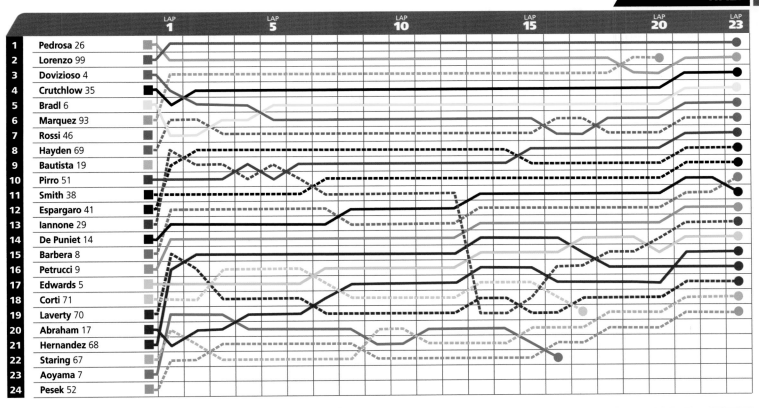

	Rider	
1	Pedrosa	26
2	Lorenzo	99
3	Dovizioso	4
4	Crutchlow	35
5	Bradl	6
6	Marquez	93
7	Rossi	46
8	Hayden	69
9	Bautista	19
10	Pirro	51
11	Smith	38
12	Espargaro	41
13	Iannone	29
14	De Puniet	14
15	Barbera	8
16	Petrucci	9
17	Edwards	5
18	Corti	71
19	Laverty	70
20	Abraham	17
21	Hernandez	68
22	Staring	67
23	Aoyama	7
24	Pesek	52

RACE

	Rider	Motorcycle	Race Time	Time +	Fastest Lap	Avg. Speed	B
1	Lorenzo	Yamaha	41m 39.733s		1m 47.929s	107.932mph	M/M
2	Pedrosa	Honda	41m 45.133s	5.400s	1m 47.898s	107.684mph	M/M
3	Crutchlow	Yamaha	41m 46.145s	6.412s	1m 48.397s	107.621mph	M/M
4	Bradl	Honda	41m 59.054s	19.321s	1m 48.599s	107.124mph	M/M
5	Dovizioso	Ducati	41m 59.273s	19.540s	1m 48.707s	107.062mph	M/M
6	Hayden	Ducati	42m 06.054s	26.321s	1m 48.768s	106.814mph	M/M
7	Pirro	Ducati	42m 17.877s	38.144s	1m 49.560s	106.317mph	M/M
8	Espargaro	ART	42m 19.535s	39.802s	1m 49.586s	106.254mph	M/S
9	Smith	Yamaha	42m 19.976s	40.243s	1m 49.536s	106.192mph	M/M
10	Barbera	FTR	42m 28.125s	48.392s	1m 50.030s	105.882mph	M/S
11	De Puniet	ART	42m 28.213s	48.480s	1m 49.910s	105.882mph	M/S
12	Petrucci	Ioda-Suter	42m 53.441s	1m 13.708s	1m 50.954s	104.825mph	M/S
13	Iannone	Ducati	42m 54.334s	1m 14.601s	1m 50.027s	104.763mph	M/M
14	Edwards	FTR Kawasaki	43m 00.982s	1m 21.249s	1m 50.830s	104.515mph	M/S
15	Abraham	ART	43m 05.471s	1m 25.738s	1m 51.318s	104.328mph	M/S
16	Hernandez	ART	43m 07.072s	1m 27.339s	1m 51.659s	104.266mph	M/S
17	Laverty	PBM	43m 07.491s	1m 27.758s	1m 51.618s	104.266mph	M/S
18	Staring	FTR Honda	43m 24.157s	1m 44.424s	1m 52.116s	103.583mph	M/S
19	Pesek	Ioda-Suter	43m 24.960s	1m 45.227s	1m 52.140s	103.583mph	S/S
NF	Marquez	Honda	36m 16.625s	3 Laps	1m 47.639s	107.746mph	M/M
NF	Corti	FTR Kawasaki	31m 57.481s	6 Laps	1m 51.630s	104.018mph	M/S
NF	Aoyama	FTR	30m 15.606s	7 Laps	1m 52.265s	103.334mph	M/S
NF	Rossi	Yamaha		0 Lap			M/M
NF	Bautista	Honda		0 Lap			M/M

CHAMPIONSHIP

	Rider	Nation	Team	Points
1	Pedrosa	SPA	Repsol Honda Team	103
2	Lorenzo	SPA	Yamaha Factory Racing	91
3	Marquez	SPA	Repsol Honda Team	77
4	Crutchlow	GBR	Monster Yamaha Tech 3	71
5	Dovizioso	ITA	Ducati Team	50
6	Rossi	ITA	Yamaha Factory Racing	47
7	Hayden	USA	Ducati Team	45
8	Bautista	SPA	GO&FUN Honda Gresini	38
9	Bradl	GER	LCR Honda MotoGP	30
10	Espargaro	SPA	Power Electronics Aspar	28
11	Smith	GBR	Monster Yamaha Tech 3	24
12	Pirro	ITA	Ignite Pramac Racing	22
13	Iannone	ITA	Energy T.I. Pramac Racing	21
14	Barbera	SPA	Avintia Blusens	13
15	De Puniet	FRA	Power Electronics Aspar	11
16	Spies	USA	Ignite Pramac Racing	9
17	Petrucci	ITA	Came IodaRacing Project	8
18	Laverty	GBR	Paul Bird Motorsport	3
19	Edwards	USA	NGM Mobile Forward Racing	3
20	Hernandez	COL	Paul Bird Motorsport	3
21	Abraham	CZE	Cardion AB Motoracing	2
22	Aoyama	JPN	Avintia Blusens	1

a run-on at the first corner of lap 13. Perplexed, as there had been no hint of grip problems in practice or warm-up. Only just resumed training after his Jerez crashes, so not race fit.

14 COLIN EDWARDS Ran a new swinging arm, which he reckoned was an improvement, but still found it impossible to get off the brake as early as he wanted in order to run through corners at the same pace as the other CRT bikes.

15 KAREL ABRAHAM Gave himself problems with average qualifying, followed by a bad start. Took the last point thanks to Marquez's crash and passing Hernandez in the closing stages.

16 YONNY HERNANDEZ Went well in the first half of the race, then hit chatter which put him out of the points.

17 MICHAEL LAVERTY Happier in practice than during the race. Never found a setting he was happy with, the particular problem being corner entry, but maintained his 100 per cent finishing record.

18 BRYAN STARING A difficult weekend, learning a track like Mugello with just one bike, and hampered by a crash in practice.

19 LUKAS PESEK His first finish since Qatar. Still more confident riding alone, hence his qualifying can be impressive, than dicing with other CRTs.

NON-FINISHERS

MARC MARQUEZ Survived the fastest crash in GP history almost unscathed, plus two more slower get-offs in practice. Up to second in the race, having set fastest lap after stalking his team-mate, but crashed again two laps from home at Savelli.

CLAUDIO CORTI Retired when his traction control stopped working, having clocked he was sliding considerably more than Edwards, his team-mate. Also stung by a bee during the race!

HIROSHI AOYAMA Broke his left thumb and did some serious damage to the ligaments in his left knee in a heavy practice crash. Started the race but, not surprisingly, had to pull out.

ALVARO BAUTISTA Came together with Rossi at the third corner, putting both of them in the barrier.

VALENTINO ROSSI Sideswiped by Bautista at the third corner. Race Direction called it a racing incident.

NON-STARTERS

BEN SPIES Again tried to compete, but had to pull out after the first day for more work on his shoulder.

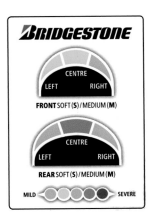

GRAN PREMI APEROL DE CATALUNYA

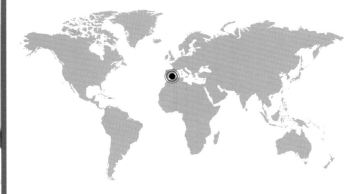

HOME COMFORT

Jorge Lorenzo rode like a champion to hold off a race-long challenge from Dani Pedrosa

It felt as though the race had been decided on Saturday, when Dani Pedrosa pulverised the absolute lap record to take pole position by the astounding margin of over 0.6s. It looked like the most local of local men would celebrate his 200th Grand Prix with a dominant win. As usual with bike racing, though, just when the plot seems settled the unexpected happens. And it did.

Race day was considerably hotter than the rest of the weekend, with Bridgestone reporting track temperatures peaking at 57°C during the race. That plot says the Hondas like the heat better than the Yamahas because they need to get energy into the rear tyre to find grip, whereas the Yamahas lose edge grip – in other words, more reasons for Dani to capitalise on his pole position. And again the plot wasn't entirely correct. It is true that the Catalunya circuit's tarmac gets very slick as it heats up, which may account for the rash of early crashes: six riders were out within five laps.

One of those crashes excited more interest than the rest: Alvaro Bautista's. He tried to go inside Rossi's Yamaha on the first lap, at Turn 10, the left-hander at the end of the back straight, only to slide off. His bike nearly collected Valentino, who had to take avoiding action. Given the events of the first lap at Mugello two weeks previously, when Bautista had been grudgingly exonerated after another first-lap incident, Rossi had plenty to say this time. The word 'stupid' was used and, after referring to Mugello and other previous incidents, Valentino suggested Race Direction have a word.

Unlike Mugello, there was no suggestion that Valentino had had his chances of a rostrum ruined; the heat and lack of grip saw to that. He finished in a very solid fourth place, however, after Cal Crutchlow slid

ABOVE Jorge Lorenzo did it again – a start-to-finish victory for the second race running

RIGHT The Repsol Hondas were this far apart for most of the race, and closer when Marquez tried to make a move...

off early on. Rossi's complaints about the levels of grip made Lorenzo's race even more remarkable. Jorge took the lead at the first corner when Pedrosa had a minor wobble and he was never headed. That makes it sound easy. It wasn't. For 17 of the 25 laps the gap between Lorenzo and Pedrosa hovered around, but usually under, half a second. Third-place man Marc Marquez was a similar distance behind, and that's how it stayed for nearly the whole race. Catalunya does this; we've often seen riders very close together but unable to make a move. Have a look at the lap chart to see how little things changed after the early skirmishes.

Not surprisingly, Jorge said it was one of his best races. One slip, one mistake, he reported, would have been enough to give away victory. All but one rider set their best time in the first four laps, with Dani saying the temperature change meant the Honda shook its head when he got on the throttle, so he had to be careful. The only man who didn't seem affected by the track conditions was the World Champion.

Marc Marquez spent most, if not all of the race following Dani, looking and learning. No-one expected him to go the whole distance without making some attempt at taking second off his team-mate, and sure

'A PERFECT DAY, TO BE HONEST I DIDN'T EXPECT TO WIN'
JORGE LORENZO

enough it came on the penultimate lap at Turn 4. Leaving aside the fact that Turn 4 is not a place where many would think of passing, Marquez made what he called a 'big mistake' and locked the front. Somehow he saved it and managed to avoid Pedrosa by the slimmest of margins. It took slow-motion TV replays to confirm they hadn't touched. Marc got his apology in as they waited for the rostrum: 'Before you see the video…'

While the racing was tense rather than thrilling, there were a few interesting sub-plots to the main event. Javier del Amor turned up to look after the Avintia team's guests and conduct tours of the pit garage. When Hiro Aoyama put himself out of contention Javier was sent home to get his leathers, and the recently retired Spanish Championship racer qualified, kept the bike on its wheels and scored the final point.

Bradley Smith, with a mangled little finger and broken scaphoid from Mugello, jumped across a four-second gap in the closing stages to take sixth off Andrea Dovizioso. More importantly, he was only 32 seconds behind the winner, an improvement of 10 seconds that put him firmly in the area where, as Bradley described it, you're riding it properly. After the post-race test he had a skin graft on his finger and a screw put in his scaphoid.

All that remained was for Jorge Lorenzo to take Anna Vives, the young lady who designed his special home-event crash helmet paint scheme, to the rostrum with him. Anna, who has Down's Syndrome, is well known in Catalunya as a role model for people with disabilities. Jorge's empathy with Anna was obvious, revealing another side to this complex young man. No-one appeared to complain about the extra person on the podium; Jorge was in control of everything.

ABOVE Despite his injuries from Mugello, Bradley Smith finished an impressive sixth

BELOW Bryan Staring opened his account with two points for 14th place on the FTR Honda

THE CHANGE

The first test of the season took place on the Monday and Tuesday after the GP, followed by a couple more days at Aragon. It was also the first chance to see Suzuki's bike, ridden by Randy de Puniet. The in-line four was respectably quick, but the factory shocked everyone by announcing that they wouldn't be returning to full-time competition until 2015. Hopefully, there will be wild-card entries in 2014.

It was also an important test for two factories, Ducati and Yamaha, as both tried to find ways to get competitive with the leaders, or in Yamaha's case to bring Valentino Rossi up to speed. They had very different outcomes.

Ducati's works riders, Dovizioso and Hayden, tried the new chassis for the first time and were underwhelmed. Dovi conceded it might have made a small improvement in corner exit but in no way addressed the fundamental problems. Nicky Hayden simply saw no progress. This was not the reaction the factory expected. There had been reasons for smiles in the Ducati pit at the opening races of the year – front

rows, Dovi leading in France – but all of a sudden optimism was in short supply.

It was different over at the factory Yamaha pit. Rossi was positively effusive about the test. This wasn't the usual 'we work in a good way' PR fluff; this was genuine optimism. It seemed as if Valentino's crew had sorted out the issue with the front end that stopped him braking as he wanted to,

which particularly affected him in qualifying. He also used the same swinging arm as Lorenzo for the first time – perhaps an indication that he had stopped trying to reinvent his 2010 M1?

And, almost unnoticed, Honda sent their riders, including Stefan Bradl, out on the 2014 RCV. There were no problems.

ABOVE AND RIGHT
Jorge Lorenzo celebrates a home win with the designer of his special crash helmet paint scheme, Anna Vives

OFFICIAL TIMEKEEPER

GRAN PREMI APEROL DE CATALUNYA
CIRCUIT DE CATALUNYA

ROUND 6
June 16

RACE RESULTS

CIRCUIT LENGTH 2.937 miles
NO. OF LAPS 25
RACE DISTANCE 73.431 miles
WEATHER Dry, 31°C
TRACK TEMPERATURE 52°C
WINNER Jorge Lorenzo
FASTEST LAP 1m 42.552s, 103.085mph, Marc Marquez
LAP RECORD 1m 42.358s, 103.304mph, Dani Pedrosa, 2008

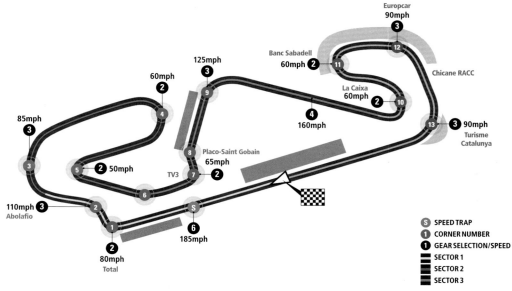

QUALIFYING

	Rider	Nation	Motorcycle	Team	Time	Pole +
1	Pedrosa	SPA	Honda	Repsol Honda Team	1m 40.893s	
2	Crutchlow	GBR	Yamaha	Monster Yamaha Tech 3	1m 41.501s	0.608s
3	Lorenzo	SPA	Yamaha	Yamaha Factory Racing	1m 41.566s	0.673s
4	Bautista	SPA	Honda	GO&FUN Honda Gresini	1m 41.714s	0.821s
5	Hayden	USA	Ducati	Ducati Team	1m 41.800s	0.907s
6	Marquez	SPA	Honda	Repsol Honda Team	1m 41.842s	0.949s
7	Rossi	ITA	Yamaha	Yamaha Factory Racing	1m 41.959s	1.066s
8	Iannone	ITA	Ducati	Energy T.I. Pramac Racing	1m 41.963s	1.070s
9	Dovizioso	ITA	Ducati	Ducati Team	1m 42.053s	1.160s
10	Bradl	GER	Honda	LCR Honda MotoGP	1m 42.090s	1.197s
11	Smith	GBR	Yamaha	Monster Yamaha Tech 3	1m 42.548s	1.655s
12	Espargaro	SPA	ART	Power Electronics Aspar	1m 42.878s	1.985s
13	De Puniet	FRA	ART	Power Electronics Aspar	1m 43.186s	Q1
14	Pirro	ITA	Ducati	Ignite Pramac Racing	1m 43.330s	Q1
15	Barbera	SPA	FTR	Avintia Blusens	1m 43.659s	Q1
16	Edwards	USA	FTR Kawasaki	NGM Mobile Forward Racing	1m 43.983s	Q1
17	Abraham	CZE	ART	Cardion AB Motoracing	1m 44.362s	Q1
18	Petrucci	ITA	Ioda-Suter	Came IodaRacing Project	1m 44.369s	Q1
19	Corti	ITA	FTR Kawasaki	NGM Mobile Forward Racing	1m 44.603s	Q1
20	Laverty	GBR	PBM	Paul Bird Motorsport	1m 44.630s	Q1
21	Hernandez	COL	ART	Paul Bird Motorsport	1m 44.913s	Q1
22	Staring	AUS	FTR Honda	GO&FUN Honda Gresini	1m 45.441s	Q1
23	Pesek	CZE	Ioda-Suter	Came IodaRacing Project	1m 46.302s	Q1
24	Del Amor	SPA	FTR	Avintia Blusens	1m 48.952s	Q1

FINISHERS

1 JORGE LORENZO It looked like a repeat of Mugello, but was actually a better race. Never headed but had to ride at 100 per cent all race long as the Hondas were never more than half a second back, at least until two-thirds distance. Closed the gap to Pedrosa at the top of the table to seven points.

2 DANI PEDROSA Set pole with the fastest-ever lap of the Circuit de Catalunya, but race day was a case of dealing with the conditions and not making a mistake. He'd expected to do better.

3 MARC MARQUEZ Shadowed his team-mate all the way and nearly hit him when he locked the front a couple of laps from the flag. Said he was surprised to finish on the rostrum – no-one else seemed in the least bit shocked.

4 VALENTINO ROSSI Was hoping to fight for the rostrum but was again handicapped by his qualifying. Nevertheless, was able to lap as quickly as the leaders on worn tyres and, more significantly, thought he'd found some answers at the Monday test.

5 STEFAN BRADL Saw the crashing going on around him and realised he would have to be less aggressive than usual in the opening laps to conserve his tyres. An excellent follow-up result to his fourth place at Mugello.

6 BRADLEY SMITH His best finish so far but, much more importantly, reduced the usual gap to the leader from 40 to 30 seconds – and all with a cracked scaphoid and mangled finger from his Mugello crashes. In the closing stages he got across a four-second gap to take sixth off Dovizioso.

7 ANDREA DOVIZIOSO Not happy. Knew this was going to be a difficult weekend on a track that would expose the Ducati's problems. It was even worse than he expected, thanks to the heat: 'I really didn't think I'd do such slow lap times.'

8 ALEIX ESPARGARO Another top CRT finish, again equalling the best finish by a CRT, but he spent the whole race worrying about the lack of grip from the front tyre.

9 COLIN EDWARDS The team's best finish in MotoGP. When the dust from the early crashing settled, Colin found himself behind Espargaro and doing similar lap times. When the grip went right down, and he saw he was in the top ten, he just concentrated on getting to the flag.

10 MICHELE PIRRO Riding as a replacement for Ben Spies for the second time. Ran off track on the first lap while avoiding Hernandez, rejoined last and worked hard to get back to the pack.

Like every Ducati rider, suffered severely from grip and pumping problems.

11 DANILO PETRUCCI Followed Barbera after a good start until the Spaniard crashed. Like many others, then concentrated on picking up useful points.

12 CLAUDIO CORTI First points in MotoGP, and the first time both Forward Racing bikes scored, although Claudio didn't really enjoy the race.

13 YONNY HERNANDEZ Best finish of the season so far, but still troubled by the rapid rear-tyre wear that has been a perennial problem. Used the Monday test to address the issue.

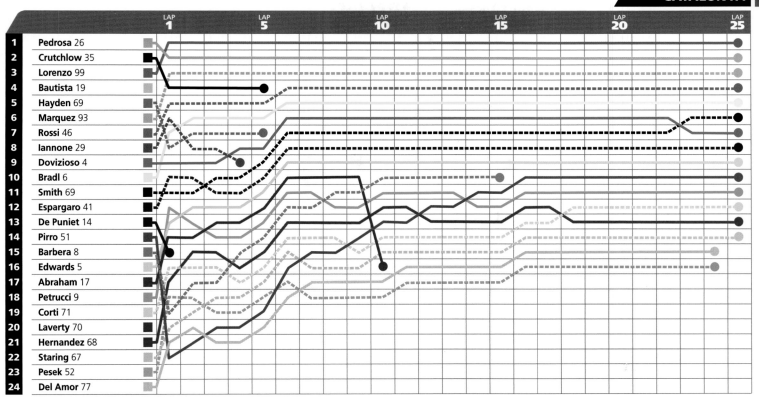

Lap positions chart — riders listed 1–24:

	Rider	
1	Pedrosa	26
2	Crutchlow	35
3	Lorenzo	99
4	Bautista	19
5	Hayden	69
6	Marquez	93
7	Rossi	46
8	Iannone	29
9	Dovizioso	4
10	Bradl	6
11	Smith	69
12	Espargaro	41
13	De Puniet	14
14	Pirro	51
15	Barbera	8
16	Edwards	5
17	Abraham	17
18	Petrucci	9
19	Corti	71
20	Laverty	70
21	Hernandez	68
22	Staring	67
23	Pesek	52
24	Del Amor	77

RACE

	Rider	Motorcycle	Race Time	Time +	Fastest Lap	Avg. Speed	
1	Lorenzo	Yamaha	43m 06.479s		1m 42.638s	102.153mph	H/M
2	Pedrosa	Honda	43m 08.242s	1.763s	1m 42.609s	102.091mph	H/M
3	Marquez	Honda	43m 08.305s	1.826s	1m 42.552s	102.091mph	H/M
4	Rossi	Yamaha	43m 12.353s	5.874s	1m 42.807s	101.967mph	H/M
5	Bradl	Honda	43m 33.235s	26.756s	1m 43.364s	101.097mph	H/M
6	Smith	Yamaha	43m 38.707s	32.228s	1m 43.830s	100.911mph	H/M
7	Dovizioso	Ducati	43m 39.171s	32.692s	1m 43.494s	100.911mph	H/M
8	Espargaro	ART	44m 05.094s	58.615s	1m 44.665s	99.916mph	M/S
9	Edwards	FTR Kawasaki	44m 09.621s	1m 03.142s	1m 44.712s	99.730mph	H/M
10	Pirro	Ducati	44m 16.253s	1m 09.774s	1m 44.213s	99.482mph	H/M
11	Petrucci	Ioda-Suter	44m 30.856s	1m 24.377s	1m 45.505s	98.922mph	H/S
12	Corti	FTR Kawasaki	44m 40.158s	1m 33.679s	1m 45.594s	98.612mph	H/M
13	Hernandez	ART	44m 51.834s	1m 45.355s	1m 45.820s	98.177mph	H/S
14	Staring	FTR Honda	44m 57.224s	1m 50.745s	1m 46.604s	97.990mph	H/M
15	Del Amor	FTR	44m 49.011s	1 Lap	1m 49.283s	94.324mph	H/S
16	Pesek	Ioda-Suter	44m 53.698s	1 Lap	1m 46.850s	94.200mph	H/S
NF	Barbera	FTR	26m 30.243s	10 Laps	1m 45.138s	99.730mph	H/M
NF	Abraham	ART	17m 56.247s	15 Laps	1m 44.771s	98.239mph	H/M
NF	Crutchlow	Yamaha	8m 38.236s	20 Laps	1m 42.696s	101.967mph	H/M
NF	Hayden	Ducati	8m 42.346s	20 Laps	1m 43.364s	101.159mph	H/M
NF	Iannone	Ducati	6m 59.934s	21 Laps	1m 43.484s	100.662mph	H/M
NF	De Puniet	ART	1m 51.160s	24 Laps		95.070mph	H/S
NF	Bautista	Honda		0 Lap			H/M
NF	Laverty	PBM		0 Lap			H/M

CHAMPIONSHIP

	Rider	Nation	Team	Points
1	Pedrosa	SPA	Repsol Honda Team	123
2	Lorenzo	SPA	Yamaha Factory Racing	116
3	Marquez	SPA	Repsol Honda Team	93
4	Crutchlow	GBR	Monster Yamaha Tech 3	71
5	Rossi	ITA	Yamaha Factory Racing	60
6	Dovizioso	ITA	Ducati Team	59
7	Hayden	USA	Ducati Team	45
8	Bradl	GER	LCR Honda MotoGP	41
9	Bautista	SPA	GO&FUN Honda Gresini	38
10	Espargaro	SPA	Power Electronics Aspar	36
11	Smith	GBR	Monster Yamaha Tech 3	34
12	Pirro	ITA	Ignite Pramac Racing	28
13	Iannone	ITA	Energy T.I. Pramac Racing	21
14	Barbera	SPA	Avintia Blusens	13
15	Petrucci	ITA	Came IodaRacing Project	13
16	De Puniet	FRA	Power Electronics Aspar	11
17	Edwards	USA	NGM Mobile Forward Racing	10
18	Spies	USA	Ignite Pramac Racing	9
19	Hernandez	COL	Paul Bird Motorsport	6
20	Corti	ITA	NGM Mobile Forward Racing	4
21	Laverty	GBR	Paul Bird Motorsport	3
22	Staring	AUS	GO&FUN Honda Gresini	2
23	Abraham	CZE	Cardion AB Motoracing	2
24	Aoyama	JPN	Avintia Blusens	1
25	Del Amor	SPA	Avintia Blusens	1

14 BRYAN STARING Scored his first World Championship points, but not overjoyed with his own performance.

15 JAVIER DEL AMOR The story of the weekend! Took over the injured Aoyama's bike on Saturday lunchtime and scored a World Championship point on Sunday. Not bad for a retired racer who was expecting to show Avintia team guests around the pit garage.

16 LUKAS PESEK Fell early on and remounted after a lengthy argument with the marshals.

NON-FINISHERS

HECTOR BARBERA Crashed when he lost the front nine laps from home while pressing to close the gap to Edwards.

KAREL ABRAHAM Pulled out of the race with a mechanical fault while holding tenth place.

CAL CRUTCHLOW Pushing hard to stay with the top three, who were slowly but surely pulling away, when he crashed on lap six after clipping the kerb on the inside of Turn 9. Blamed himself, but pointed out the need to solve the problem of lack of grip at the start of races.

NICKY HAYDEN Fast all weekend, but then hung on to the brake a fraction too long and crashed at Turn 9 on lap six. Uncharacteristically furious and spent some time thumping the air fence, but later said it had been his mistake.

ANDREA IANNONE Yet another early crasher, going down at Turn 10 when he lost the front on lap five.

RANDY DE PUNIET Noticed a lack of power on the first lap and then had the motor lock as he crossed the line.

MICHAEL LAVERTY Lost his 100 per cent finishing record when he ran on at Turn 9 and toppled over in the gravel.

ALVARO BAUTISTA Crashed out at the end of the back straight on the first lap, narrowly avoiding collecting Rossi's Yamaha.

NON-STARTERS

HIROSHI AOYAMA Crashed on Saturday morning, taking the tip off the ring finger on his left hand and damaging the middle digit. Operated on the next day and replaced by del Amor.

BEN SPIES Still unfit after his shoulder operation and over-optimistic attempts to return to racing.

BRIDGESTONE

CENTRE / LEFT / RIGHT
FRONT MEDIUM (M) / HARD (H)

CENTRE / LEFT / RIGHT
REAR SOFT (S) / MEDIUM (M) / HARD (H)

MILD ⬤◯◯◯◯ SEVERE

ROUND 7

YAMAHA
MONSTER ENERGY
YAMALUBE
ENEOS
SEMAKIN DI DEPAN
VR46
46

IVECO TT ASSEN

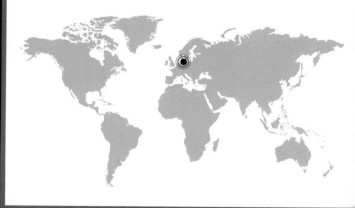

REELING IN THE YEARS

Valentino Rossi won for the first time in nearly three years but was almost eclipsed by Jorge Lorenzo's heroics

It was only right that the grand old theatre of the Assen circuit hosted the most dramatic Grand Prix of recent times, and in front of a full house, as Valentino Rossi ended his personal drought of almost a thousand days without a win. And he did it in style, just like he always did.

The optimism emanating from his camp following a crucial test after the previous race was entirely justified. Rossi started with his best qualifying of the year, the front of the second row, and followed it with a race that reminded everyone of the glory days. In the Ducati years, an American journalist regularly used to say: 'Who's that guy in Rossi's leathers?' Watching Valentino at Assen, it was easy to understand what he meant. The old body language was suddenly back: committed, confident, the shapes only Vale makes on a bike. He was relaxed enough to bide his time as the Repsol Hondas led the way and, when he was happy with the grip of his tyres, he passed them on successive laps to take the lead. A Mexican wave of mass adulation followed him round the circuit, culminating in a mighty roar that almost levitated the wavy roof of the grandstand as he exited the Timmer chicane in the lead. He even set the fastest lap, not something he's ever made a habit of, fifth time round, a lap which included taking the lead off Pedrosa going into the chicane.

For once, though, there was nearly as much attention on a rider other than Rossi. Jorge Lorenzo played out his own drama, although it looked at first as if it might be a tragedy. Jorge dominated the first session with a time that wasn't bettered in free practice. He was looking to do the same in the wet second session when he put his rear wheel on standing

water coming out of Meeuwenmeer. Data from his Alpinestars leathers' airbag said he was doing 149mph, that his 'flight time' – terrible phrase – was over 0.6s and that the first impact was on his left arm. Given the forces involved, Jorge was lucky only his collarbone was broken.

The break would need plating, an operation was scheduled almost immediately at a local hospital, and the paddock got on with calculating by how many points Dani Pedrosa would extend his championship lead. Then it transpired that the determinedly democratic Dutch weren't going to let Lorenzo queue jump, so a flight to Barcelona was organised. Next morning the rumour mill was buzzing. Jorge had had the operation at 2am (the timing would turn out to be crucial) and was returning to Assen 'to be with his team'. He duly arrived on Friday afternoon, accompanied by speculation that he was going to attempt to race.

The rumours turned out to be correct. Crucially, more than 24 hours had passed since he'd had a general anaesthetic and he was able to perform

OPPOSITE The crash that broke Jorge Lorenzo's collarbone on Thursday; he put his back tyre on the painted kerb and crashed at 149mph

ABOVE It's Saturday and 24 hours after having his collarbone pinned, Lorenzo rolls out of his pit garage

RIGHT Cal Crutchlow on his way to his first MotoGP pole position, the first by a Briton in a decade

Valentino Rossi was moved to cross the pit garage before the sighting lap and shake Jorge's hand. Marc Marquez was also hurting. He'd launched himself over the highside at Ramshoek in FP3 on his out-lap on slicks during a predominantly wet session and broken a finger and a toe. It all looked set for Dani Pedrosa to take advantage of his championship rivals' misfortune.

It still looked that way when Dani got the holeshot from the second row (he'd crashed in qualifying). Even when Valentino eased his way into the lead it still looked good. Lorenzo was back in fourth with the attendant Cal Crutchlow surely about to go past, but it didn't quite work out for Dani. It took Cal a long time to overtake Jorge, but once he did he set out to catch the Hondas. Why was he so far back after his first pole position in MotoGP? It was his old problem with the bike not stopping or turning with a full tank. He even had the embarrassment of Lorenzo coming past in the opening laps. But once he was comfortable, Cal put on another startling charge in the closing stages. As he closed on the top three, Pedrosa started running into grip problems and his times slowed abruptly. Cal caught and passed him despite running wide at De Strubben and having to do the work all over again. He then closed down Marquez, who was starting to feel his injuries. Going into the first corner of the last lap, Marquez slowed more than expected and Cal missed him by millimetres. 'I wanted you to see what Dani sees on the TV,' joked Cal, referring to the incident at Barcelona between Dani and Marc.

So Rossi went untroubled to his 80th win, to the joy of the crowd, as Lorenzo rode to a heroic fifth place, thus losing only two points to a very frustrated Pedrosa.

ABOVE The satellite Pramac Yamahas of Andrea Iannone and Michele Pirro circulated together in a good impression of the factory team

BELOW The factory Ducatis were together all race until a coming together in the last corner. Bradley Smith went past both of them

the physical tests demanded by the medical authorities. He rode in warm-up and thought at first he was attempting the impossible, but surprised himself by finding a way to ride that minimised the pain. He passed another test before the race. This wasn't bravado or machismo insisted Jorge, it was a calculated risk by a professional sportsman. And it was a gamble that paid off.

Even by the standards of MotoGP men, whose ability to compartmentalise pain is a constant source of wonder, this was a jaw-dropping endeavour.

'IT'S GOOD FOR THE RACING WHEN HE'S UP AT THE FRONT'
MARC MARQUEZ

OPPOSITE It's been a while. Valentino Rossi on top of the rostrum for the first time since the Malaysian GP in 2010

WHY IT HAD TO BE ASSEN

Before Assen Valentino had yet to come near to challenging his team-mate in either a race or qualifying, and he was behind a Yamaha satellite team rider in the championship. At Qatar he said he'd set himself the target of a rostrum finish on his first race back with Yamaha but that his 'target to be happy' was to win a race this season. He also said he went best on 'the tracks I grew up on'.

That meant the races at the heart of the European season, the places where he'd run up so many wins: Mugello, Catalunya, Assen. Last time out at Barcelona Vale had shown with a fine fourth that he could still lap as fast as the front men on a tricky track, especially in the closing stages. But another average qualifying performance there severely compromised his chances of a rostrum. His early-season pronouncements about the new qualifying format were a distraction from the real issue, pushing hard with the new-generation front tyre (the one that only Casey and Dani didn't

want, remember); last time Vale was on a Yamaha he had the old, stiff carcass. This is a different issue from the choice of softer/harder tread compounds on race day; both grades of tread rubber are applied to the same carcass. That hadn't stopped him trying, through set-up, to turn the 2013 M1 into a replica of his old Yamaha, although the fact he tried Jorge's swingarm in the test may have been indicative of a new approach. However, front-fork modifications produced a mood swing. Specifically, Valentino said he'd found some answers to the problems he had under braking.

Was all he really needed a bit of that rare commodity nowadays, testing? The bottom line was this: if Valentino Rossi couldn't beat a Spaniard or two at Assen, while riding a motorcycle he was happy with, then when could he? The next three tracks looked Honda friendly, as did Motegi and Valencia. Vale is not fond of new tracks, so Silverstone, Indy

and Aragon were bad bets. Could he really rely on a major piece of theatre at home in Misano, or Phillip Island, or Sepang late in the season? Any way you cut it, Assen was always going to be a critical, perhaps even pivotal, point of his season.

IVECO TT
ASSEN
TT CIRCUIT ASSEN

ROUND **7**
June 29

RACE RESULTS

CIRCUIT LENGTH 2.822 miles

NO. OF LAPS 26

RACE DISTANCE 73.379 miles

WEATHER Dry, 18°C

TRACK TEMPERATURE 18°C

WINNER Valentino Rossi

FASTEST LAP 1m 34.894s,
107.062mph, Valentino Rossi

LAP RECORD 1m 34.548s,
107.460mph, Dani Pedrosa, 2012

Circuit map with corner markings:
- Mandeveen — 10
- De Bult 70mph — 2
- Stekkenwal — 8, 80mph 3
- 11 — 2 65mph Duikersloot
- 9
- 12 — Meeuwenmeer
- Ruskenhoek — 7, 14
- 15 — 13, 6 165mph Hoge Heide
- Ramshoek
- 6 — S, 170mph 6
- 4 130mph
- Ossebroeken — 3, 4
- 17, 16 — 2 85mph
- 18 — Geert Timmer Bocht
- Madijk — 2, 5
- 45mph 1 De Strubben
- 1, 5 165mph
- 3 70mph Haarbocht

S SPEED TRAP
1 CORNER NUMBER
1 GEAR SELECTION/SPEED
SECTOR 1
SECTOR 2
SECTOR 3

QUALIFYING

	Rider	Nation	Motorcycle	Team	Time	Pole +
1	Crutchlow	GBR	Yamaha	Monster Yamaha Tech 3	1m 34.398s	
2	Marquez	SPA	Honda	Repsol Honda Team	1m 34.755s	0.357s
3	Bradl	GER	Honda	LCR Honda MotoGP	1m 34.878s	0.480s
4	Rossi	ITA	Yamaha	Yamaha Factory Racing	1m 34.974s	0.576s
5	Pedrosa	SPA	Honda	Repsol Honda Team	1m 35.006s	0.608s
6	Smith	GBR	Yamaha	Monster Yamaha Tech 3	1m 35.454s	1.056s
7	Espargaro	SPA	ART	Power Electronics Aspar	1m 35.500s	1.102s
8	Bautista	SPA	Honda	GO&FUN Honda Gresini	1m 35.508s	1.110s
9	De Puniet	FRA	ART	Power Electronics Aspar	1m 35.622s	1.224s
10	Hayden	USA	Ducati	Ducati Team	1m 35.908s	1.510s
11	Pirro	ITA	Ducati	Ignite Pramac Racing	1m 36.866s	2.468s
12	Lorenzo	SPA	Yamaha	Yamaha Factory Racing		
13	Iannone	ITA	Ducati	Energy T.I. Pramac Racing	1m 36.432s	Q1
14	Barbera	SPA	FTR	Avintia Blusens	1m 36.490s	Q1
15	Dovizioso	ITA	Ducati	Ducati Team	1m 36.524s	Q1
16	Petrucci	ITA	Ioda-Suter	Came IodaRacing Project	1m 36.695s	Q1
17	Abraham	CZE	ART	Cardion AB Motoracing	1m 36.791s	Q1
18	Edwards	USA	FTR Kawasaki	NGM Mobile Forward Racing	1m 37.143s	Q1
19	Staring	AUS	FTR Honda	GO&FUN Honda Gresini	1m 37.315s	Q1
20	Corti	ITA	FTR Kawasaki	NGM Mobile Forward Racing	1m 37.625s	Q1
21	Hernandez	COL	ART	Paul Bird Motorsport	1m 37.781s	Q1
22	Laverty	GBR	PBM	Paul Bird Motorsport	1m 38.378s	Q1
23	Pesek	CZE	Ioda-Suter	Came IodaRacing Project	1m 38.704s	Q1
24	Silva	SPA	FTR	Avintia Blusens	1m 39.077s	Q1

FINISHERS

1 VALENTINO ROSSI After two and a half dry seasons, Vale finally made it 80 race wins in the top class. The vital advances made at the post-Barcelona test allowed him to qualify better than he had all year, start well and, for the first time, do what he wanted on the bike.

2 MARC MARQUEZ Despite a thumping crash in free practice he kept up his record of finishing on the podium. Never had the pace to challenge Rossi and had to work hard to fight off Crutchlow in the final laps when his injured right arm was preventing him braking properly.

3 CAL CRUTCHLOW First pole position – and the first by a British rider in over a decade. Suffered his usual problems in the first five laps and found himself behind Lorenzo. Once past, he caught the Hondas easily and passed the troubled Pedrosa. Scared everyone at the start of the last lap when he nearly touched Marquez and ran on.

4 DANI PEDROSA Got one of his trademark holeshots but quickly ran into tyre problems. Reported lack of grip both front and rear to top a troubled weekend. Sub-20°C track temperatures did not help. Should have taken advantage of Lorenzo's problems but only managed to extend his lead by two points.

5 JORGE LORENZO Broke his collarbone on Thursday, had it plated Friday morning, raced on Saturday: a heroic effort, and calculated to limit the damage to the championship. Astonishingly, he only gave up two points to title-leader Pedrosa.

6 STEFAN BRADL Great qualifying for his first ever front row in MotoGP followed by a good start, but soon shuffled back to sixth. Swapped from Nissin to Brembo brakes; comfortable on them in qualifying but they didn't appear to help in the race.

7 ALVARO BAUTISTA Happy to finish after the last two races. Never happy with his set-up. Took time to get heat into his tyres, then had a problem with his rear brake.

8 ALEIX ESPARGARO Eighth again but only 32 seconds behind the winner! Said it was his best race in MotoGP. Assen may suit the ART but this was still a brilliant ride, though somewhat overshadowed by other goings-on.

9 BRADLEY SMITH Thought the operation to pin his scaphoid after the Barcelona test would mean a pain-free Assen. He was wrong. Superb in qualifying, suffered in the race, but mugged both factory Ducatis on the last corner.

10 ANDREA DOVIZIOSO The stress of the Ducati job showed. Got a penalty point for kicking Barbera in qualifying,

then followed Hayden for the whole race before trying a hard pass on the last corner that allowed Smith past both of them.

11 NICKY HAYDEN Not particularly bothered by Dovi's last-corner pass, but distinctly bothered by the fact they finished over 30 seconds behind the winner. Like the rest of the team, depressed by the post-Barcelona test of the 'lab bike'.

12 RANDY DE PUNIET Regained confidence in the front end, but a wheelie off the line put him behind the satellite Ducatis. When he got past them, the trio in front were too far ahead.

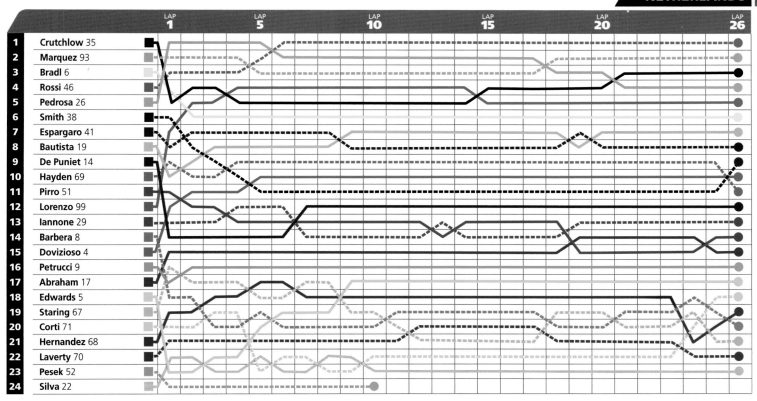

		LAP 1	LAP 5	LAP 10	LAP 15	LAP 20	LAP 26
1	Crutchlow 35						
2	Marquez 93						
3	Bradl 6						
4	Rossi 46						
5	Pedrosa 26						
6	Smith 38						
7	Espargaro 41						
8	Bautista 19						
9	De Puniet 14						
10	Hayden 69						
11	Pirro 51						
12	Lorenzo 99						
13	Iannone 29						
14	Barbera 8						
15	Dovizioso 4						
16	Petrucci 9						
17	Abraham 17						
18	Edwards 5						
19	Staring 67						
20	Corti 71						
21	Hernandez 68						
22	Laverty 70						
23	Pesek 52						
24	Silva 22						

RACE

	Rider	Motorcycle	Race Time	Time +	Fastest Lap	Avg. Speed	B
1	Rossi	Yamaha	41m 25.202s		1m 34.894s	106.254mph	S/MS
2	Marquez	Honda	41m 27.372s	2.170s	1m 34.921s	106.192mph	S/MS
3	Crutchlow	Yamaha	41m 29.275s	4.073s	1m 34.978s	106.068mph	S/MS
4	Pedrosa	Honda	41m 33.034s	7.832s	1m 35.101s	105.944mph	S/MS
5	Lorenzo	Yamaha	41m 40.712s	15.510s	1m 35.066s	105.633mph	S/MS
6	Bradl	Honda	41m 52.721s	27.519s	1m 35.588s	105.074mph	S/MS
7	Bautista	Honda	41m 56.800s	31.598s	1m 35.719s	104.950mph	S/MS
8	Espargaro	ART	41m 57.607s	32.405s	1m 36.076s	104.887mph	S/S
9	Smith	Yamaha	41m 58.953s	33.751s	1m 36.002s	104.825mph	S/MS
10	Dovizioso	Ducati	41m 59.003s	33.801s	1m 35.952s	104.825mph	S/MS
11	Hayden	Ducati	41m 59.573s	34.371s	1m 35.980s	104.825mph	S/MS
12	De Puniet	ART	42m 22.876s	57.674s	1m 36.824s	103.831mph	S/S
13	Iannone	Ducati	42m 26.626s	1m 01.424s	1m 36.756s	103.707mph	S/MS
14	Pirro	Ducati	42m 26.763s	1m 01.561s	1m 36.820s	103.707mph	S/MS
15	Abraham	ART	42m 29.628s	1m 04.426s	1m 36.829s	103.583mph	S/S
16	Petrucci	Ioda-Suter	42m 36.316s	1m 11.114s	1m 37.465s	103.334mph	S/S
17	Edwards	FTR Kawasaki	42m 40.451s	1m 15.249s	1m 37.335s	103.148mph	S/S
18	Corti	FTR Kawasaki	42m 50.086s	1m 24.884s	1m 37.930s	102.775mph	S/S
19	Hernandez	ART	42m 51.056s	1m 25.854s	1m 37.509s	102.713mph	XS/S
20	Barbera	FTR	42m 51.180s	1m 25.978s	1m 37.765s	102.713mph	S/S
21	Staring	FTR Honda	42m 51.458s	1m 26.256s	1m 37.825s	102.713mph	S/S
22	Laverty	PBM	42m 51.812s	1m 26.610s	1m 38.045s	102.713mph	S/S
23	Silva	FTR	43m 03.375s	1m 38.173s	1m 38.084s	102.216mph	S/S
NF	Pesek	Ioda-Suter	16m 51.798s	16 Laps	1m 39.172s	100.414mph	XS/S

CHAMPIONSHIP

	Rider	Nation	Team	Points
1	Pedrosa	SPA	Repsol Honda Team	136
2	Lorenzo	SPA	Yamaha Factory Racing	127
3	Marquez	SPA	Repsol Honda Team	113
4	Crutchlow	GBR	Monster Yamaha Tech 3	87
5	Rossi	ITA	Yamaha Factory Racing	85
6	Dovizioso	ITA	Ducati Team	65
7	Bradl	GER	LCR Honda MotoGP	51
8	Hayden	USA	Ducati Team	50
9	Bautista	SPA	GO&FUN Honda Gresini	47
10	Espargaro	SPA	Power Electronics Aspar	44
11	Smith	GBR	Monster Yamaha Tech 3	41
12	Pirro	ITA	Ignite Pramac Racing	30
13	Iannone	ITA	Energy T.I. Pramac Racing	24
14	De Puniet	FRA	Power Electronics Aspar	15
15	Barbera	SPA	Avintia Blusens	13
16	Petrucci	ITA	Came IodaRacing Project	13
17	Edwards	USA	NGM Mobile Forward Racing	10
18	Spies	USA	Ignite Pramac Racing	9
19	Hernandez	COL	Paul Bird Motorsport	6
20	Corti	ITA	NGM Mobile Forward Racing	4
21	Laverty	GBR	Paul Bird Motorsport	3
22	Abraham	CZE	Cardion AB Motoracing	3
23	Staring	AUS	GO&FUN Honda Gresini	2
24	Aoyama	JPN	Avintia Blusens	1
25	Del Amor	SPA	Avintia Blusens	1

13 ANDREA IANNONE Suffered like every other Ducati rider on a circuit where there isn't much hard braking. Never managed to improve the bike from the first session on.

14 MICHELE PIRRO Replaced Ben Spies on the 'lab bike' using Spies's engines. Went with the other Ducatis at the start but backed off when arm pump made itself felt as early as the second lap.

15 KAREL ABRAHAM Happy to take a point given there was only one retirement from the race. Raced with the satellite Ducatis but couldn't stay with them on the straights.

16 DANILO PETRUCCI Raced the harder front tyre, despite never using it in practice. Chatter in the second half of the race put him out of the points.

17 COLIN EDWARDS Got pushed out a couple of times in the first lap, but came back well despite finding the bike very heavy in changes of direction.

18 CLAUDIO CORTI Similar problems to his team-mate Edwards. Won the four-man dice he was involved in all race.

19 YONNY HERNANDEZ Not happy with being out of the points but content that his lap times were consistent, thanks to work done at the Barcelona test.

20 HECTOR BARBERA Penalised in qualifying for blocking Dovizioso. Qualified best of the FTR riders but was overtaken by both the Forward Racing bikes in the race.

21 BRYAN STARING Involved in a four-bike dice for most of the race. Blamed his finishing position on lack of consistency.

22 MICHAEL LAVERTY Very fast in the wet but found the chassis settings from the Barcelona test did not translate directly to Assen. Lack of dry testing time didn't help.

23 IVAN SILVA Back in the Avintia team as a replacement for Hiro Aoyama.

NON-FINISHERS

LUKAS PESEK Stopped with serious arm-pump problems.

NON-STARTERS

BEN SPIES Still recovering from his serious shoulder problems. Again replaced by Pirro.

HIROSHI AOYAMA Still recovering from the operation on the fingers of his left hand after his Barcelona crash. Replaced by Silva.

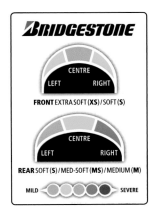

BRIDGESTONE

FRONT EXTRA SOFT (XS) / SOFT (S)

REAR SOFT (S) / MED-SOFT (MS) / MEDIUM (M)

MILD ⬭⬭⬭⬭⬭ SEVERE

eni MOTORRAD GRAND PRIX DEUTSCHLAND

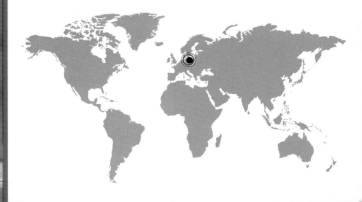

THE MEN WHO FELL TO EARTH

Injury for Lorenzo and Pedrosa, disappointment for Rossi, joy for Marquez

As usual, the story of the German round was the story of the three Spaniards who've dominated the season. This time, however, only Marc Marquez emerged with any reason to smile. Actually, he had every reason to smile. He had the perfect weekend: pole position, the win and the fastest lap – and he went to the top of the points table. His compatriots Pedrosa and Lorenzo suffered a weekend full of pain, and neither made it to the grid.

The first corner at Sachsenring has never been kind to Dani Pedrosa. His 2008 championship bid effectively ended there and it looked as if the same fate might have befallen his 2013 effort when he highsided horribly on Saturday morning. Dani was far from the only casualty of a vicious weekend, however. Jorge Lorenzo, perhaps a victim of the same over-confidence that hurt him at Assen, bent the plate on his collarbone while attempting to going fastest in the second session, as he had in FP1.

Pedrosa came down hard on his head and left shoulder. Initial investigation, both at the track and at Chemnitz hospital, revealed no fractures but he had low blood pressure and was complaining of dizziness. He intended to take part on Sunday but his symptoms recurred after he'd been cleared to ride and his permission was revoked. For Jorge, there was to be no repeat of the iron-man antics of Assen two weeks previously. He again returned to Barcelona for an operation that was, of course, considerably more complicated than the original one.

A combination of cool conditions and the nature of the Sachsenring track saw a rash of crashes, many at the top of the Waterfall, the off-camber, downhill right-hander that follows a succession of lefts – although it should be noted that neither Jorge nor Dani were victims

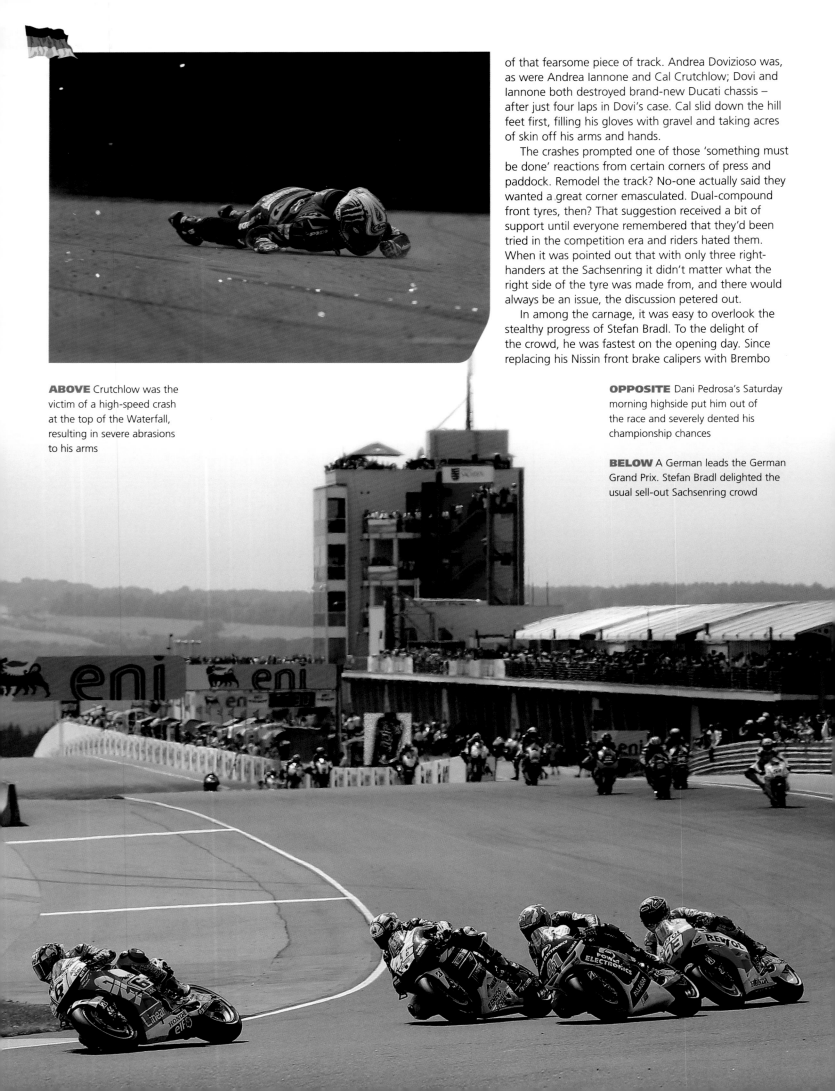

of that fearsome piece of track. Andrea Dovizioso was, as were Andrea Iannone and Cal Crutchlow; Dovi and Iannone both destroyed brand-new Ducati chassis – after just four laps in Dovi's case. Cal slid down the hill feet first, filling his gloves with gravel and taking acres of skin off his arms and hands.

The crashes prompted one of those 'something must be done' reactions from certain corners of press and paddock. Remodel the track? No-one actually said they wanted a great corner emasculated. Dual-compound front tyres, then? That suggestion received a bit of support until everyone remembered that they'd been tried in the competition era and riders hated them. When it was pointed out that with only three right-handers at the Sachsenring it didn't matter what the right side of the tyre was made from, and there would always be an issue, the discussion petered out.

In among the carnage, it was easy to overlook the stealthy progress of Stefan Bradl. To the delight of the crowd, he was fastest on the opening day. Since replacing his Nissin front brake calipers with Brembo

ABOVE Crutchlow was the victim of a high-speed crash at the top of the Waterfall, resulting in severe abrasions to his arms

OPPOSITE Dani Pedrosa's Saturday morning highside put him out of the race and severely dented his championship chances

BELOW A German leads the German Grand Prix. Stefan Bradl delighted the usual sell-out Sachsenring crowd

the young German was showing distinct signs of overcoming the front-end difficulties that had afflicted him since Aragon the previous season. HRC people had started to indicate their worry that he had hit a level and seemed unable to solve his problem and progress. The change of brakes certainly helped. At Assen he started from the front row for the first time in his MotoGP career and in Germany he seemed on course to do it again until he slipped off at the bottom of the Omega.

In Holland, his race had done little to back up his qualifying performance; indeed it was his second-worst finish of the season so far, but at home he overcame the problems that had seen him crash three times in the first four races of the season. Frustratingly, the rostrum was just out of reach but the usual packed house got to cheer him passing Rossi on the first lap and leading until the sixth when he succumbed to Marc Marquez's inevitable progress. However, Bradl's performance, which had been flat-lining for months, was most definitely on the upswing.

It looked like Valentino Rossi would be able to say the same thing. He started from the front row for the

'HE CONTROLLED THE GAP TO ME VERY WELL, HE DESERVED TO WIN'
CAL CRUTCHLOW

ABOVE Despite riding hurt, Cal Crutchlow charged hard at the end of the race after passing five riders and came closer than he's ever been to winning a GP

BELOW Marc Marquez's victory put him back to the top of the championship table

OPPOSITE Aleix Espargaro split the factory Ducatis, indeed it took a mighty last-lap effort from Dovizioso to take seventh off him

first time since the Portuguese GP of 2010, got the holeshot and looked ready to take on Marquez, just as he'd done at Qatar. It didn't happen; instead of the regal progress of Assen, he was caught, passed and gapped by a very sore Cal Crutchlow on a supposedly lower-spec Yamaha. Valentino was distinctly unimpressed, despite scoring back-to-back rostrums. Crutchlow wasn't, not surprisingly since it was the first time he'd done it.

The other Spaniard who had a good weekend was Aleix Espargaro. The softer rear tyre (compared to the prototypes) used by the CRT machines enabled Aleix to start from fifth on the grid, a personal best and the best ever by a CRT rider. However, it was his race performance, including a round-the-outside move on the leaders at Turn 1 that seriously impressed Cal Crutchlow, which caught the eye. Espargaro ran in the top three for a couple of laps before being shuffled down the order to take yet another eighth place. His Aprilia is definitely a considerably higher spec than the others on the grid, but the way he'd put his team-mate de Puniet firmly in the shade all year is the real indicator of Aleix's pace. His misfortune is to be the fourth-fastest Spaniard in the class and to have a very fast younger brother.

To compound the discomfort of Pedrosa and Lorenzo, the next Grand Prix was only a week away, at Laguna Seca. The prospect of a long-haul flight followed by a very physical, left-handed track was not attractive for someone with nasty left-shoulder injuries and, in Dani's case, symptoms of something potentially more serious. One thing was obvious: with Marquez taking such comprehensive advantage of their absence, both would be forced to try and ride in California.

BACK TO THE FUTURE

There were more senior Japanese personnel in the Sachsenring paddock than is usual for anywhere except Motegi. The reason? Meetings of the Grand Prix Commission had been set up to finalise the technical regulations for next season onwards and to negotiate the contracts to go with those changes. The results of their deliberations were released over the following couple of weeks, indicating a little more wrangling over detail. Carmelo Ezpeleta's willingness to move towards the CRT format had already forced the factories' hands; if they wanted MotoGP to remain a pure prototype series they would have to supply the bikes. For 2014 Honda will supply customer bikes, Yamaha will lease M1 engines, and Ducati may even lease this year's bikes. Against the costs of those options, there will also be interest in Aprilia's ART.

The Commission confirmed that there would be two types of motorcycle on the grid in 2014: those with factory status and those without. Both types will have to use the series' specified official ECU with data-logger. Each manufacturer (and that word includes chassis makers) may enter up to four bikes designated as having 'factory' status. These bikes will have to use the official ECU but will be able to use the manufacturer's own software. The penalty for that concession is that factory bikes will be limited to 20 litres of fuel and 5 engines. The others will use the official software, have 24 litres of petrol per race and up to 12 engines for the season.

The concept of a claiming rule, already watered down, will thankfully not survive beyond this season. It was never going to be used and served only to complicate matters. From 2014 onwards we will be back to talking about factory or works machines and privateers, the crucial difference being the software and fuel allowance. Some of the privateers will buy their own machines, while others will build chassis for leased engines.

eni MOTORRAD GRAND PRIX DEUTSCHLAND
SACHSENRING CIRCUIT

ROUND **8**
July 14

RACE RESULTS

CIRCUIT LENGTH 2.281 miles

NO. OF LAPS 30

RACE DISTANCE 68.432 miles

WEATHER Dry, 23°C

TRACK TEMPERATURE 42°C

WINNER Marc Marquez

FASTEST LAP 1m 22.066s, 100.041mph, Marc Marquez

LAP RECORD 1m 21.846s, 100.351mph, Dani Pedrosa, 2011

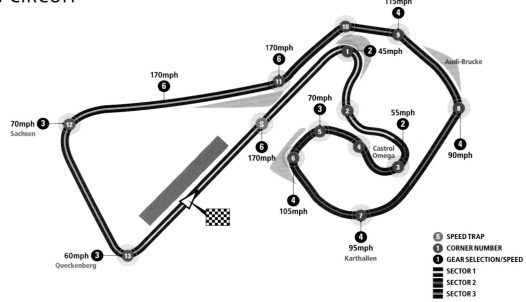

115mph — 4
170mph — 6
170mph — 6
70mph — 3 Sachsen 12
70mph — 3
105mph — 4
60mph — 3 Queckenberg
95mph — 4 Karthallen
90mph — 4
55mph — 2 Castrol Omega
45mph — 2
Audi-Brucke

S SPEED TRAP
1 CORNER NUMBER
1 GEAR SELECTION/SPEED
■ SECTOR 1
■ SECTOR 2
■ SECTOR 3

QUALIFYING

	Rider	Nation	Motorcycle	Team	Time	Pole +
1	**Marquez**	SPA	Honda	Repsol Honda Team	**1m 21.311s**	
2	Crutchlow	GBR	Yamaha	Monster Yamaha Tech 3	**1m 21.434s**	0.123s
3	Rossi	ITA	Yamaha	Yamaha Factory Racing	**1m 21.493s**	0.182s
4	Bradl	GER	Honda	LCR Honda MotoGP	**1m 21.862s**	0.551s
5	Espargaro	SPA	ART	Power Electronics Aspar	**1m 21.887s**	0.576s
6	Hayden	USA	Ducati	Ducati Team	**1m 22.157s**	0.846s
7	Smith	GBR	Yamaha	Monster Yamaha Tech 3	**1m 22.297s**	0.986s
8	Bautista	SPA	Honda	GO&FUN Honda Gresini	**1m 22.484s**	1.173s
9	Dovizioso	ITA	Ducati	Ducati Team	**1m 22.561s**	1.250s
10	Corti	ITA	FTR Kawasaki	NGM Mobile Forward Racing	**1m 23.059s**	1.748s
11	Petrucci	ITA	Ioda-Suter	Came IodaRacing Project	**1m 23.361s**	2.050s
12	Pedrosa	SPA	Honda	Repsol Honda Team		
13	De Puniet	FRA	ART	Power Electronics Aspar	**1m 23.152s**	Q1
14	Barbera	SPA	FTR	Avintia Blusens	**1m 23.333s**	Q1
15	Pirro	ITA	Ducati	Ignite Pramac Racing	**1m 23.349s**	Q1
16	Laverty	GBR	PBM	Paul Bird Motorsport	**1m 23.549s**	Q1
17	Hernandez	COL	ART	Paul Bird Motorsport	**1m 23.565s**	Q1
18	Edwards	USA	FTR Kawasaki	NGM Mobile Forward Racing	**1m 23.631s**	Q1
19	Abraham	CZE	ART	Cardion AB Motoracing	**1m 23.752s**	Q1
20	Aoyama	JPN	FTR	Avintia Blusens	**1m 23.820s**	Q1
21	Pesek	CZE	Ioda-Suter	Came IodaRacing Project	**1m 24.395s**	Q1
22	Staring	AUS	FTR Honda	GO&FUN Honda Gresini	**1m 27.273s**	Q1
23	Iannone	ITA	Ducati	Energy T.I. Pramac Racing		Q1

FINISHERS

1 MARC MARQUEZ Took full advantage of the absence of the World Champion and the championship leader to win from pole and go back to the top of the table. Had to get past Rossi plus fast starters Bradl and Espargaro and then fight off Crutchlow in the closing laps.

2 CAL CRUTCHLOW Started from the front row for the fourth time this year and took his fourth podium of the year; no Brit had done that since Sheene in '82. Again lost ground in the first few laps and then charged at the end to within 1.5s of Marquez before the Spaniard responded.

3 VALENTINO ROSSI Nowhere near as happy as in the Netherlands. Started from the front row for the first time since Portugal 2010 but was caught, passed and dropped by Crutchlow on the satellite Yamaha.

4 STEFAN BRADL Delighted the crowd by leading his home race for five laps, but five laps later had been relegated to fourth place. Identified corner speed in the second section as the place where he lost out to the competition: 'A weak point for us.'

5 ALVARO BAUTISTA A better result than practice suggested thanks to a great start and dogged concentration to overcome a horrible lack of traction in the second sector, from the Omega curve up the hill

and through the first three slow lefts. Happy to put in a good weekend's work after the travails of the previous races.

6 BRADLEY SMITH The finishing position was impressive but the gap to the winner, 25 seconds, was more so, an improvement of 7s on his previous best. Not bad with a weak left wrist from the screw in his scaphoid inserted after Catalunya.

7 ANDREA DOVIZIOSO Started the weekend with one new chassis and one standard but wrote off the new one on Friday morning with a massive crash at the Waterfall. Then it was the same old story, lack of front-end grip on a track where it's essential to know what the front is gripping.

8 ALEIX ESPARGARO A stellar weekend: qualified fifth, his best-ever starting position and the best ever by a rider on a CRT bike. Tried to go round the outside at Turn 1 and was in the top three for the first couple of laps, until the soft tyre lost its edge, but it took a serious effort from Dovi on the last lap to take seventh off him.

9 NICKY HAYDEN Looked like a good weekend up to Sunday morning, starting from the second row on a track he likes. Then he had a crash in warm-up and had to use his second bike for the race. Nowhere near as fast as on his preferred bike, with lack of rear grip the main difference.

10 MICHELE PIRRO Again replaced Spies on the Pramac bike and raced at similar lap times and in close proximity to Hayden, which pleased him, as did his consistency. However, he never got a good feeling with the bike, as his fifth-row qualifying demonstrated.

11 HECTOR BARBERA An encouraging weekend. Gambled with a front-end change for the race, which worked despite a slow start. Finished right on the tail of Pirro's Ducati having passed both Forward Racing bikes.

12 RANDY DE PUNIET Went back to the 2012 chassis on Sunday morning in an attempt to get the feel he'd been looking for all year. It worked, but it took him a few laps of the race to get used to it.

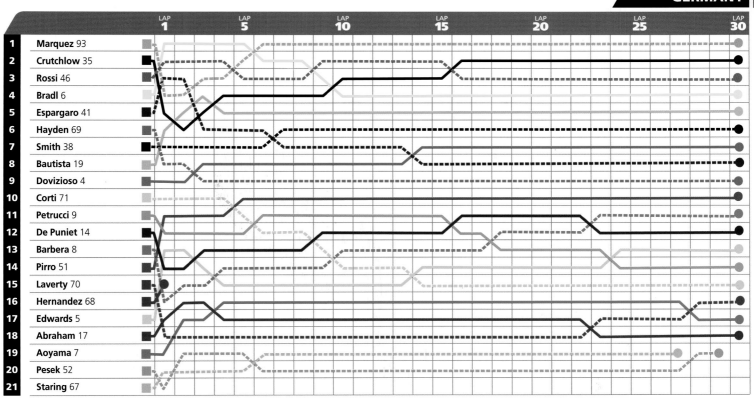

		LAP 1	LAP 5	LAP 10	LAP 15	LAP 20	LAP 25	LAP 30
1	Marquez 93							
2	Crutchlow 35							
3	Rossi 46							
4	Bradl 6							
5	Espargaro 41							
6	Hayden 69							
7	Smith 38							
8	Bautista 19							
9	Dovizioso 4							
10	Corti 71							
11	Petrucci 9							
12	De Puniet 14							
13	Barbera 8							
14	Pirro 51							
15	Laverty 70							
16	Hernandez 68							
17	Edwards 5							
18	Abraham 17							
19	Aoyama 7							
20	Pesek 52							
21	Staring 67							

RACE

	Rider	Motorcycle	Race Time	Time +	Fastest Lap	Avg. Speed	B
1	Marquez	Honda	41m 14.653s		1m 22.066s	99.544mph	H/M
2	Crutchlow	Yamaha	41m 16.212s	1.559	1m 22.094s	99.482mph	H/M
3	Rossi	Yamaha	41m 24.273s	9.620	1m 22.275s	99.109mph	H/M
4	Bradl	Honda	41m 28.645s	13.992	1m 22.439s	98.984mph	H/M
5	Bautista	Honda	41m 36.428s	21.775	1m 22.657s	98.674mph	H/M
6	Smith	Yamaha	41m 39.733s	25.080	1m 22.863s	98.549mph	H/M
7	Dovizioso	Ducati	41m 44.680s	30.027	1m 22.967s	98.301mph	H/M
8	Espargaro	ART	41m 44.977s	30.324	1m 22.980s	98.301mph	H/S
9	Hayden	Ducati	42m 00.008s	45.355	1m 23.228s	97.742mph	H/M
10	Pirro	Ducati	42m 01.795s	47.142	1m 23.589s	97.680mph	H/M
11	Barbera	FTR	42m 02.477s	47.824	1m 23.403s	97.617mph	H/S
12	De Puniet	ART	42m 03.176s	48.523	1m 23.584s	97.617mph	S/S
13	Edwards	FTR Kawasaki	42m 09.081s	54.428	1m 23.663s	97.369mph	H/S
14	Petrucci	Ioda-Suter	42m 14.976s	1m 00.323	1m 23.833s	97.120mph	H/S
15	Corti	FTR Kawasaki	42m 20.183s	1m 05.530	1m 23.869s	96.934mph	H/M
16	Laverty	PBM	42m 23.806s	1m 09.153	1m 24.354s	96.810mph	H/S
17	Aoyama	FTR	42m 30.254s	1m 15.601	1m 23.904s	96.561mph	H/S
18	Abraham	ART	42m 34.336s	1m 19.683	1m 24.175s	96.437mph	H/S
19	Pesek	Ioda-Suter	41m 38.078s	1 Lap	1m 25.027s	95.318mph	S/S
NF	Staring	FTR Honda	38m 34.021s	3 Laps	1m 24.916s	95.753mph	S/S
NF	Hernandez	ART	1m 28.380s	29 Laps		92.895mph	S/M

CHAMPIONSHIP

	Rider	Nation	Team	Points
1	Marquez	SPA	Repsol Honda Team	138
2	Pedrosa	SPA	Repsol Honda Team	136
3	Lorenzo	SPA	Yamaha Factory Racing	127
4	Crutchlow	GBR	Monster Yamaha Tech 3	107
5	Rossi	ITA	Yamaha Factory Racing	101
6	Dovizioso	ITA	Ducati Team	74
7	Bradl	GER	LCR Honda MotoGP	64
8	Bautista	SPA	GO&FUN Honda Gresini	58
9	Hayden	USA	Ducati Team	57
10	Espargaro	SPA	Power Electronics Aspar	52
11	Smith	GBR	Monster Yamaha Tech 3	51
12	Pirro	ITA	Ignite Pramac Racing	36
13	Iannone	ITA	Energy T.I. Pramac Racing	24
14	De Puniet	FRA	Power Electronics Aspar	19
15	Barbera	SPA	Avintia Blusens	18
16	Petrucci	ITA	Came IodaRacing Project	15
17	Edwards	USA	NGM Mobile Forward Racing	13
18	Spies	USA	Ignite Pramac Racing	9
19	Hernandez	COL	Paul Bird Motorsport	6
20	Corti	ITA	NGM Mobile Forward Racing	5
21	Laverty	GBR	Paul Bird Motorsport	3
22	Abraham	CZE	Cardion AB Motoracing	3
23	Staring	AUS	GO&FUN Honda Gresini	2
24	Aoyama	JPN	Avintia Blusens	1
25	Del Amor	SPA	Avintia Blusens	1

13 COLIN EDWARDS Started well but had trouble turning the bike in the first few laps. Equalled his qualifying times once the fuel load went down but ran out of grip on the left side in the last six or seven laps.

14 DANILO PETRUCCI Happy for the first half of the race but then chatter started, which both slowed and distracted him.

15 CLAUDIO CORTI Confused by the way the bike behaved in the race and suspicious of the tyre, but happy to grab a point.

16 MICHAEL LAVERTY Another solid race but failed to score points. Was one of many practice fallers at the Waterfall.

17 HIROSHI AOYAMA Back after the hand injury sustained at Mugello.

18 KAREL ABRAHAM Suffering with flu. Sat out one practice session and had to be lifted from his bike after the race.

19 LUKAS PESEK Never tried the hard front so raced with the softer option, which compromised his pace in the second half of the race. Happy to finish.

NON-FINISHERS

BRYAN STARING Four crashes in the weekend, including one in the race when he was letting the top three lap him.

YONNY HERNANDEZ Crashed for the third time in the weekend on the opening lap. Team-owner Paul Bird was not amused, especially by the one in warm-up.

NON-STARTERS

BEN SPIES Still undergoing treatment on his shoulder. Replaced by factory tester Michele Pirro.

DANI PEDROSA Crashed heavily at Turn 1 on Saturday morning, hitting his head hard and cracking his collarbone. Cleared to ride but suffered a return of dizziness and low blood pressure so his clearance was withdrawn.

JORGE LORENZO Fell at the top of the Waterfall corner in FP2 and bent the plate on the collarbone he'd broken in Assen. This time he returned to Barcelona after definitively withdrawing from the race.

ANDREA IANNONE Dislocated his shoulder in a Turn 1 crash during fourth free practice. Decided not to race in the hope of being fit for Laguna Seca the following weekend.

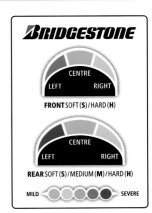

BRIDGESTONE

FRONT SOFT (**S**) / HARD (**H**)

REAR SOFT (**S**) / MEDIUM (**M**) / HARD (**H**)

MILD ——— SEVERE

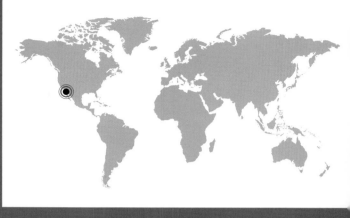

RED BULL
U.S. GRAND PRIX

REPEAT PRESCRIPTION

Marc Marquez took advantage of the walking wounded to win consecutive races for the first time

There was only a week between the German and American rounds, so there was no reason to expect a challenge from either Dani Pedrosa or Jorge Lorenzo. Both injured their left collarbones at the Sachsenring, in Lorenzo's case bending a surgical plate that had been inserted only two weeks previously. Despite having a bigger plate, more screws and some bone cement inserted, Jorge turned up and rode all the sessions. Pedrosa, on the other hand, kept his cards very close to his chest. Or rather the Honda team surrounded him with a wall of silence. The official line was that Dani had partly broken his left collarbone, the one that had been operated on five times before. There was also talk of muscle torn away from the shoulder.

Both riders travelled to the USA later than is usual, preferring to stay in Spain for therapy rather than trying to lessen the effects of jet lag. The phrase 'damage limitation' was used a lot. Honda didn't send Pedrosa out for the morning session on either Friday or Saturday. Laguna is close to the coast and it is quite usual for the track to be cold and misty when proceedings get under way – and Dani would learn very little and risk a lot on a cold track. Both men were obviously in pain and clearly would not be able to contend for the win at the toughest track of the year for a rider with a damaged left shoulder: tight, left-handed, with several hard-braking spots and nowhere to rest. The question now was who would take most advantage.

The first man to make his presence felt was Stefan Bradl. Since he'd swapped to Brembo brakes at Assen he'd made it on to the front row for the first time and led his home race. In the USA, he started fast and stayed fast. He was second fastest in both FP2 and FP4, took

ABOVE Stefan Bradl's run of top form continued. He started from pole position for the first time in MotoGP

LEFT The satellite Hondas lead the charge through Turn 1

OPPOSITE When Rossi pushed Marquez wide at the top of the Corkscrew, it looked like a repeat of the 2008 incident between Valentino and Casey Stoner. Any similarity between the events are definitely deliberate

his first pole on Saturday and started Sunday by being quickest in warm-up. This was no lucky pole – Marquez crashed trying to better Stefan's time – it was the culmination of good, solid, professional work throughout the weekend. Helped, of course, by the confidence built over the previous two races. It also came as the paddock was awash with the latest batch of rumours concerning the future of Cal Crutchlow. The Laguna version said that he would be taking Bradl's ride. When Stefan admitted in a press conference that he hadn't got a contract for 2014 the gossip gained substance, trumping the Cal to Ducati rumours which were in pole position after Nicky Hayden announced that Ducati had decided to dispense with his services for next season.

However, Cal had a very quiet weekend. Distracted by the speculation about his future? Maybe. But it left Valentino Rossi to carry the Yamaha banner. He might only have finished third but Vale was much happier than he'd been with the same position the previous week. He fought off Bautista's challenge for the last rostrum place but could do nothing about the Hondas in front of him. He tried though, oh how he tried. When

ABOVE What? Only one Spaniard on the rostrum! Bradl and Rossi flank Marquez

OPPOSITE For Jorge Lorenzo, Laguna Seca was always about damage limitation. He finished a brave sixth

BELOW Alex de Angelis stood in for Ben Spies. Here he leads Hector Barbera, who broke Espargaro's season-long streak of CRT class wins

Marquez went to the inside in the right-hand kink over the brow approaching the Corkscrew Rossi went deep in the corner, leaving Marc nowhere to go. Well, that's what Valentino thought. Marquez refused to concede the corner and both men turned in very late and then, inevitably, ran over the inside of the kerb. It was almost identical to the Rossi–Stoner incident of 2008, an event that haunted Casey. To call Marquez's move audacious is to be guilty of the wildest understatement. When, post-event, pictures came to light of him sitting on his scooter

on the very spot on the outside of the track it seemed as if the move might even have been premeditated.

Marquez went on to reel in the impressive Bradl and become the first rookie to win the big race at Laguna. He also took another record off Freddie Spencer – for youngest rider to win back-to-back races in the top class. Bradl took second for his first rostrum and to make a strong case to Honda. Valentino was happy with third place on a track that played to the strengths of the Hondas. He had no option but to be happy with Marquez, although there were some within Yamaha with short memories who were very unhappy. First Valentino playfully strangled the Spaniard in parc fermé before the two hugged each other. Marquez, smiley as ever, said he would 'pay copyright' for the pass. Vale managed to keep smiling and say he now had credit with Marc for the rest of the season when it came to a marginal passing move.

Rossi took out any frustration he felt on Livio Suppo, Honda team principal: 'So. You and Stoner broke my balls for two or three years about that overtake, because I cut the corner, you know? So what do you say today? Have to be disqualified, eh? Have to be disqualified?'

Suppo was unmoved: 'Thank you for the question. Thank you to Marc, after a few years, we pay back.'

Still no love lost there.

Almost unnoticed, the collarbone casualties rolled in fifth and sixth, which meant a significant increase in Marc Marquez's championship lead to 16 points over Pedrosa, with Lorenzo another 10 points further back at the half-way point of the season. The question everyone was silently asking was would the situation have been vastly different if the two older Spaniards had been unhurt?

'I ALREADY SAID TO HIM [ROSSI] THAT I WILL PAY COPYRIGHT...'

MARC MARQUEZ

MOTOR HEADS

For 2013, the engine allocation for factory machines was reduced by one, to five motors for the season. At the half-way point the usual pattern was emerging: Honda were cruising, Yamaha were worrying and engines were the least of Ducati's worries.

All four Honda riders have used three engines. In each case, the first two have been used for around 40 sessions, including four races. Every Honda rider's third motor has been raced once and used for, on average, around 10 sessions. One Honda engine has been withdrawn, meaning it cannot be used again. That was Alvaro Bautista's third motor, used for 12 sessions, including one race. Don't read too much into that. Last year Hiroshi Aoyama had a motor withdrawn early in the season, so presumably one of the junior satellite team's motors is routinely sent home for forensic analysis of wear rates.

Over at Yamaha things were a little trickier. All four riders have used four engines, and both factory riders have had one withdrawn: Rossi's second engine after 28 sessions, three of which were races; Lorenzo's first after just 15 practice sessions plus two races. That leaves each Yamaha rider with just one new motor to take to complete the season. At current rates that is possible, but there is absolutely no room for any losses of the sort experienced by Lorenzo last season when one of his engines blew up on its side in an Assen gravel trap after he was torpedoed by Bautista.

All the Ducati riders still have two motors to take and one withdrawn from service. Of the CRT riders, allowed 12 motors for the year, Petrucci and Barbera have had six engines withdrawn and may run into trouble before the end of the year. The penalty for taking an extra motor over and above the allocation is to start the race where the offence occurs from pit lane.

- **S** SPEED TRAP
- **1** CORNER NUMBER
- **1** GEAR SELECTION/SPEED
- SECTOR 1
- SECTOR 2
- SECTOR 3

RED BULL
U.S. GRAND PRIX
LAGUNA SECA

ROUND 9
July 21

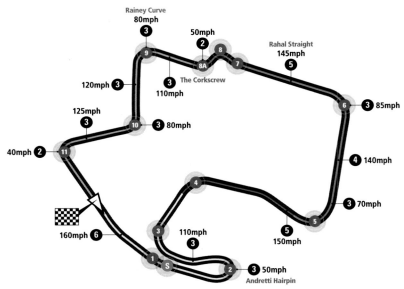

RACE RESULTS

CIRCUIT LENGTH 2.243 miles

NO. OF LAPS 32

RACE DISTANCE 71.781 miles

WEATHER Dry, 23°C

TRACK TEMPERATURE 49°C

WINNER Marc Marquez

FASTEST LAP 1m 21.539s, 98.984mph, Marc Marquez

LAP RECORD 1m 21.229s, 99.414mph, Dani Pedrosa, 2012

QUALIFYING

	Rider	Nation	Motorcycle	Team	Time	Pole +
1	**Bradl**	GER	Honda	LCR Honda MotoGP	1m 21.176s	
2	**Marquez**	SPA	Honda	Repsol Honda Team	1m 21.193s	0.017s
3	**Bautista**	SPA	Honda	GO&FUN Honda Gresini	1m 21.373s	0.197s
4	**Rossi**	ITA	Yamaha	Yamaha Factory Racing	1m 21.418s	0.242s
5	**Crutchlow**	GBR	Yamaha	Monster Yamaha Tech 3	1m 21.420s	0.244s
6	**Lorenzo**	SPA	Yamaha	Yamaha Factory Racing	1m 21.453s	0.277s
7	**Pedrosa**	SPA	Honda	Repsol Honda Team	1m 21.728s	0.552s
8	**Dovizioso**	ITA	Ducati	Ducati Team	1m 22.026s	0.850s
9	**Smith**	GBR	Yamaha	Monster Yamaha Tech 3	1m 22.075s	0.899s
10	**Hayden**	USA	Ducati	Ducati Team	1m 22.090s	0.914s
11	**Espargaro**	SPA	ART	Power Electronics Aspar	1m 22.099s	0.923s
12	**De Puniet**	FRA	ART	Power Electronics Aspar		
13	**Barbera**	SPA	FTR	Avintia Blusens	1m 22.808s	Q1
14	**De Angelis**	RSM	Ducati	Ignite Pramac Racing	1m 23.253s	Q1
15	**Edwards**	USA	FTR Kawasaki	NGM Mobile Forward Racing	1m 23.272s	Q1
16	**Petrucci**	ITA	Ioda-Suter	Came IodaRacing Project	1m 23.323s	Q1
17	**Corti**	ITA	FTR Kawasaki	NGM Mobile Forward Racing	1m 23.616s	Q1
18	**Hernandez**	COL	ART	Paul Bird Motorsport	1m 23.875s	Q1
19	**Abraham**	CZE	ART	Cardion AB Motoracing	1m 23.919s	Q1
20	**Laverty**	GBR	PBM	Paul Bird Motorsport	1m 23.987s	Q1
21	**Aoyama**	JPN	FTR	Avintia Blusens	1m 24.235s	Q1
22	**Staring**	AUS	FTR Honda	GO&FUN Honda Gresini	1m 24.756s	Q1
23	**Pesek**	CZE	Ioda-Suter	Came IodaRacing Project	1m 24.809s	Q1

FINISHERS

1 MARC MARQUEZ Back-to-back wins to break another of Spencer's records, becoming the first rookie to win here, and consolidating his place at the top of the table. Took second off Rossi with a premeditated replica of the infamous pass Vale made on Stoner in 2008, down the Corkscrew, then hauled in Bradl for victory.

2 STEFAN BRADL A brilliant weekend that started with pole position and ended with his first rostrum finish, after leading for half the race. It was the first pole by a German in the top class and the first rostrum since 1971.

3 VALENTINO ROSSI Top Yamaha by a distance and much happier with third than he was in Germany, on the grounds this track favours the Hondas. Couldn't catch Bradl, but controlled Bautista. Became the oldest rider ever to score three consecutive rostrums in the top class.

4 ALVARO BAUTISTA A solid weekend so nearly capped off with a rostrum, but Rossi was too clever. Nevertheless, a massive confidence boost for Alvaro and the team after recent events.

5 DANI PEDROSA Wrapped in cotton wool and secrecy by Honda for the entire weekend. Cleverly sat out morning sessions to reduce the risk of a cold track

crash and save energy for the race. Clearly in pain from the shoulder hurt in Germany but able to overtake Lorenzo.

6 JORGE LORENZO After two general anaesthetics in two weeks and no training for almost three weeks, this was always going to be an exercise in damage limitation. Not surprisingly, Jorge suffered on the most physical track of the year but achieved his objective of scoring points.

7 CAL CRUTCHLOW A bad weekend and the first time he hasn't finished a race as top satellite bike rider. Struggled all weekend but took solace from the thought that in previous years he would have crashed trying to make up for the lack of grip.

8 NICKY HAYDEN Another tough weekend not helped by overheating his rear brake early on and then having his left handlebar and lever rearranged when Dovizioso moved across involuntarily on the front straight. Recovered to retake eighth after going through Turn 2 in fourth due to a bent clutch lever.

9 ANDREA DOVIZIOSO Spent most of the race with his team-mate, as has become the norm. There was a scary coming-together on the front straight late on but he was unable to defend his advantage over Hayden.

10 HECTOR BARBERA Top CRT for the first time this season after a splendid

battle with Edwards and de Angelis. Hector and Alex swapped places four times on the last lap in a replay of their old 250 battles.

11 ALEX DE ANGELIS Rode Ben Spies's standard 2013 Ducati as a replacement because factory tester Pirro was committed to a test. Had a mainly lonely race until he indulged in a bit of fairing bashing with Barbera in the closing laps.

12 COLIN EDWARDS Only a second off being top CRT. Started well, pushed for a few laps and then took stock of his position. Used de Angelis as a reference but couldn't fight off Barbera at the end.

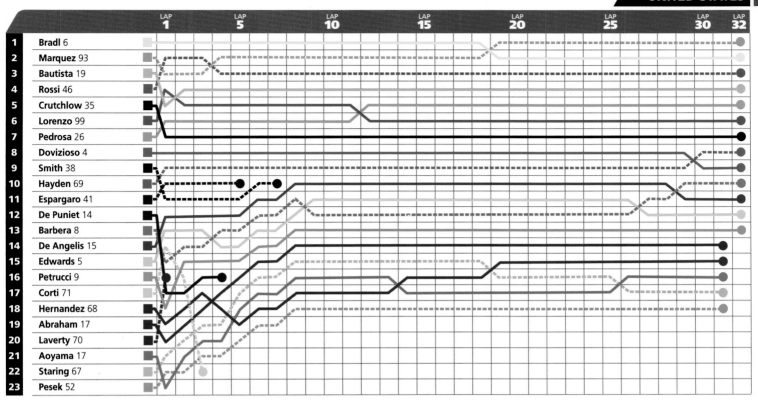

		LAP 1	LAP 5	LAP 10	LAP 15	LAP 20	LAP 25	LAP 30	LAP 32
1	Bradl 6								
2	Marquez 93								
3	Bautista 19								
4	Rossi 46								
5	Crutchlow 35								
6	Lorenzo 99								
7	Pedrosa 26								
8	Dovizioso 4								
9	Smith 38								
10	Hayden 69								
11	Espargaro 41								
12	De Puniet 14								
13	Barbera 8								
14	De Angelis 15								
15	Edwards 5								
16	Petrucci 9								
17	Corti 71								
18	Hernandez 68								
19	Abraham 17								
20	Laverty 70								
21	Aoyama 17								
22	Staring 67								
23	Pesek 52								

RACE

	Rider	Motorcycle	Race Time	Time +	Fastest Lap	Avg. Speed	B
1	Marquez	Honda	44m 00.695s		1m 21.539s	97.804mph	M/S
2	Bradl	Honda	44m 02.993s	2.298s	1m 21.781s	97.742mph	M/S
3	Rossi	Yamaha	44m 05.193s	4.498s	1m 22.088s	97.680mph	M/S
4	Bautista	Honda	44m 05.252s	4.557s	1m 22.102s	97.680mph	M/S
5	Pedrosa	Honda	44m 09.952s	9.257s	1m 22.240s	97.493mph	M/S
6	Lorenzo	Yamaha	44m 13.665s	12.970s	1m 22.219s	97.369mph	M/S
7	Crutchlow	Yamaha	44m 15.999s	15.304s	1m 22.187s	97.245mph	M/S
8	Hayden	Ducati	44m 34.658s	33.963s	1m 22.651s	96.561mph	M/S
9	Dovizioso	Ducati	44m 34.824s	34.129s	1m 22.657s	96.561mph	M/S
10	Barbera	FTR	45m 03.064s	1m 02.369s	1m 23.720s	95.567mph	M/XS
11	De Angelis	Ducati	45m 03.299s	1m 02.604s	1m 23.430s	95.567mph	M/S
12	Edwards	FTR Kawasaki	45m 04.288s	1m 03.593s	1m 23.849s	95.505mph	M/S
13	Petrucci	Ioda-Suter	45m 21.145s	1m 20.450s	1m 23.937s	94.946mph	M/XS
14	Abraham	ART	44m 05.885s	1 Lap	1m 24.549s	94.573mph	M/S
15	Hernandez	ART	44m 15.867s	1 Lap	1m 24.801s	94.200mph	M/XS
16	Aoyama	FTR	44m 16.857s	1 Lap	1m 24.777s	94.200mph	M/S
17	Staring	FTR Honda	44m 25.931s	1 Lap	1m 24.836s	93.889mph	M/XS
18	Pesek	Ioda-Suter	45m 06.444s	1 Lap	1m 25.259s	92.460mph	M/XS
NF	Smith	Yamaha	9m 51.183s	25 Laps	1m 22.821s	95.567mph	M/S
NF	Espargaro	ART	7m 03.642s	27 Laps	1m 22.793s	95.256mph	M/XS
NF	De Puniet	ART	5m 46.737s	28 Laps	1m 23.624s	93.144mph	M/XS
NF	Corti	FTR Kawasaki	14m 27.083s	29 Laps	1m 25.679s	27.900mph	M/S
NF	Laverty	PBM		1m 33.622s	31 Laps	86.246mph	M/XS

CHAMPIONSHIP

	Rider	Nation	Team	Points
1	Marquez	SPA	Repsol Honda Team	163
2	Pedrosa	SPA	Repsol Honda Team	147
3	Lorenzo	SPA	Yamaha Factory Racing	137
4	Rossi	ITA	Yamaha Factory Racing	117
5	Crutchlow	GBR	Monster Yamaha Tech 3	116
6	Bradl	GER	LCR Honda MotoGP	84
7	Dovizioso	ITA	Ducati Team	81
8	Bautista	SPA	GO&FUN Honda Gresini	71
9	Hayden	USA	Ducati Team	65
10	Espargaro	SPA	Power Electronics Aspar	52
11	Smith	GBR	Monster Yamaha Tech 3	51
12	Pirro	ITA	Ignite Pramac Racing	36
13	Iannone	ITA	Energy T.I. Pramac Racing	24
14	Barbera	SPA	Avintia Blusens	24
15	De Puniet	FRA	Power Electronics Aspar	19
16	Petrucci	ITA	Came IodaRacing Project	18
17	Edwards	USA	NGM Mobile Forward Racing	17
18	Spies	USA	Ignite Pramac Racing	9
19	Hernandez	COL	Paul Bird Motorsport	7
20	De Angelis	RSM	Ignite Pramac Racing	5
21	Corti	ITA	NGM Mobile Forward Racing	5
22	Abraham	CZE	Cardion AB Motoracing	5
23	Laverty	GBR	Paul Bird Motorsport	3
24	Staring	AUS	GO&FUN Honda Gresini	2
25	Aoyama	JPN	Avintia Blusens	1
26	Del Amor	SPA	Avintia Blusens	1

13 DANILO PETRUCCI Started well, racing with Edwards and Barbera, but lost touch when he missed a gear. In the second half his tyre went off and back pain from his German crash was a problem too. Deeply affected by the death earlier in the day of his fellow Umbrian Andrea Antonelli in the Russian round of the World Supersport Championship.

14 KAREL ABRAHAM A lonely race to two points, but Karel's health problems persisted and he stayed in the States for tests to try to get fully fit again.

15 YONNY HERNANDEZ Very careful not to repeat the crashes of the previous weekend. Salvaged a point for the team.

16 HIROSHI AOYAMA Couldn't hold on to the bike properly in the last ten laps due to his injured hand, but spent most of the race in the fight for the last point, despite being last on the first lap.

17 BRYAN STARING Much happier than in previous races. Good race pace on his first visit to Laguna but slowed by his foot injury in the second half of the race.

18 LUKAS PESEK Finished despite his motor losing power, which detached him from the final group.

NON-FINISHERS

BRADLEY SMITH His engine cut out on lap eight. Improved throughout the weekend and was shadowing the factory Ducatis when he stopped.

ALEIX ESPARGARO Decided to run the harder tyre to cope with elevated temperatures but crashed out, his first failure to finish in a season and a half.

RANDY DE PUNIET His engine stopped on lap four, having felt down on power in the opening laps following a Saturday crash. The first time this season the team failed to score a point.

CLAUDIO CORTI Put out of the race by his third engine failure of the season.

MICHAEL LAVERTY Fell at Turn 2 on the second lap.

NON-STARTERS

BEN SPIES At the track, and saying he would be back at the next race after a full recovery from his shoulder injury. Replaced by de Angelis.

ANDREA IANNONE Recovering from the shoulder dislocation he'd suffered in Germany the previous weekend.

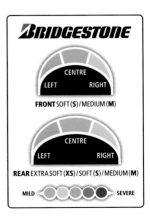

BRIDGESTONE

FRONT SOFT (**S**) / MEDIUM (**M**)

REAR EXTRA SOFT (**XS**) / SOFT (**S**) / MEDIUM (**M**)

MILD — SEVERE

ROUND 10

LOTUS
SHOEI
Red Bull
93
GAS
REPSOL
HONDA
93
HRC
REPSOL
RC213V
HONDA
REPSOL

RED BULL INDIANAPOLIS GRAND PRIX

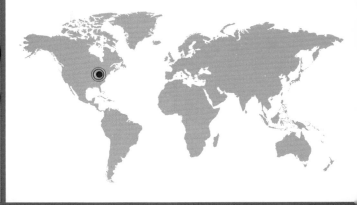

A CHIP ON THE SHOULDER

Marquez took advantage of his injured countrymen as Ben Spies's season went from bad to even worse

It felt like a return to the start of the season – as if the last few races hadn't happened. Rossi was never in contention but was fast on worn tyres, Crutchlow had problems at the start of the race, Bradl lost the front a lot and Marquez blazed his way to another win. No matter that the Indianapolis track was its usual treacherous self or that both Lorenzo and Pedrosa were at least partially recovered from surgery, it was another one of Marc's commonplace miracles.

As the two other Spaniards slowly recuperated from their shoulder problems two more riders took their places in the list of those whose season has been severely compromised by dislocations and breaks. Karel Abraham hit the deck in FP1 and did unspecified if painful damage to his left shoulder. He tried to ride in warm-up without painkillers but could only manage three laps, so sensibly withdrew with an eye on his home race the following week. The second victim was Ben Spies, attempting to race for the first time since he withdrew at Mugello. The long-term problem was the shoulder injured at Sepang in 2012, plus some previous damage. It had been repaired in what turned into a major procedure, serious enough to require transplant tissue, and then it seems that in the second race of the year, in Texas, Ben reinjured it. The attempted comeback at Mugello had been wildly over-optimistic. This time Ben injured the other – left – shoulder, dislocating the collarbone badly enough to need surgery. The surgeons took the opportunity to do a clean-up job on the other shoulder as well.

The Friday morning crash gave rise to nearly as many rumours as Ben's medical condition post-Texas. It happened in a straight line, with Ben sitting up. He had forgotten that the traction control does not activate until

ABOVE Wild card Blake Young on the Attack Performance Racing Kawasaki qualified but didn't make it round the first lap

RIGHT Lorenzo leads round Turns 3 and 4 in the shadow of Indy's impressive Hall of Fame and museum

OPPOSITE Ben Spies tried to come back for the first time since Mugello only to seriously injure his other collarbone. It was MotoGP's last sighting of Ben

the bike has shifted out of second gear; a touch too much throttle and he was over the bars. There followed a strange pantomime of sickbed press conference – no photos please – and recriminations among notably unhappy Ducati people. There was a strong feeling that this story wasn't over yet, and we all wondered about Ben's future.

By contrast, Lorenzo returned from the summer break looking healthy, claiming he'd been able to train as he'd wanted. Pedrosa, on the other hand, had discovered that his injury was worse than first thought. His collarbone was, in fact, broken all the way through, not cracked, but thankfully the bone was not displaced and therefore needed no surgery. The downside was that the only treatment was for him to keep still and do nothing. Dani did not seem optimistic about the race and talked more of restoring his confidence than winning.

Jorge Lorenzo did all he could to execute his usual plan of doing a disappearing act from the start, but he wasn't allowed to. On the first lap he took over half a second out of the field, but that was as big as his lead ever got. Inevitably, Marquez overhauled him and, more surprisingly, so did Pedrosa. A distinctly displeased Jorge reported a sudden drop-off in tyre performance that consigned him to a relatively distant third.

Apart from Lorenzo, the Yamahas appeared to lose their way. Cal Crutchlow at last got the factory seat-tank unit he'd been pleading for and immediately found it wasn't the magic bullet he'd hoped it would be. His team-mate Bradley Smith had trouble with the low-grip track but started and finished the race well. Valentino Rossi also finished well, getting over his old problem

'WE DID
THE PERFECT
WEEKEND'
MARC MARQUEZ

ABOVE The last corner of the best fight of the race was for fourth between Rossi, Crutchlow and Bautista. Valentino made experience pay

BELOW Colin Edwards was fastest CRT in qualifying and narrowly lost out to Espargaro (who else?) in the race

with corner entry and braking to smash and grab fourth off Crutchlow in the final corner, with Bautista as collateral damage.

More last-corner action came courtesy of Nicky Hayden. As was now customary, the two factory Ducatis circulated in line astern for most of the race. Back in Assen, Andrea Dovizioso had nerfed Hayden out of the way at the final corner with enough force to take them both wide and allow Smith past. This time Nicky, at a track only a couple of hours' drive from his family home, repaid the compliment – with interest. He dived inside Dovi with enough force to send them both leaping over

the steel-plate L-section that delineated the edge of the track. Just as at Assen, Bradley Smith beat them both in the drag race to the line, although he had to make a last-minute adjustment to avoid the flagman. To his credit Dovizioso didn't make an issue of it, probably because he was far more concerned with the distance they were behind the winner than with losing a couple of points. He even offered the opinion that professional motocrossers wouldn't have been able to jump their bikes that well.

Marc Marquez had taken the lead in the championship by a slender two points in Germany after Pedrosa and Lorenzo's collarbone-breaking accidents. At Laguna Seca, a week later, he took full advantage and opened the lead up to 16 points. Now, after the summer break and with his two protagonists almost restored to full health, he had another five points over Pedrosa. In a championship that was always going to be decided by who made the fewest mistakes, that many points looked perilously close to a decisive advantage. More to the point, Marquez looked like no other rookie the championship had ever seen, and the Honda, thanks to a few subtle tweaks, now looked a superior motorcycle, able to run with the Yamahas on any track. As the majority of tracks in the second half of the season were deemed to be Honda-friendly circuits, it was possible, without any great leap of the imagination, to make a strong case for Marquez becoming World Champion. There was only one counter-argument: surely he couldn't continue riding on, and mainly over, the edge and get away with it for the rest of the year? Could he?

COMING TO AMERICA

Speculation over the future of the Indianapolis GP was temporarily halted when it was announced that the event would continue into 2014. The worn state of the infield section of the track attracted nearly as much criticism as the previous year, while any further extension of the contract would depend on some serious resurfacing work. It would also depend on the US GP at Laguna Seca and the GP of the Americas at the new Circuit of the Americas in Austin, Texas. Three GPs in the USA was not a situation many thought could last, especially with South America ready to host races in Argentina and, maybe, Brazil, plus pressure from the manufacturers to race in booming markets in Asia, especially Indonesia.

With the Texas track having just started a ten-year contract, one of the others was obviously vulnerable. Laguna, although popular, can only accommodate the top class and a relatively small audience simply because of space constraints. It must also be said that the track had been

given a free pass on safety issues over the years as safety was sidelined in order to bring MotoGP back to the USA. Along with other issues, this was thought to be the reason that the Laguna race would be the casualty.

On the rider market, during the summer break Cal Crutchlow and Ducati announced that, as rumoured, he would be replacing Nicky Hayden in the factory team for the 2014 and

'15 seasons. Stefan Bradl's form – remember that second place on the rostrum at Laguna – earned him an extension of his contract with the LCR team, while the Gresini team moved into pole position in the race to sign Scott Redding. The best comment of the weekend came, of course, from Crutchlow. Was moving to Ducati really a good idea? 'I like the colour.'

BELOW The factory Ducatis aviate off the steel kerbing at the last corner of the last lap thanks to Nicky Hayden's extremely enthusiastic passing manoeuvre

RED BULL
INDIANAPOLIS GRAND PRIX
INDIANAPOLIS MOTOR SPEEDWAY

ROUND 10
August 18

RACE RESULTS

CIRCUIT LENGTH 2.620 miles
NO. OF LAPS 27
RACE DISTANCE 70.740 miles
WEATHER Dry, 27°C
TRACK TEMPERATURE 39°C
WINNER Marc Marquez
FASTEST LAP 1m 39.044s, 95.194mph, Marc Marquez (Record)
PREVIOUS LAP RECORD 1m 39.088s, 95.177mph, Dani Pedrosa, 2012

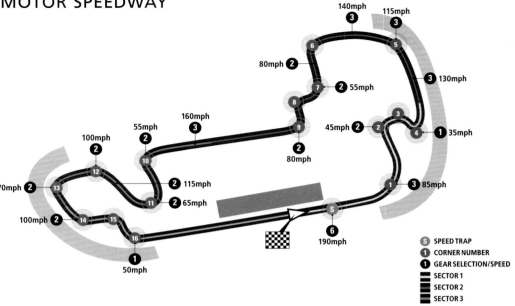

S SPEED TRAP
1 CORNER NUMBER
1 GEAR SELECTION/SPEED
SECTOR 1
SECTOR 2
SECTOR 3

QUALIFYING

	Rider	Nation	Motorcycle	Team	Time	Pole +
1	Marquez	SPA	Honda	Repsol Honda Team	1m 37.958s	
2	Lorenzo	SPA	Yamaha	Yamaha Factory Racing	1m 38.471s	0.513s
3	Pedrosa	SPA	Honda	Repsol Honda Team	1m 38.485s	0.527s
4	Crutchlow	GBR	Yamaha	Monster Yamaha Tech 3	1m 38.502s	0.544s
5	Bautista	SPA	Honda	GO&FUN Honda Gresini	1m 38.872s	0.914s
6	Hayden	USA	Ducati	Ducati Team	1m 39.142s	1.184s
7	Smith	GBR	Yamaha	Monster Yamaha Tech 3	1m 39.255s	1.297s
8	Bradl	GER	Honda	LCR Honda MotoGP	1m 39.313s	1.355s
9	Rossi	ITA	Yamaha	Yamaha Factory Racing	1m 39.356s	1.398s
10	Dovizioso	ITA	Ducati	Ducati Team	1m 39.555s	1.597s
11	Iannone	ITA	Ducati	Energy T.I. Pramac Racing	1m 40.042s	2.084s
12	Edwards	USA	FTR Kawasaki	NGM Mobile Forward Racing	1m 40.372s	2.414s
13	Espargaro	SPA	ART	Power Electronics Aspar	1m 40.444s	Q1
14	Petrucci	ITA	Ioda-Suter	Came IodaRacing Project	1m 41.122s	Q1
15	De Puniet	FRA	ART	Power Electronics Aspar	1m 41.154s	Q1
16	Corti	ITA	FTR Kawasaki	NGM Mobile Forward Racing	1m 41.334s	Q1
17	Barbera	SPA	FTR	Avintia Blusens	1m 41.527s	Q1
18	Laverty	GBR	PBM	Paul Bird Motorsport	1m 41.618s	Q1
19	Aoyama	JPN	FTR	Avintia Blusens	1m 41.665s	Q1
20	Staring	AUS	FTR Honda	GO&FUN Honda Gresini	1m 41.786s	Q1
21	Hernandez	COL	ART	Paul Bird Motorsport	1m 41.807s	Q1
22	Pesek	CZE	Ioda-Suter	Came IodaRacing Project	1m 41.868s	Q1
23	Abraham	CZE	ART	Cardion AB Motoracing	1m 42.165s	Q1
24	Young	USA	APR	Attack Performance Racing	1m 44.472s	Q1

FINISHERS

1 MARC MARQUEZ Three wins in a row, wins at all three American tracks, fastest in every session, new lap record, new pole-position record, and an increase in his championship lead. On a slippy, difficult track he did not put a wheel wrong all weekend. It was impossible to believe we were looking at a rookie.

2 DANI PEDROSA Still hurting, having to adjust his riding style to cope, and seemingly quite surprised to finish second. Took second place off Lorenzo two laps from the flag in typical fashion, blasting past on the front straight.

3 JORGE LORENZO Did what he had to do to try for the win: got the holeshot and held off the Hondas for nearly half the race. Surprised by a sudden drop-off in tyre performance after 11 laps that meant Marquez came past, and he was then unable to hold off Pedrosa. Still not fully fit.

4 VALENTINO ROSSI The old problems in qualifying returned, relegating him to ninth on the grid. After a slowish start he reminded us how good he is on worn tyres, closing down the Crutchlow/Bautista fight for fourth and taking the place on the last lap with a hard but fair move.

5 CAL CRUTCHLOW Got the factory fuel tank he'd been after, which partially did

what he hoped and improved his pace in the opening laps. Battled with Bautista for most of the race until Rossi closed them down. For Cal it was a good result at a track he doesn't like and he went back to top satellite in the table.

6 ALVARO BAUTISTA Another strong race, only losing out to the Yamahas in the final laps. Spent most of the race disputing fourth with Crutchlow before Rossi arrived late on. Pushing hard early in the race took its toll on his front tyre and he couldn't defend his place in the closing laps.

7 STEFAN BRADL Disappointment, after a good run of races. Three crashes

in practice, all thanks to the old front-end problems, resulted in a set-up that was safe but very difficult for changing direction. It was, said Stefan, 'heavy'.

8 BRADLEY SMITH Not happy with finishing so far behind the winner after a great start, but taking advantage of the Ducati coming-together on the last corner improved his mood. Complained of problems with the rear of the bike from early on.

9 NICKY HAYDEN Got his own back for Assen with a last-corner lunge that put both Ducatis off the circuit. Nicky said it was his fault but didn't appear to be suffering any guilt.

10 ANDREA DOVIZIOSO After they lost rear grip early, the Ducatis again ended up circulating together. Dovi got the worse of a Hayden lunge on the last corner, but given they were 40 seconds behind the winner he wasn't particularly bothered.

11 ANDREA IANNONE Much happier than one might expect from his finishing position. First race since he'd dislocated his shoulder in Germany.

12 ALEIX ESPARGARO Top CRT again despite pain in his hand from a big crash on Saturday. Had a painkilling injection before the race but found it difficult to change direction, let alone ride in his usual aggressive style.

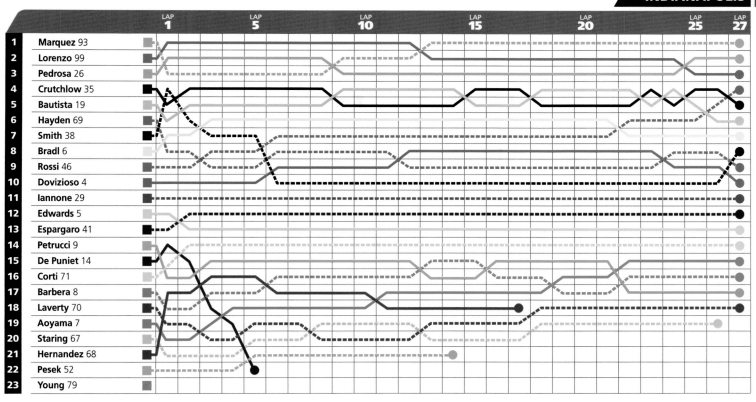

		LAP 1	LAP 5	LAP 10	LAP 15	LAP 20	LAP 25	LAP 27
1	Marquez 93							
2	Lorenzo 99							
3	Pedrosa 26							
4	Crutchlow 35							
5	Bautista 19							
6	Hayden 69							
7	Smith 38							
8	Bradl 6							
9	Rossi 46							
10	Dovizioso 4							
11	Iannone 29							
12	Edwards 5							
13	Espargaro 41							
14	Petrucci 9							
15	De Puniet 14							
16	Corti 71							
17	Barbera 8							
18	Laverty 70							
19	Aoyama 7							
20	Staring 67							
21	Hernandez 68							
22	Pesek 52							
23	Young 79							

RACE

	Rider	Motorcycle	Race Time	Time +	Fastest Lap	Avg. Speed	
1	Marquez	Honda	44m 52.463s		1m 39.044s	94.573mph	H/M
2	Pedrosa	Honda	44m 55.958s	3.495s	1m 39.133s	94.448mph	H/M
3	Lorenzo	Yamaha	44m 58.167s	5.704s	1m 39.248s	94.324mph	H/M
4	Rossi	Yamaha	45m 12.358s	19.895s	1m 39.630s	93.827mph	H/M
5	Crutchlow	Yamaha	45m 12.418s	19.955s	1m 39.442s	93.827mph	H/M
6	Bautista	Honda	45m 12.524s	20.061s	1m 39.226s	93.827mph	H/M
7	Bradl	Honda	45m 17.305s	24.842s	1m 39.447s	93.703mph	H/M
8	Smith	Yamaha	45m 33.153s	40.690s	1m 40.325s	93.144mph	H/M
9	Hayden	Ducati	45m 33.164s	40.701s	1m 40.085s	93.144mph	H/M
10	Dovizioso	Ducati	45m 33.286s	40.823s	1m 40.209s	93.144mph	H/M
11	Iannone	Ducati	45m 52.131s	59.668s	1m 40.299s	92.522mph	H/M
12	Espargaro	ART	45m 59.113s	1m 06.650s	1m 41.059s	92.274mph	H/S
13	Edwards	FTR Kawasaki	46m 01.925s	1m 09.462s	1m 41.130s	92.149mph	H/M
14	Corti	FTR Kawasaki	46m 07.670s	1m 15.207s	1m 41.438s	91.963mph	H/M
15	Aoyama	FTR	46m 12.622s	1m 20.159s	1m 41.608s	91.839mph	H/S
16	Barbera	FTR	46m 18.342s	1m 25.879s	1m 41.599s	91.590mph	H/M
17	Petrucci	Ioda-Suter	46m 22.079s	1m 29.616s	1m 41.835s	91.466mph	H/S
18	Laverty	PBM	46m 28.851s	1m 36.388s	1m 41.925s	91.279mph	H/S
19	Staring	FTR Honda	45m 03.610s	1 Lap	1m 42.671s	90.658mph	H/S
NF	Hernandez	ART	29m 11.700s	10 Laps	1m 42.065s	91.466mph	H/S
NF	Pesek	Ioda-Suter	24m 30.146s	13 Laps	1m 42.655s	89.788mph	H/S
NF	De Puniet	ART	8m 51.913s	22 Laps	1m 42.733s	88.608mph	H/S
NF	Young	APR					H/M

CHAMPIONSHIP

	Rider	Nation	Team	Points
1	Marquez	SPA	Repsol Honda Team	188
2	Pedrosa	SPA	Repsol Honda Team	167
3	Lorenzo	SPA	Yamaha Factory Racing	153
4	Rossi	ITA	Yamaha Factory Racing	130
5	Crutchlow	GBR	Monster Yamaha Tech 3	127
6	Bradl	GER	LCR Honda MotoGP	93
7	Dovizioso	ITA	Ducati Team	87
8	Bautista	SPA	GO&FUN Honda Gresini	81
9	Hayden	USA	Ducati Team	72
10	Smith	GBR	Monster Yamaha Tech 3	59
11	Espargaro	SPA	Power Electronics Aspar	56
12	Pirro	ITA	Ignite Pramac Racing	36
13	Iannone	ITA	Energy T.I. Pramac Racing	29
14	Barbera	SPA	Avintia Blusens	24
15	Edwards	USA	NGM Mobile Forward Racing	20
16	De Puniet	FRA	Power Electronics Aspar	19
17	Petrucci	ITA	Came IodaRacing Project	18
18	Spies	USA	Ignite Pramac Racing	9
19	Corti	ITA	NGM Mobile Forward Racing	7
20	Hernandez	COL	Paul Bird Motorsport	7
21	De Angelis	RSM	Ignite Pramac Racing	5
22	Abraham	CZE	Cardion AB Motoracing	5
23	Laverty	GBR	Paul Bird Motorsport	3
24	Staring	AUS	GO&FUN Honda Gresini	2
25	Aoyama	JPN	Avintia Blusens	2
26	Del Amor	SPA	Avintia Blusens	1

13 COLIN EDWARDS Quickest CRT in qualifying and less than three seconds behind the top CRT in the race despite a couple of moments, which he likened to his famous save at Jerez. Only lost touch with Espargaro in the closing laps.

14 CLAUDIO CORTI A solid race. Tried to follow his team-mate but had two big moments and lost touch with Edwards. Happier when the fuel load went down and had no problems with the front in the second half of the race.

15 HIROSHI AOYAMA More like his old self now his hand has healed after the Mugello accident. Came out on top of the three-man dice for the last point.

16 HECTOR BARBERA Another man who couldn't get the front-end feel he needed. Struggled all weekend.

17 DANILO PETRUCCI His race was completely compromised by the choice of the soft rear tyre for the race. The only rider to race with it but couldn't even take advantage of the extra grip in the opening laps.

18 MICHAEL LAVERTY Found Indianapolis a tricky problem to solve, and never comfortable with the front end.

19 BRYAN STARING Unhappy not to be able to replicate the pace he'd shown in practice and qualifying.

NON-FINISHERS

YONNY HERNANDEZ Looking good in the race when his engine started losing power at around half-distance. Forced to pull in.

LUKAS PESEK Pulled in when he realised he was making mistakes but unsure what the problem actually was – a worry with his home race next on the calendar.

RANDY DE PUNIET Had problems all weekend. In the race found the power delivery and traction control were both playing up so he pulled in.

BLAKE YOUNG Wild-card entry, as he was at the other GPs on American tracks. Qualified here but crashed on the first lap.

NON-STARTERS

BEN SPIES Crashed and dislocated his collarbone in FP3, fortunately not on the shoulder he had repaired over the winter. The injury looked bad enough to keep him out of the next two races – at least.

KAREL ABRAHAM Hurt his shoulder in a Friday morning crash. Attempted to ride in warm-up but was half a second slower than anyone, so decided to try to get fit for his home GP the following weekend.

BRIDGESTONE

FRONT SOFT (S) / HARD (H)

REAR SOFT (S) / MEDIUM (M) / HARD (H)

MILD ●●●●● SEVERE

**bwin GRAND PRIX
ČESKÉ REPUBLIKY**

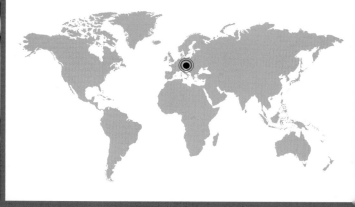

ACCEPTING THE INEVITABLE?

Marquez won his fourth race in a row, but at least it was closer than usual

Returning to Europe for the first time since the summer break clarified a few things – specifically, that the Honda was now a slightly better all-round racing motorcycle than the Yamaha, and that the only man who could bridge the gap was Jorge Lorenzo. Unfortunately for Jorge, the man he was trying to catch, Marc Marquez, showed no signs of slowing down. Lorenzo was now left with one tactic to try to beat him, namely getting the holeshot and opening up a lead in the early stages that he could manage to the end of the race. Like most things in racing, that was much easier said than done. Nevertheless Jorge did it, and would continue to do it.

He didn't achieve pole position, though, because that went to Cal Crutchlow at the track where 12 months previously he'd scored his first rostrum finish in MotoGP. Lorenzo was relegated to the middle of the second row behind three Hondas, including Bautista's satellite bike. So Jorge made what he later described as the best start of his career to lead into the first corner. He pulled out a gap of over a second on the first lap, making it 1.3s at the end of the second, but that was as far ahead of Marc Marquez as he managed to get. Jorge continued to lead until seven laps from the flag.

It was another display of impeccable riding from the World Champion on a track that again showed up the differences between the Hondas and the Yamaha. Once Smith and Crutchlow had succumbed to early crashes (although Cal remounted), and Rossi had drifted back to his now customary skirmish with Bautista, the front three underlined their superiority to the rest of the field and how closely they were

'THE CHAMPIONSHIP IS NOT LOST
BUT IT'S VERY DIFFICULT NOW'
JORGE LORENZO

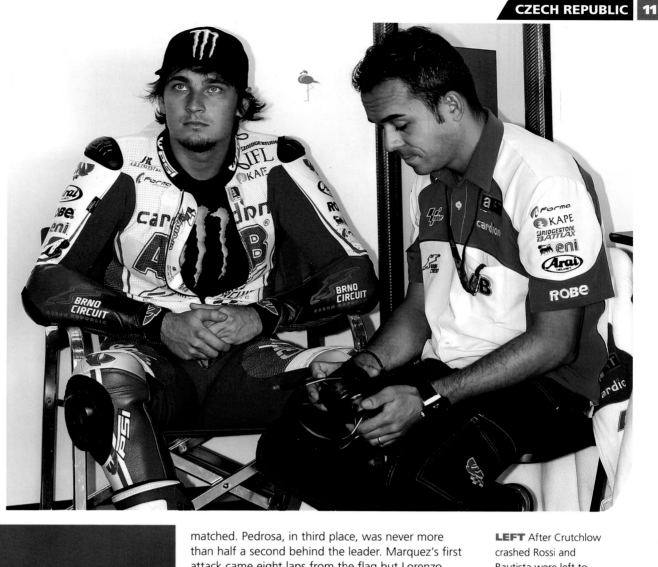

matched. Pedrosa, in third place, was never more than half a second behind the leader. Marquez's first attack came eight laps from the flag but Lorenzo had it covered; next time round Marc did get past but again Jorge was back in front two laps later. Marquez's next attack was decisive. Four laps out he retook the lead and although Lorenzo strained every sinew to stay with the Honda, Pedrosa took second a couple of laps from the flag and instantly closed on his team-mate. Dani admitted leaving it too late – another lap and he might indeed have been the winner, but he took too long to push past Lorenzo. Pedrosa wasn't too upset, though, seemingly more than content to have recovered from his injury and been truly competitive all weekend.

Rossi won his battle with Bautista thanks to a last-lap pass that suggested his Saturday moan about the new qualifying system being 'unfair' was more a symptom of his frustration than a serious comment. It may also have been a reflection of the growing realisation that Marquez and Honda had the upper hand. Rossi and Lorenzo now had to face the reality of being beaten on a 'Yamaha track' and facing a run of 'Honda tracks' to finish the season.

Even though the result looked very similar to more than one previous race, there were several new, hard conclusions to be drawn. Marquez's four wins in a row was another rookie record and extended his lead to 26 points – more than a race's worth for the first time. Lorenzo looked and sounded devastated. That, he said, was the end of his championship. The way Jorge had been unable to push right to the end

LEFT After Crutchlow crashed Rossi and Bautista were left to fight out fourth place, with Rossi just prevailing

ABOVE Karel Abraham rode his home GP despite suffering badly from the shoulder injury sustained at Indianapolis

underlined the areas in which the Honda could now outperform even a perfectly ridden Yamaha on a track historically thought to favour the latter. The fact that the Honda was the quicker bike was no surprise; 'twas ever thus. The fact that Jorge complained about his bike's behaviour under braking was a tacit admission that Yamaha were now losing out in areas where they used to enjoy the advantage.

Then there was the matter of the seamless-shift gearbox. Both factory Yamaha riders tested it at Brno during the summer break and immediately started strenuous public lobbying to be given it as soon as possible, no doubt because the factory wasn't intending to introduce it until 2014. It wouldn't have improved lap times, explained Jorge, but it would have been kinder to his rear tyre, enabling him to maintain his speed in the final laps. Not that he slowed down much, more that it became harder to maintain his pace and counter the Hondas.

This was one of those races that was measured in hundredths of a second over the whole 22 laps. The difference between the leading trio came down to Lorenzo being unable to stay in the 1m 56s bracket for the whole race and Pedrosa lacking that final fraction of a per cent of his usual confidence. A competitor can afford neither of those when faced with Marc Marquez. It is a measure of what Marquez had already achieved that no-one was particularly surprised to see the rookie win, setting the fastest lap of the race on the way, on a track that the form book said did not favour his motorcycle. The only person who seemed remotely bemused by the result was Marquez himself.

ABOVE Lukas Pesek's depressing season with the Ioda team didn't improve at his home race

BELOW Dani Pedrosa left it a lap too late to follow his team-mate Marquez past the Yamaha of Lorenzo

OPPOSITE Veteran Austrian Martin Bauer rode his first Grand Prix on the S&B Team's Suter BMW

RENT A RACER

Colin Edwards and the Forward Racing Team had a good weekend. Edwards finished second CRT for the second race running, right on the rear wheel of Espargaro, and he also learned that their job next year might be a little easier than they'd thought. Yamaha announced that the package the team would lease next season would include more than the M1 engine.

When the deal was announced it was for engines only, but now Yamaha had decided to kick-start the project by including the frame and swinging arm as well. The team will still have to build its own airbox, tank and bodywork, and source suspension, brakes, etc. In 2015, the deal will return to a basic engine-only lease. The question being asked was would an M1 with 24 litres of fuel be able to race with a factory bike on 21 litres? No rider was announced, but the team were known to be in discussions with Aleix Espargaro, and Colin Edwards was keen to re-sign. Other candidates included the team's other current rider, Claudio Corti, and Nicky Hayden, who had been told by Ducati that his services would not be required in 2014.

Honda's customer bike had so far secured two orders. The first was from Team Gresini to replace their Honda FireBlade-powered FTR, with Moto2 ace Scott Redding expected to be announced as the rider before his home GP the following weekend. The second came from the Cardion team to replace their ART Aprilia. Rider Karel Abraham has spent much of his two seasons on the ART injured and almost missed his home race because of the shoulder damage sustained in Indianapolis.

bwin GRAND PRIX ČESKÉ REPUBLIKY
AUTODROM BRNO
ROUND **11**
August 25

S SPEED TRAP
1 CORNER NUMBER
1 GEAR SELECTION/SPEED
SECTOR 1
SECTOR 2
SECTOR 3

RACE RESULTS

CIRCUIT LENGTH 3.357 miles
NO. OF LAPS 22
RACE DISTANCE 73.860 miles
WEATHER Dry, 17°C
TRACK TEMPERATURE 23°C
WINNER Marc Marquez
FASTEST LAP 1m 56.135s,
104.018mph, Marc Marquez (Record)
PREVIOUS LAP RECORD 1m 56.274s,
103.945mph, Jorge Lorenzo, 2012

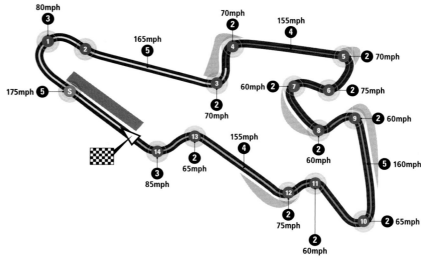

QUALIFYING

	Rider	Nation	Motorcycle	Team	Time	Pole +
1	Crutchlow	GBR	Yamaha	Monster Yamaha Tech 3	1m 55.527s	
2	Bautista	SPA	Honda	GO&FUN Honda Gresini	1m 55.754s	0.227s
3	Marquez	SPA	Honda	Repsol Honda Team	1m 55.863s	0.336s
4	Pedrosa	SPA	Honda	Repsol Honda Team	1m 55.868s	0.341s
5	Lorenzo	SPA	Yamaha	Yamaha Factory Racing	1m 55.949s	0.422s
6	Smith	GBR	Yamaha	Monster Yamaha Tech 3	1m 56.014s	0.487s
7	Rossi	ITA	Yamaha	Yamaha Factory Racing	1m 56.186s	0.659s
8	Bradl	GER	Honda	LCR Honda MotoGP	1m 56.477s	0.950s
9	Dovizioso	ITA	Ducati	Ducati Team	1m 56.825s	1.298s
10	Hayden	USA	Ducati	Ducati Team	1m 56.979s	1.452s
11	Iannone	ITA	Ducati	Energy T.I. Pramac Racing	1m 57.455s	1.928s
12	Edwards	USA	FTR Kawasaki	NGM Mobile Forward Racing	1m 58.392s	2.865s
13	Espargaro	SPA	ART	Power Electronics Aspar	1m 58.378s	Q1
14	Pirro	ITA	Ducati	Ignite Pramac Racing	1m 58.812s	Q1
15	De Puniet	FRA	ART	Power Electronics Aspar	1m 58.953s	Q1
16	Hernandez	COL	ART	Paul Bird Motorsport	1m 58.983s	Q1
17	Petrucci	ITA	Ioda-Suter	Came IodaRacing Project	1m 59.057s	Q1
18	Corti	ITA	FTR Kawasaki	NGM Mobile Forward Racing	1m 59.062s	Q1
19	Barbera	SPA	FTR	Avintia Blusens	1m 59.128s	Q1
20	Pesek	CZE	Ioda-Suter	Came IodaRacing Project	2m 00.522s	Q1
21	Laverty	GBR	PBM	Paul Bird Motorsport	2m 00.584s	Q1
22	Aoyama	JPN	FTR	Avintia Blusens	2m 00.653s	Q1
23	Abraham	CZE	ART	Cardion AB Motoracing	2m 00.792s	Q1
24	Staring	AUS	FTR Honda	GO&FUN Honda Gresini	2m 00.827s	Q1
25	Bauer	AUT	S&B Suter	Remus Racing Team	2m 01.135s	Q1

FINISHERS

1 MARC MARQUEZ The records keep tumbling – four wins in a row for the first time since 2008 and the first rookie ever to take five wins in a season. Followed Lorenzo for most of the race before passing him and pulling out a lead that was just big enough.

2 DANI PEDROSA Pleased with his race, and talked about the improvement in his mental approach and his recovery from injury. However, couldn't compete on the brakes and thought he'd waited just too long to make his final attack.

3 JORGE LORENZO An amazing start from the second row put him in front, where he stayed for most of the race. Couldn't open a gap, though, and four laps from the flag Marquez came past – and next time round so did Pedrosa. Had no strength left and his rear tyre had degraded.

4 VALENTINO ROSSI Once the Tech 3 Yamahas had fallen, Rossi was left to spend most of the race fighting with Bautista. Won the fight after a last-lap pass, as at Indianapolis. Not happy with fourth but pleased to have halved the gap to the winner from the previous race.

5 ALVARO BAUTISTA Again beaten by Rossi in a close fight, but pleased to better his own qualifying pace. Also pleased with the major improvement on last year's pace, due mainly to the direction of work started at Laguna.

6 STEFAN BRADL A lonely race thanks to lack of edge grip on both sides of the tyres – not a good thing on Brno's fast curves.

7 ANDREA DOVIZIOSO The usual story: only able to race with his team-mate and too far behind the winner to be happy. Was pleased with 1m 58s lap times he put in at the end of the race, though.

8 NICKY HAYDEN Switched to the softer front tyre on the grid, a gamble he was pleased with. Decided against trying a pass on his team-mate at the end, probably a good thing after Indianapolis.

9 ANDREA IANNONE Two crashes during the weekend didn't help his shoulder injury and after ten laps he was in trouble, especially on the brakes and under acceleration – 'I couldn't stay on the bike at all.' Ground out an impressive result nevertheless.

10 ALEIX ESPARGARO Made major changes for race day after his qualifying crash. Top CRT again, despite rear tyre trouble in the second half of the race.

11 COLIN EDWARDS Top CRT in qualifying and closing on Espargaro at the flag. Comfortable on the bike at last.

12 MICHELE PIRRO Replaced Spies on the standard bike, which he found lacking in front-end feel compared to the 'lab bike' he usually rides. Even a switch to the softer front tyre didn't help, and he did not want to take risks with a three-day test coming up.

13 DANILO PETRUCCI Started the weekend with chatter and a stomach upset, finished with a good race.

14 HIROSHI AOYAMA Started way back on the grid thanks to a fall in qualifying, but had a good race which culminated in passing de Puniet on the last lap. Scored points for the second race in a row.

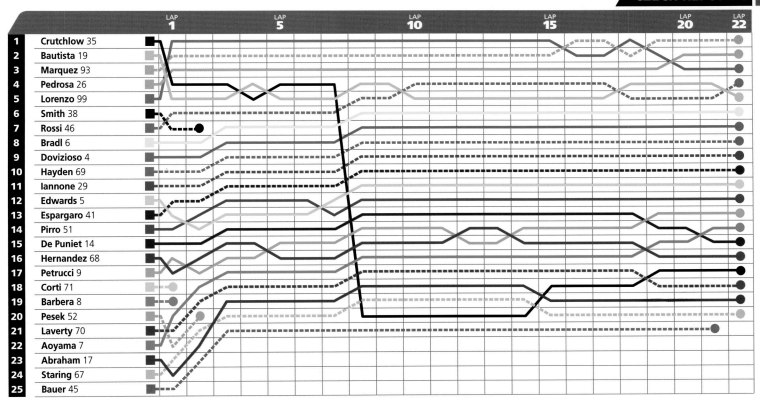

| | Rider | | | | | | LAP 1 | LAP 5 | LAP 10 | LAP 15 | LAP 20 | LAP 22 |

RACE

	Rider	Motorcycle	Race Time	Time +	Fastest Lap	Avg. Speed	B
1	Marquez	Honda	42m 50.729s		1m 56.135s	103.396mph	H/M
2	Pedrosa	Honda	42m 51.042s	0.313s	1m 56.151s	103.396mph	H/M
3	Lorenzo	Yamaha	42m 53.006s	2.277s	1m 56.359s	103.334mph	H/M
4	Rossi	Yamaha	43m 00.830s	10.101s	1m 56.557s	103.023mph	H/M
5	Bautista	Honda	43m 00.907s	10.178s	1m 56.575s	103.023mph	H/M
6	Bradl	Honda	43m 10.536s	19.807s	1m 56.710s	102.588mph	H/M
7	Dovizioso	Ducati	43m 25.744s	35.015s	1m 57.536s	102.029mph	H/M
8	Hayden	Ducati	43m 26.083s	35.354s	1m 57.466s	101.967mph	S/M
9	Iannone	Ducati	43m 41.878s	51.149s	1m 57.986s	101.408mph	H/M
10	Espargaro	ART	43m 47.121s	56.392s	1m 58.383s	101.159mph	H/S
11	Edwards	FTR Kawasaki	43m 48.149s	57.420s	1m 58.621s	101.159mph	H/S
12	Pirro	Ducati	43m 56.159s	1m 05.430s	1m 58.771s	100.849mph	H/M
13	Petrucci	Ioda-Suter	44m 03.093s	1m 12.364s	1m 59.347s	100.600mph	S/S
14	Aoyama	FTR	44m 04.229s	1m 13.500s	1m 58.875s	100.538mph	H/S
15	De Puniet	ART	44m 04.857s	1m 14.128s	1m 58.861s	100.476mph	H/S
16	Hernandez	ART	44m 05.720s	1m 14.991s	1m 59.353s	100.476mph	H/S
17	Crutchlow	Yamaha	44m 11.369s	1m 20.640s	1m 56.396s	100.227mph	H/M
18	Laverty	PBM	44m 25.191s	1m 34.462s	1m 59.668s	99.730mph	H/S
19	Abraham	ART	44m 40.442s	1m 49.713s	2m 00.722s	99.171mph	S/S
20	Staring	FTR Honda	44m 40.753s	1m 50.024s	2m 00.805s	99.171mph	H/S
21	Bauer	S&B Suter	44m 38.367s	1 Lap	2m 01.560s	94.759mph	H/S
NF	Smith	Yamaha	4m 00.917s	20 Laps	1m 56.956s	100.289mph	H/M
NF	Pesek	Ioda-Suter	4m 09.332s	20 Laps	2m 00.500s	96.934mph	H/S
NF	Corti	FTR Kawasaki	2m 07.548s	21 Laps		94.697mph	H/S
NF	Barbera	FTR	2m 07.725s	21 Laps		94.573mph	H/S

CHAMPIONSHIP

	Rider	Nation	Team	Points
1	Marquez	SPA	Repsol Honda Team	213
2	Pedrosa	SPA	Repsol Honda Team	187
3	Lorenzo	SPA	Yamaha Factory Racing	169
4	Rossi	ITA	Yamaha Factory Racing	143
5	Crutchlow	GBR	Monster Yamaha Tech 3	127
6	Bradl	GER	LCR Honda MotoGP	103
7	Dovizioso	ITA	Ducati Team	96
8	Bautista	SPA	GO&FUN Honda Gresini	92
9	Hayden	USA	Ducati Team	80
10	Espargaro	SPA	Power Electronics Aspar	62
11	Smith	GBR	Monster Yamaha Tech 3	59
12	Pirro	ITA	Ignite Pramac Racing	40
13	Iannone	ITA	Energy T.I. Pramac Racing	36
14	Edwards	USA	NGM Mobile Forward Racing	25
15	Barbera	SPA	Avintia Blusens	24
16	Petrucci	ITA	Came IodaRacing Project	21
17	De Puniet	FRA	Power Electronics Aspar	20
18	Spies	USA	Ignite Pramac Racing	9
19	Corti	ITA	NGM Mobile Forward Racing	7
20	Hernandez	COL	Paul Bird Motorsport	7
21	De Angelis	RSM	Ignite Pramac Racing	5
22	Abraham	CZE	Cardion AB Motoracing	5
23	Aoyama	JPN	Avintia Blusens	4
24	Laverty	GBR	Paul Bird Motorsport	3
25	Staring	AUS	GO&FUN Honda Gresini	2
26	Del Amor	SPA	Avintia Blusens	1

15 RANDY DE PUNIET Happier with the bike than he'd been for a while, but his tyre performance dropped off quickly.

16 YONNY HERNANDEZ Dropped out of contention for a points-scoring place in the final few laps when he ran into rear-grip problems.

17 CAL CRUTCHLOW After the second pole of his MotoGP career, the Brit was fourth and fighting with Bautista and Rossi when he lost the front and crashed. Had been pushing to close the gap to the leaders before the chance of a rostrum disappeared. Remounted to finish the race.

18 MICHAEL LAVERTY Again struggled for front-end feel in practice. Couldn't go with the CRT pack at the start.

19 KAREL ABRAHAM Struggled all weekend after his Indianapolis crash. Seriously considered pulling out, but gritted his teeth to finish. Doubtful for Silverstone.

20 BRYAN STARING Started the weekend with chatter problems, felt better in the race, then his tyre degraded in the closing stages.

21 MARTIN BAUER Wild-card entry on the Suter BMW. On the pace in practice, but fell on the first lap after a coming-together with Abraham. Remounted to finish his first GP.

NON-FINISHERS

BRADLEY SMITH Crashed at Turn 9 early on, after a superb qualifying performance for sixth on the grid. The data suggest the rookie error of getting on the gas a little too early might have been the cause. Unable to rejoin because of a broken handlebar.

LUKAS PESEK Having his best weekend for a while, then crashed at Turn 1. Blamed chatter.

CLAUDIO CORTI Crashed with Barbera on the second lap, sustaining concussion. Spent the night in hospital as a precaution.

HECTOR BARBERA Crashed with Corti on the second lap and lost second place in the CRT standings to Edwards.

NON-STARTERS

BEN SPIES Out for a considerable period of time after a double shoulder operation following his Indianapolis crash. Replaced by Pirro. Seems doubtful we'll see Ben again this year.

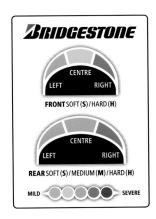

HERTZ BRITISH GRAND PRIX

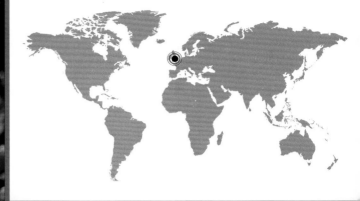

SUMMERTIME BLUES

Lorenzo struck back as Marquez's luck held, the Honda rider taking second despite injury and penalty

Everyone had a good time at Silverstone this year, with the exception of Cal Crutchlow. A change of date saw the race benefit from golden late-summer weather and a large, enthusiastic crowd who were treated to a record-shattering, eye-watering qualifying session and then warmed up on Sunday by a fine Moto2 win from Scott Redding. The paddock was equally delighted to return to the old pits complex and get away from the overbearing, soulless grandeur of The Wing.

Unfortunately, come Sunday afternoon, the packed grandstands were well aware that it was unlikely Crutchlow would figure in the race. In morning warm-up he'd suffered his third crash of the weekend, hurting his arm and narrowly avoiding being collected by Marquez's bike. Marc had the same crash while Cal's bike was being cleared and it was only thanks to the smart work of the spotter that Crutchlow and the marshals weren't hit by the Honda as it cannoned off the Yamaha. Initially, it appeared that Marquez had come off worse; he was holding his shoulder as he was led away in a manner that usually translates as a broken collarbone. It looked as if the prayers of Lorenzo and Pedrosa had been answered. However, the diagnosis was a dislocated collarbone – not, as sometimes reported, a dislocated shoulder – and to the surprise of most of the paddock he was declared fit to race.

All champions need a little luck, and again Marquez was fortunate in that the injury appeared not to handicap him a great deal in the race. And many considered him more than a little lucky to get away with only two penalty points for the incident.

Yet again Jorge Lorenzo led from the start and circulated in his now customary immaculate fashion. Marquez followed, but Dani Pedrosa, victim of lacklustre

'I'M PLEASED THE WEEKEND IS OVER, AT LEAST WE FINISHED THE RACE'
CAL CRUTCHLOW

qualifying, got tangled up in the first corner and had to fight back from sixth place. As the two leaders pulled away, Bradl again exhibiting early pace in third, Dani put in a superb run of laps to get up to the duo, setting the fastest lap of the race on the way. It looked for all the world as if he'd got the pace to breeze past for the win. But it was not to be. Once more Pedrosa was betrayed by his inability to move around on the bike, looking for grip once the tyres had gone off. There was no attack; he had to settle for third.

That left Lorenzo and Marquez to fight it out. Two laps from the flag Marquez pushed past; Lorenzo repaid the favour next time round. On the next, and final, lap Marquez again found a way to take the lead but left a minuscule gap as he pulled the bike from left to right lean between Brooklands and Luffield. Jorge, who later claimed he had settled for second at this point, put his Yamaha on the inside and they came round Woodcote, the final corner, side by side. At the line, Lorenzo led by under a tenth of a second for his first win since Catalunya. On a track that surely favoured the Honda and where Marquez had obliterated the pole-position record, it was as fine a piece of riding as anyone could wish to see – a fact underlined by the relative positions of the other Yamahas.

Marquez said his shoulder hadn't given him difficulties until late in the race, when he started having problems in

ABOVE Marquez's Honda cannons off the fallen Crutchlow's Yamaha during Sunday-morning warm-up

LEFT After three falls Cal Crutchlow couldn't build on his front-row start and came home seventh

ABOVE Bradley Smith's decision to use the softer rear tyre didn't do him any favours in his now customary fight with the Ducatis

BELOW It was this close at the flag: Jorge won by less than a tenth of a second

RIGHT Michael Laverty got the PBM to the flag in his and the bike's first British GP

changes of direction. Lorenzo backed this up, saying on the penultimate lap he'd observed that Marc was struggling in places.

For the eleventh time this season Aleix Espargaro was first CRT home in tenth place. This class win was even more praiseworthy than usual due to a big crash on Saturday in which he wrenched his neck horribly and broke a finger. A properly beaten-up Cal Crutchlow finished seventh while his team-mate Bradley Smith could only manage ninth behind Nicky Hayden's Ducati. Unusually, both the harder and softer rear tyre options were realistic race choices and Brad went for the softer one. When the track didn't heat up as expected he was in trouble, although he was in his usual fight with the factory Ducatis. Dovizioso seemed to have that fight won, but then he crashed two laps from home. Hayden had destroyed his preferred bike in warm-up, but Smith was the more worried of the two after Dovi's crash and settled for what he could get. The British fans made do with cheering Valentino Rossi's last-lap overtake of Alvaro Bautista for fourth place and the news that Scott Redding had signed to ride MotoGP for Fausto Gresini's team in 2014.

Up to this point in the season, Marc Marquez had avoided talking about the championship either directly or obliquely, retreating into the comfort of the standard 'taking it race by race', 'Dani and Jorge will be fast, they have so much experience' clichés. Now he allowed a thought about the title to escape, remarking that his 20 points were good for the championship. His lead over Pedrosa was up to 30 points, but Lorenzo in third was now only another nine points adrift. Despite six races remaining, that gap looked too much even for a man riding as near to perfectly as it's possible to imagine.

CHEST PAIN

Airbags in leathers have been around on the racetrack since 2007, with systems from Italian manufacturers Dainese and Alpinestars in use in GPs. Current systems use complex algorithms to deploy airbags milliseconds after electronics in the hump of the leathers detect a crash. The chapter on the Mugello race (round 5) includes data from Marc Marquez's high-speed crash there to give an idea of the forces and time intervals involved.

Up to now, such airbags have protected the collarbone and shoulder joint specifically. Dainese claim that none of the 306 crashes by users of their D-air Racing system between 2007 and August 2013 have resulted in fractures to those areas. At Silverstone, they unveiled their latest development, the D-air Racing Thorax, with a substantially larger airbag that hugs the wearer's trunk. The test pilot has been Moto3 ace Luis Salom who has used it for over a year.

The technical challenge was to incorporate a higher-volume gas generator to reach the inflation pressures necessary while keeping the rider feeling that the system wasn't hindering his riding in any way. Other racers will get the D-air Racing Thorax in due course, and road riders are already able to buy the D-air Street, the only motorcycle airbag system with TüV safety approval.

HERTZ BRITISH GRAND PRIX
SILVERSTONE

ROUND 12
September 1

RACE RESULTS

CIRCUIT LENGTH 3.666 miles
NO. OF LAPS 20
RACE DISTANCE 73.322 miles
WEATHER Dry, 18°C
TRACK TEMPERATURE 29°C
WINNER Jorge Lorenzo
FASTEST LAP 2m 01.941s, 108.181mph, Dani Pedrosa (Record)
PREVIOUS LAP RECORD 2m 02.888s, 107.398mph, Jorge Lorenzo, 2012

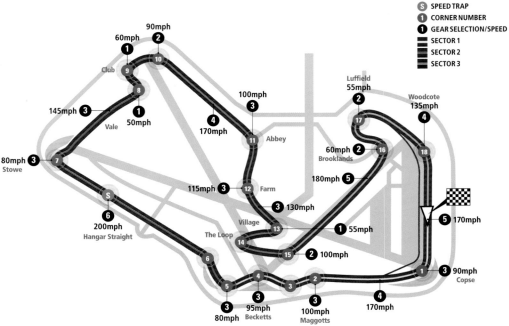

- **S** SPEED TRAP
- **1** CORNER NUMBER
- **1** GEAR SELECTION/SPEED
- SECTOR 1
- SECTOR 2
- SECTOR 3

QUALIFYING

	Rider	Nation	Motorcycle	Team	Time	Pole +
1	Marquez	SPA	Honda	Repsol Honda Team	2m 00.691s	
2	Lorenzo	SPA	Yamaha	Yamaha Factory Racing	2m 00.819s	0.128s
3	Crutchlow	GBR	Yamaha	Monster Yamaha Tech 3	2m 01.425s	0.734s
4	Bradl	GER	Honda	LCR Honda MotoGP	2m 01.558s	0.867s
5	Pedrosa	SPA	Honda	Repsol Honda Team	2m 01.624s	0.933s
6	Rossi	ITA	Yamaha	Yamaha Factory Racing	2m 02.109s	1.418s
7	Dovizioso	ITA	Ducati	Ducati Team	2m 02.123s	1.432s
8	Bautista	SPA	Honda	GO&FUN Honda Gresini	2m 02.252s	1.561s
9	Hayden	USA	Ducati	Ducati Team	2m 02.289s	1.598s
10	Smith	GBR	Yamaha	Monster Yamaha Tech 3	2m 02.409s	1.718s
11	Edwards	USA	FTR Kawasaki	NGM Mobile Forward Racing	2m 04.032s	3.341s
12	Espargaro	SPA	ART	Power Electronics Aspar		
13	De Puniet	FRA	ART	Power Electronics Aspar	2m 04.114s	Q1
14	Barbera	SPA	FTR	Avintia Blusens	2m 04.236s	Q1
15	Pirro	ITA	Ducati	Ignite Pramac Racing	2m 04.680s	Q1
16	Iannone	ITA	Ducati	Energy T.I. Pramac Racing	2m 04.692s	Q1
17	Hernandez	COL	ART	Paul Bird Motorsport	2m 04.749s	Q1
18	Petrucci	ITA	Ioda-Suter	Came IodaRacing Project	2m 04.798s	Q1
19	Laverty	GBR	PBM	Paul Bird Motorsport	2m 04.936s	Q1
20	Corti	ITA	FTR Kawasaki	NGM Mobile Forward Racing	2m 05.356s	Q1
21	Aoyama	JPN	FTR	Avintia Blusens	2m 05.622s	Q1
22	Pesek	CZE	Ioda-Suter	Came IodaRacing Project	2m 07.261s	Q1
23	Staring	AUS	FTR Honda	GO&FUN Honda Gresini	2m 07.300s	Q1

FINISHERS

1 JORGE LORENZO Looked shell-shocked after losing pole to Marquez but rode one of the best races of his life to beat Marc by a wheel after an epic race in front of a record crowd. The pair swapped places twice in the final three corners. Wouldn't entertain talk of the championship, just of more race wins.

2 MARC MARQUEZ Broke the pole position record by 1.3 seconds on Saturday. Started Sunday by crashing under yellow flags, getting himself a dislocated collarbone and two points on his licence – and then only lost the race by a fraction of a second.

3 DANI PEDROSA Made up for lacklustre qualifying and a bad start with a lap-record-breaking charge up to the leaders. Unfortunately he lost grip on the right of the tyre and struggled to stay with his rivals for the rest of the race.

4 VALENTINO ROSSI His race followed the usual pattern: average qualifying followed by difficulties in the first laps and then good pace in the closing stages and another fourth place after yet another fight with Bautista. It was, he said, better than his fourth at Brno because he'd never had a good race at this track.

5 ALVARO BAUTISTA Lost fourth to Rossi on the last lap after again spending most of the race in close company with the Yamaha. Happy with his race, happy with his consistency and with the way he and the team could now find improvements through the weekend.

6 STEFAN BRADL Disappointed to finish too far behind Bautista. Again the problem was edge grip that didn't allow him to drive out of corners in the way he's used to doing. Good on used tyres in practice, very good on the brakes, but hit problems in the race.

7 CAL CRUTCHLOW Injured at his home race for the third straight year. Two big crashes within 45 minutes on Saturday followed by another in warm-up suggested he was never going to be up with the leaders – abrasions and swelling to his right arm meant he had to have the right sleeve of his leathers seriously altered overnight.

8 NICKY HAYDEN Used his second bike after a high-speed crash at Farm Curve in the warm-up. Able to fight with team-mate Dovizioso and Bradley Smith, despite using an older engine.

9 BRADLEY SMITH Went for the softer tyre which proved to be a mistake. Still managed to fight with the Ducatis for the whole race. The problem is Bradley's lack of confidence when track temperatures drop.

10 ALEIX ESPARGARO Top CRT again, but admitted to being distracted by speculation over his future and not as close to the prototypes as he'd expected. Lucky to get away from a horrible crash in qualifying with a broken finger.

11 ANDREA IANNONE Still in some pain from the shoulder he dislocated in Germany and glad to see the last of three races on consecutive weekends. Made up for his poor qualifying with a storming first lap after which he simply defended his position.

12 MICHELE PIRRO Fell in warm-up and had to use his second bike for the race. Not keen on the standard bike at

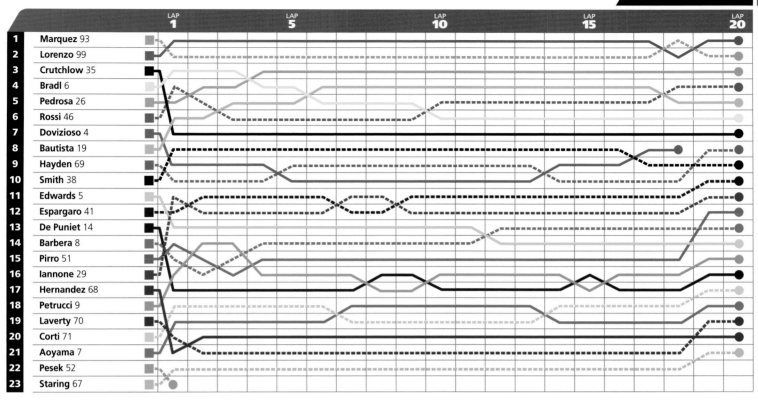

		LAP 1	LAP 5	LAP 10	LAP 15	LAP 20
1	Marquez 93					
2	Lorenzo 99					
3	Crutchlow 35					
4	Bradl 6					
5	Pedrosa 26					
6	Rossi 46					
7	Dovizioso 4					
8	Bautista 19					
9	Hayden 69					
10	Smith 38					
11	Edwards 5					
12	Espargaro 41					
13	De Puniet 14					
14	Barbera 8					
15	Pirro 51					
16	Iannone 29					
17	Hernandez 68					
18	Petrucci 9					
19	Laverty 70					
20	Corti 71					
21	Aoyama 7					
22	Pesek 52					
23	Staring 67					

RACE

	Rider	Motorcycle	Race Time	Time +	Fastest Lap	Avg. Speed	
1	Lorenzo	Yamaha	40m 52.515s		2m 02.116s	107.621mph	M/M
2	Marquez	Honda	40m 52.596s	0.081s	2m 01.996s	107.621mph	M/M
3	Pedrosa	Honda	40m 54.066s	1.551s	2m 01.941s	107.559mph	M/M
4	Rossi	Yamaha	41m 05.748s	13.233s	2m 02.685s	107.000mph	M/M
5	Bautista	Honda	41m 05.813s	13.298s	2m 02.124s	107.000mph	M/MS
6	Bradl	Honda	41m 12.742s	20.227s	2m 02.659s	106.689mph	M/MS
7	Crutchlow	Yamaha	41m 18.814s	26.299s	2m 02.797s	106.441mph	M/M
8	Hayden	Ducati	41m 28.508s	35.993s	2m 03.442s	106.068mph	S/MS
9	Smith	Yamaha	41m 28.634s	36.119s	2m 03.173s	106.006mph	M/MS
10	Espargaro	ART	41m 45.711s	53.196s	2m 03.926s	105.322mph	M/S
11	Iannone	Ducati	41m 51.573s	59.058s	2m 03.986s	105.074mph	S/M
12	Pirro	Ducati	41m 53.225s	1m 00.710s	2m 05.046s	105.012mph	S/MS
13	Barbera	FTR	41m 54.205s	1m 01.690s	2m 04.645s	104.950mph	M/S
14	Edwards	FTR Kawasaki	41m 54.358s	1m 01.843s	2m 04.620s	104.950mph	M/MS
15	Petrucci	Ioda-Suter	42m 01.348s	1m 08.833s	2m 04.956s	104.639mph	S/S
16	De Puniet	ART	42m 01.578s	1m 09.063s	2m 04.967s	104.639mph	M/MS
17	Corti	FTR Kawasaki	42m 08.989s	1m 16.474s	2m 05.408s	104.328mph	M/MS
18	Aoyama	FTR	42m 09.050s	1m 16.535s	2m 05.293s	104.328mph	S/S
19	Laverty	PBM	42m 24.572s	1m 32.057s	2m 06.299s	103.707mph	M/S
20	Hernandez	ART	42m 28.739s	1m 36.224s	2m 06.356s	103.520mph	M/S
21	Staring	FTR Honda	42m 53.150s	2m 00.635s	2m 07.663s	102.526mph	S/S
NF	Dovizioso	Ducati	37m 17.411s	2 Laps	2m 03.574s	106.130mph	M/MS
NF	Pesek	Ioda-Suter	2m 14.233s	19 Laps		98.301mph	S/S

CHAMPIONSHIP

	Rider	Nation	Team	Points
1	Marquez	SPA	Repsol Honda Team	233
2	Pedrosa	SPA	Repsol Honda Team	203
3	Lorenzo	SPA	Yamaha Factory Racing	194
4	Rossi	ITA	Yamaha Factory Racing	156
5	Crutchlow	GBR	Monster Yamaha Tech 3	136
6	Bradl	GER	LCR Honda MotoGP	113
7	Bautista	SPA	GO&FUN Honda Gresini	103
8	Dovizioso	ITA	Ducati Team	96
9	Hayden	USA	Ducati Team	88
10	Espargaro	SPA	Power Electronics Aspar	68
11	Smith	GBR	Monster Yamaha Tech 3	66
12	Pirro	ITA	Ignite Pramac Racing	44
13	Iannone	ITA	Energy T.I. Pramac Racing	41
14	Edwards	USA	NGM Mobile Forward Racing	27
15	Barbera	SPA	Avintia Blusens	27
16	Petrucci	ITA	Came IodaRacing Project	22
17	De Puniet	FRA	Power Electronics Aspar	20
18	Spies	USA	Ignite Pramac Racing	9
19	Corti	ITA	NGM Mobile Forward Racing	7
20	Hernandez	COL	Paul Bird Motorsport	7
21	De Angelis	RSM	Ignite Pramac Racing	5
22	Abraham	CZE	Cardion AB Motoracing	5
23	Aoyama	JPN	Avintia Blusens	4
24	Laverty	GBR	Paul Bird Motorsport	3
25	Staring	AUS	GO&FUN Honda Gresini	2
26	Del Amor	SPA	Avintia Blusens	1

the best of times and less keen on it with wrong settings. Found his rhythm and made progress from mid-distance.

13 HECTOR BARBERA Following two disappointing races he was happy to recover his form. Second CRT after a good fight with Edwards.

14 COLIN EDWARDS In the points for the fifth race in a row. Thought he would be nearer the top CRTs after good qualifying but lost traction and edge grip after just eight laps.

15 DANILO PETRUCCI Started well and hung on to the Ducatis of Pirro and Iannone for a while before grip levels

went down. Then it was a matter of defending against Barbera and de Puniet. Said latter part of the race was so hard it felt like the last lap on every lap.

16 RANDY DE PUNIET Much happier after good practice, but didn't start well and then had gear-selection problems.

17 CLAUDIO CORTI Not fully recovered from his Brno crash so couldn't do too much on a track that is one of his favourites.

18 HIROSHI AOYAMA Only found a set-up he was happy with on Sunday morning, and was then unhappy with the result.

19 MICHAEL LAVERTY Tried new forks in his PBM-framed Aprilia but still looking for that elusive feel.

20 YONNY HERNANDEZ Fast on Friday but thoroughly detuned by three crashes, including one in Sunday morning warm-up.

21 BRYAN STARING Another Saturday crasher. His hand went numb after three laps of the race but he got to the finish.

NON-FINISHERS

LUKAS PESEK Crashed on the first lap without injury.

ANDREA DOVIZIOSO First DNF of the season. Pressing hard to try to get a gap on his team-mate and Smith when he lost the front at Farm, two laps after passing Brad's Yamaha — the same place where Hayden had crashed in warm-up.

NON-STARTERS

BEN SPIES Out of GPs long term while recovering from his shoulder surgeries after Indianapolis. Replaced by Michele Pirro.

KAREL ABRAHAM Missed Silverstone to help recovery from his Indianapolis crash.

BRIDGESTONE

FRONT SOFT **(S)** / MEDIUM **(M)**

REAR SOFT **(S)** / MED-SOFT **(MS)** / MEDIUM **(M)**

MILD ○○○○● SEVERE

GP APEROL DI SAN MARINO E RIVIERA DI RIMINI

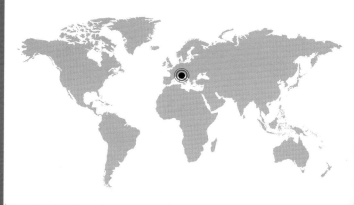

SMOOTH OPERATOR

Lorenzo was given a seamless-shift gearbox and made it back-to-back wins

Yamaha's factory riders, Jorge Lorenzo and Valentino Rossi, finally got what they'd been asking for in the shape of the seamless-shift gearbox they'd tested at Brno. For once, being given what they'd wished for turned out to be a good thing. If Jorge's win at Silverstone had seemed nearly perfect, he now showed us what the genuine article looked like. But the ease with which he dealt with the Hondas on Sunday belied a difficult weekend that again pointed up the largely unsung but vital relationship between the rider and his race engineer, Ramon Forcada.

In qualifying Lorenzo found himself second on the grid – no big deal – but he was an astonishing half-second slower than pole-man Marquez on a lap that only takes 1m 33s. Overnight work cured Jorge's problem, or problems. And in Sunday morning warm-up he was a mind-boggling 0.7s quicker than Marquez. That, said Jorge, gave him the confidence to go for it, as did the new gearbox. As so often this season, Lorenzo knew he had to put in a significant gap over the Hondas early on in the race or he'd be beaten. Accordingly, he got the holeshot and reeled off a stunning set of opening laps. First time round he led by 1.235 seconds, second time by 1.723s and third time by 2.254s. By lap five he was all but three seconds ahead.

While his opponents made mistakes and got tangled up with each other, Jorge reeled off the 28 laps as perfectly as it's possible to imagine. Ignoring the first and last laps, his times varied between his best of 1m 34.020s, set on that third lap, and a worst of 1m 34.573s, which he did on both the 13th and 25th laps. That's a difference of 0.553s over 26 laps or just over 40 minutes of riding. The lap record stood at 1m 33.906s, set by Jorge himself in 2011. Only Marc Marquez got into the 1m 33s, and only on one

ABOVE Aleix Espargaro jumped the start, took a ride-through penalty yet still finished right behind top CRT man Edwards

RIGHT There was no relief from suffering for the Ducatis but at least they suffered together again

OPPOSITE Valentino Rossi also suffered at home. He finished fourth for the fourth race in a row despite qualifying on the front row

lap, but the record remained unbroken, a reflection of the distinctly worn-out nature of the tarmac.

It might not have been a spectacular race for the win but it was a magnificent demonstration of riding skill. In stark contrast to Lorenzo's ultra-controlled, precise race, Marc Marquez was also his usual self. He fell no fewer than three times in practice and made one save that defied the laws of physics. In the opening laps of the race he made a couple of errors as he struggled to cope with a full tank of fuel. These mistakes pushed him back to fourth place, behind Rossi, giving the crowd at what truly is Valentino's home track a reason to go ballistic.

Vale kept them happy for eight laps before Marquez pushed past and set off after second-placed Dani Pedrosa. The pass was made with enough force to disrupt Rossi's lap and detach him from the back of the Honda: fourth again. Marquez caught his team-mate and went past in equally rough fashion only to have Dani return the favour a few laps later; Marc then settled that argument on the same lap with yet another tough move. Was there time to go for the win, with Lorenzo four seconds up the road? No. For the second race running we heard Marquez say that 20 points were important for the championship. Lorenzo, greatly encouraged by the new gearbox, the win, and moving to second in the standings, insisted that the fight continued.

Behind what had now become the standard pattern for the top four, Stefan Bradl stalked Cal Crutchlow for the whole race and took fifth on the last lap, while Colin Edwards won the CRT fight for the first time after Aleix Espargaro was penalised for a jump start, after which he rode through the field to within 4.5 seconds of the Texan.

'I WAS CONVINCED
TO FOLLOW MY
STRATEGY OF
THE LAST COUPLE
OF RACES'
JORGE LORENZO

ABOVE The Repsol Hondas fought hard for the lower two rostrum positions

BELOW The race for top satellite bike was won by Stefan Bradl, who followed Cal Crutchlow this closely right to the last corner before making his move

OPPOSITE Jorge Lorenzo's start-to-finish win wasn't spectacular but it was perfection

The one place where there wasn't any joy was Bologna. The Ducatis suffered even more than usual at the track closest to their base. Eighth and ninth for the works bikes had to be considered normal for this season, but the gap to the winner was, frankly, embarrassing. To make matters even worse, Ben Spies, absent since his Indy crash, announced he would be out for the rest of the year. Negotiations with the Paul Bird team secured the services of Yonny Hernandez for the remainder of the season, starting at the official test on the Monday after the race. (Regular replacement and factory test rider Michele Pirro's schedule precluded him from doing the three back-to-back Asian races.) Meanwhile, rumours linking Nicky Hayden, not required by Ducati for 2014, with Aspar's team continued to gather force.

A look at the lap chart for this race might give the impression that it was somewhat boring – but only if one regards watching a 250hp-plus prototype motorcycle being driven with total precision at lap-record pace for the best part of an hour a tedious experience. Lorenzo's win was as great an example of concentration and bike control as anyone could wish to see, and all on a fuel-heavy track which would have required ignition maps that rendered the motor peaky and therefore difficult to ride smoothly when getting on the throttle. Any way you look at it, this was one of the best rides of the season.

No-one seriously thought Lorenzo's back-to-back victories would have any effect on Marc Marquez's tactics, or that the pressure would now get to him. Given events so far in the season it was difficult to imagine, but so was watching him dutifully follow the newly energised Lorenzo home for the five remaining races.

SLICK SHIFTER

What's so special about a seamless-shift gearbox, given that, as everybody is agreed, it has a very minor effect on lap times? First, it is probably useful to understand what it does. In a conventional gearbox, transmission of torque to the rear wheel is momentarily interrupted as one pair of gears, one cog on each of the gearbox's shafts, is disengaged and another pair engaged. That interruption of power delivery has all sorts of unpleasant consequences for the rider, mainly to do with the bike moving about as ratios are swapped. With a seamless box, two ratios are effectively engaged at the same time for a fraction of a revolution of the shafts. The newly engaged gear-pair effectively throws the original one out of engagement and the rider doesn't feel any loss of drive, plus the bike doesn't move about and so the tyres have an easier time. Every racer who's used such a system agrees that the stability under acceleration at significant angles of lean is significantly improved.

There is also the matter of fuel consumption. With a conventional transmission, the engine is still burning petrol during that time when no drive is being transmitted. British company Zeroshift have estimated that a seamless gearbox saves up to 7% on fuel consumption in some automotive applications, and although the overall saving in MotoGP will be much smaller, perhaps 1–2%, under current regulations that's considerable. The trick is not wasting the fuel that's burnt accelerating the crankshaft. The hardware for this has been around for over a decade; the electronics to control the torque spike generated during the instantaneous shift and to deliver a jolt-free gearchange are state-of-the-art innovations.

GP APEROL DI SAN MARINO E RIVIERA DI RIMINI
MISANO WORLD CIRCUIT MARCO SIMONCELLI

ROUND 13
September 15

RACE RESULTS

CIRCUIT LENGTH 2.626 miles
NO. OF LAPS 28
RACE DISTANCE 73.528 miles
WEATHER Dry, 24°C
TRACK TEMPERATURE 31°C
WINNER Jorge Lorenzo
FASTEST LAP 1m 33.935s, 100.600mph, Marc Marquez
LAP RECORD 1m 33.906s, 100.662mph, Jorge Lorenzo, 2011

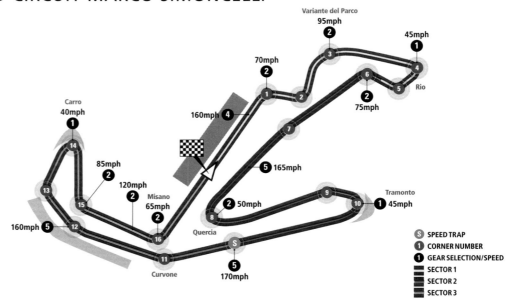

Variante del Parco 95mph
45mph
70mph
Rio
Carro 40mph
160mph
165mph
Tramonto 45mph
85mph
120mph
Misano 65mph
50mph
160mph
Quercia
170mph
Curvone

S SPEED TRAP
1 CORNER NUMBER
1 GEAR SELECTION/SPEED
SECTOR 1
SECTOR 2
SECTOR 3

QUALIFYING

	Rider	Nation	Motorcycle	Team	Time	Pole +
1	Marquez	SPA	Honda	Repsol Honda Team	1m 32.915s	
2	Lorenzo	SPA	Yamaha	Yamaha Factory Racing	1m 33.428s	0.513s
3	Rossi	ITA	Yamaha	Yamaha Factory Racing	1m 33.573s	0.658s
4	Pedrosa	SPA	Honda	Repsol Honda Team	1m 33.726s	0.811s
5	Crutchlow	GBR	Yamaha	Monster Yamaha Tech 3	1m 34.014s	1.099s
6	Espargaro	SPA	ART	Power Electronics Aspar	1m 34.028s	1.113s
7	Bradl	GER	Honda	LCR Honda MotoGP	1m 34.098s	1.183s
8	Bautista	SPA	Honda	GO&FUN Honda Gresini	1m 34.230s	1.315s
9	Dovizioso	ITA	Ducati	Ducati Team	1m 34.338s	1.423s
10	Hayden	USA	Ducati	Ducati Team	1m 34.362s	1.447s
11	Pirro	ITA	Ducati	Ignite Pramac Racing	1m 34.467s	1.552s
12	Iannone	ITA	Ducati	Energy T.I. Pramac Racing	1m 34.519s	1.604s
13	Smith	GBR	Yamaha	Monster Yamaha Tech 3	1m 34.869s	Q1
14	Edwards	USA	FTR Kawasaki	NGM Mobile Forward Racing	1m 35.174s	Q1
15	Aoyama	JPN	FTR	Avintia Blusens	1m 35.534s	Q1
16	De Puniet	FRA	ART	Power Electronics Aspar	1m 35.596s	Q1
17	Barbera	SPA	FTR	Avintia Blusens	1m 35.866s	Q1
18	Corti	ITA	FTR Kawasaki	NGM Mobile Forward Racing	1m 35.885s	Q1
19	Petrucci	ITA	Ioda-Suter	Came IodaRacing Project	1m 36.027s	Q1
20	Laverty	GBR	PBM	Paul Bird Motorsport	1m 36.788s	Q1
21	Hernandez	COL	ART	Paul Bird Motorsport	1m 36.844s	Q1
22	Abraham	CZE	ART	Cardion AB Motoracing	1m 36.877s	Q1
23	Staring	AUS	FTR Honda	GO&FUN Honda Gresini	1m 37.283s	Q1
24	Pesek	CZE	Ioda-Suter	Came IodaRacing Project	1m 37.886s	Q1

FINISHERS

1 JORGE LORENZO Shrugged off Marquez's astonishing performance in qualifying to yet again do what he had to. His team found a setting in warm-up that enabled him to get the holeshot and take well over a second out of the field on the first lap. Then opened up a small gap and while he couldn't relax he was able to control the gap. Masterful.

2 MARC MARQUEZ Ripped the pole record to shreds in qualifying, but a couple of mistakes early on put him fourth in the race. Passed Rossi, then got up to Pedrosa who gave him a good fight for second.

3 DANI PEDROSA Seriously handicapped by his usual inability to find traction on a low-grip track. Failed to qualify on the front row but fought hard in the race, especially with his team-mate in the closing stages.

4 VALENTINO ROSSI His fourth fourth place in successive races wasn't what Vale expected after his second front-row qualification of the year. Very happy with the new seamless gearbox, but the old problems under hard braking resurfaced, leading to a few small mistakes and him losing touch with the top three.

5 STEFAN BRADL A good, confidence-restoring ride after his recent disappointments and a big crash on Friday. Not sure about the tyre at first, but followed Crutchlow all race long and was able to plan his last-lap move for fifth.

6 CAL CRUTCHLOW No feeling with the bike, in pain from the arm injured at Silverstone, but still put together a solid race to boost his self-belief. Lost in free practice and didn't make Q2 directly, yet came through from Q1 and qualified fifth, then led Bradl right up to the last corner.

7 ALVARO BAUTISTA It all looked good until qualifying when he was unable to back up his practice times. Couldn't challenge Crutchlow and Bradl in the race. The team muttered about issues being out of their control.

8 ANDREA DOVIZIOSO Started behind Espargaro and therefore put off by the Spaniard's jump start. Lost places in the opening two corners before resuming his usual fight with team-mate Hayden.

9 NICKY HAYDEN Distracted by Espargaro's jump start, then ran off track while dicing with Dovizioso. Not a happy final race for Ducati on the team's home track.

10 MICHELE PIRRO Rode the 'lab bike' as a replacement for Spies. Thought he could race with the factory Ducatis but a few small mistakes, including a run-on at Quercia, caused him to lose both his focus and the tow.

11 BRADLEY SMITH Never found any feel, his usual problem on low-grip circuits. Crashed in qualifying when he over-rode trying to get into Q2. Got a good start but simply couldn't follow anyone; well beaten by the Ducatis.

12 COLIN EDWARDS Top CRT after a consistently impressive weekend. Took a while to work out why his team was giving him +7 signals (it was due to Espargaro's ride-through penalty), but put together a very strong last few laps to make sure the Aprilia couldn't catch him.

13 ALEIX ESPARGARO Stunning in qualifying and dramatic in the race. Jumped the start, did the requisite

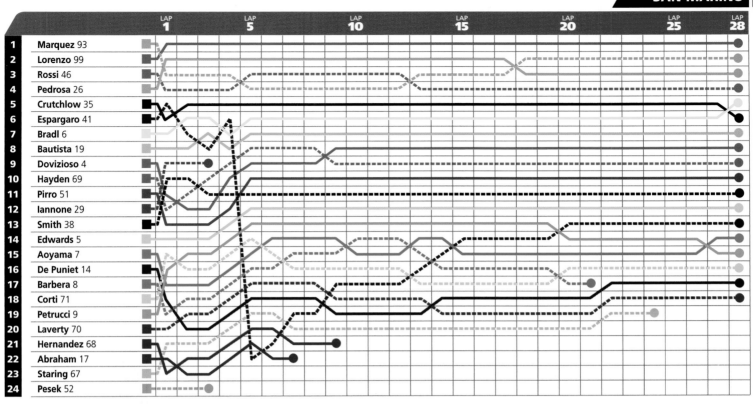

	Rider		LAP 1	LAP 5	LAP 10	LAP 15	LAP 20	LAP 25	LAP 28
1	Marquez	93							
2	Lorenzo	99							
3	Rossi	46							
4	Pedrosa	26							
5	Crutchlow	35							
6	Espargaro	41							
7	Bradl	6							
8	Bautista	19							
9	Dovizioso	4							
10	Hayden	69							
11	Pirro	51							
12	Iannone	29							
13	Smith	38							
14	Edwards	5							
15	Aoyama	7							
16	De Puniet	14							
17	Barbera	8							
18	Corti	71							
19	Petrucci	9							
20	Laverty	70							
21	Hernandez	68							
22	Abraham	17							
23	Staring	67							
24	Pesek	52							

RACE

	Rider	Motorcycle	Race Time	Time +	Fastest Lap	Avg. Speed	*B*
1	Lorenzo	Yamaha	44m 05.522s		1m 34.020s	100.041mph	H/M
2	Marquez	Honda	44m 08.901s	3.379s	1m 33.935s	99.916mph	H/M
3	Pedrosa	Honda	44m 12.890s	7.368s	1m 34.107s	99.730mph	H/M
4	Rossi	Yamaha	44m 20.584s	15.062s	1m 34.072s	99.482mph	H/M
5	Bradl	Honda	44m 27.877s	22.355s	1m 34.540s	99.171mph	M/M
6	Crutchlow	Yamaha	44m 28.121s	22.599s	1m 34.729s	99.171mph	H/M
7	Bautista	Honda	44m 36.581s	31.059s	1m 34.501s	98.860mph	M/M
8	Dovizioso	Ducati	44m 48.224s	42.702s	1m 35.217s	98.425mph	M/M
9	Hayden	Ducati	44m 50.380s	44.858s	1m 35.268s	98.363mph	M/M
10	Pirro	Ducati	44m 53.340s	47.818s	1m 35.281s	98.239mph	M/M
11	Smith	Yamaha	44m 53.533s	48.011s	1m 35.508s	98.239mph	H/M
12	Edwards	FTR Kawasaki	45m 08.676s	1m 03.154s	1m 35.823s	97.680mph	M/S
13	Espargaro	ART	45m 13.122s	1m 07.600s	1m 35.596s	97.555mph	M/S
14	Aoyama	FTR	45m 21.050s	1m 15.528s	1m 36.414s	97.245mph	M/S
15	Petrucci	Ioda-Suter	45m 23.429s	1m 17.907s	1m 36.278s	97.182mph	M/S
16	Corti	FTR Kawasaki	45m 35.177s	1m 29.655s	1m 36.686s	96.747mph	M/S
17	De Puniet	ART	45m 39.512s	1m 33.990s	1m 37.066s	96.561mph	M/S
18	Laverty	PBM	45m 42.382s	1m 36.860s	1m 37.091s	96.499mph	M/S
NF	Staring	FTR Honda	39m 34.016s	4 Laps	1m 37.467s	95.567mph	M/S
NF	Barbera	FTR	34m 13.026s	7 Laps	1m 36.411s	96.685mph	M/S
NF	Hernandez	ART	14m 50.319s	19 Laps	1m 37.272s	95.505mph	H/S
NF	Abraham	ART	11m 39.445s	21 Laps	1m 37.602s	94.573mph	M/S
NF	Iannone	Ducati	4m 53.247s	25 Laps	1m 35.247s	96.685mph	M/M
NF	Pesek	Ioda-Suter	5m 08.276s	25 Laps	1m 39.690s	91.963mph	M/S

CHAMPIONSHIP

	Rider	Nation	Team	Points
1	Marquez	SPA	Repsol Honda Team	253
2	Lorenzo	SPA	Yamaha Factory Racing	219
3	Pedrosa	SPA	Repsol Honda Team	219
4	Rossi	ITA	Yamaha Factory Racing	169
5	Crutchlow	GBR	Monster Yamaha Tech 3	146
6	Bradl	GER	LCR Honda MotoGP	124
7	Bautista	SPA	GO&FUN Honda Gresini	112
8	Dovizioso	ITA	Ducati Team	104
9	Hayden	USA	Ducati Team	95
10	Smith	GBR	Monster Yamaha Tech 3	71
11	Espargaro	SPA	Power Electronics Aspar	71
12	Pirro	ITA	Ignite Pramac Racing	50
13	Iannone	ITA	Energy T.I. Pramac Racing	41
14	Edwards	USA	NGM Mobile Forward Racing	31
15	Barbera	SPA	Avintia Blusens	27
16	Petrucci	ITA	Came IodaRacing Project	23
17	De Puniet	FRA	Power Electronics Aspar	20
18	Spies	USA	Ignite Pramac Racing	9
19	Corti	ITA	NGM Mobile Forward Racing	7
20	Hernandez	COL	Paul Bird Motorsport	7
21	Aoyama	JPN	Avintia Blusens	6
22	De Angelis	RSM	Ignite Pramac Racing	5
23	Abraham	CZE	Cardion AB Motoracing	5
24	Laverty	GBR	Paul Bird Motorsport	3
25	Staring	AUS	GO&FUN Honda Gresini	2
26	Del Amor	SPA	Avintia Blusens	1

ride-through penalty on lap five, then charged through the field and ended up only four seconds behind the top CRT.

14 HIROSHI AOYAMA Used the standard engine, not the new, pneumatic-valve version. Lost time with engine problems in practice and crashed in warm-up but found some confidence in the race and scored points after a good fight.

15 DANILO PETRUCCI Would have liked the weather to stay hot so he could've used the harder tyre. Started with a really brave outside move at the first corner but couldn't match Edwards's pace and was then mugged by Aoyama in the closing stages.

16 CLAUDIO CORTI Not happy to miss out on a point at his home GP. Chewed up the front tyre trying to make up for lack of speed and not happy to be outgunned by the similar Avintia bikes.

17 RANDY DE PUNIET A lacklustre weekend mainly due to vibration from the rear of the bike. The team thought they'd found an answer for race day, but the problem returned.

18 MICHAEL LAVERTY His best weekend for quite a while. Happier with the bike but ran on twice while dicing with de Puniet so lost touch with the group. Rode the ART, as opposed to the PBM bike, at the Monday test.

NON-FINISHERS

BRYAN STARING More bad luck. This time the Aussie was let down by his bike: the engine stopped.

HECTOR BARBERA Used a new pneumatic-valve engine, which he thought improved both top speed and acceleration. However, serious chatter forced him to pull out of the race seven laps from the flag.

YONNY HERNANDEZ Pulled in when he felt a problem with the gearbox, which turned out to be trivial. Released by the team on Monday to be the long-term replacement for Spies at Pramac Ducati.

KAREL ABRAHAM Pulled out when the pain from the shoulder he'd injured in Indianapolis became unbearable.

ANDREA IANNONE Qualified well and started the race well, but fell on the second lap as he tried to catch Bautista. Had looked the happiest Ducati rider but took a different line at Turn 6 and paid the price.

LUKAS PESEK Forced out by severe pain in his right wrist.

NON-STARTERS

BEN SPIES Still recovering from shoulder surgery and now ruled out for the season.

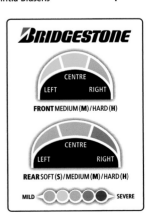

BRIDGESTONE

CENTRE
LEFT · RIGHT
FRONT MEDIUM (M) / HARD (H)

CENTRE
LEFT · RIGHT
REAR SOFT (S) / MEDIUM (M) / HARD (H)

MILD — SEVERE

GRAN PREMIO IVECO DE ARAGÓN

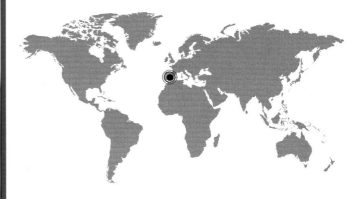

CUTTING CREW

Marc Marquez found yet another way to stir up controversy as he won, extending his championship lead while ending his team-mate's chances

It looked for a while as if the race would follow the now usual script of Lorenzo setting the pace and being hunted by the Hondas. But here, the only Spanish track on which Jorge had not won, surely the Hondas would catch him. Any deviation from that plot would be considered a surprise – and for half a dozen laps it looked as if we would get what we expected. Lorenzo did indeed get the holeshot and, risking all, he led by more than a second at the end of the first lap. Despite that typically brave opening Jorge could not increase his advantage and the two Hondas closed in, led by Dani Pedrosa.

On the sixth lap the three were together, with Pedrosa in second and looking for a way past. Marquez, in third, tried a major lunge on the brakes only to be forced to run wide when he nearly collected his team-mate. Anxious not to lose ground Marc swung back on track, again nearly colliding with Dani. Then, when Pedrosa got back on the throttle, he was pitched over the handlebars, landing heavily on his knees. Only after the race did the whole truth emerge: Marquez had actually dealt the other Honda the lightest of blows, snagging a cable running along the swinging arm with his clutch lever. It was enough to sever the cable which, unluckily for Dani, connected the rear-wheel speed sensor to the engine management system. The result of this was that when Pedrosa opened the throttle he had no traction control; the system would normally have capped the amount of power delivered in the lower gears. Dani was probably in second gear and certainly wasn't expecting over 250 horsepower to be on tap.

It was not the 28th birthday present he was hoping

'TODAY WAS
A VERY GRUELLING
RACE BECAUSE I HAD TO
MAKE TWO COMEBACKS'
MARC MARQUEZ

for. Victor the previous year, and starting from the front row for the first time since Indy, Dani looked the most likely winner as the championship headed to a run of tracks where he has always been fast. The crash effectively ended his chances of finally becoming World Champion, but with some form himself when it comes to torpedoing a team-mate (remember Estoril 2006 when he took out Nicky Hayden) he was careful not to criticise Marquez directly. When the full reasons for the crash came out Race Direction announced they would be investigating but, because of the delay, not until the next race in Malaysia.

Jorge Lorenzo did not have too much to say on the subject, being more concerned with his own race and his inability to offer any meaningful challenge to the resurgent Marquez. The coming-together of the Hondas had given Jorge a second chance to escape up the road, armed with a new lead of almost two seconds, but even that wasn't enough. Marquez closed his rival down, passed him and pulled away to his sixth win of the season and a 39-point championship lead. Jorge kept him honest but was all too aware that he didn't have the speed on this track.

The man himself was a little reflective after the race, saying he would have to be careful – although he was actually referring to a lock-up he saved while chasing Lorenzo. As for the incident with Pedrosa, he pointed out that the contact was much lighter than when Dani had passed him at Misano but admitted that, as he was behind, it was indeed his responsibility, even if the outcome was grossly out of proportion to the offence.

OPPOSITE It didn't look like they'd touched, but they had. Marquez carried on, lack of traction control put Pedrosa on the floor

LEFT It was all Lorenzo could do to keep Marquez in sight, especially up the hill to the last corner

ABOVE Australian Damian Cudlin was Yonny Hernandez's replacement in the Paul Bird Team

ABOVE The now traditional fight for fourth features all the usual suspects: Rossi, Bautista, Bradl and Crutchlow

BELOW Pol Espargaro, fresh from the Moto2 rostrum, gives some advice to elder brother Aleix on the MotoGP grid

OPPOSITE Yonny Hernandez enjoyed his first race as permanent replacement for Ben Spies in the Pramac Ducati team

The removal of one of the top three again made room for a stranger on the rostrum and, as happened in the aftermath of the rash of mid-season collarbone fractures, it was Valentino Rossi who filled the gap. He had to deal with Bautista, looking more and more impressive as the season went on, the enigmatic Bradl and Crutchlow, who yet again only had enough speed to hang on to the group rather than fight it.

The rostrum saved Valentino from becoming the only rider ever in the top class to finish fourth in five successive races. Knowing that if Pedrosa had stayed on his bike he would have had that unwanted distinction perhaps explained his less than delighted demeanour. It's not so much that he appears to have made fourth place his own, more that he's habitually nearer to the man in fifth than the one in third.

With Abraham and Spies out for the season, two new riders appeared on the grid: lanky Italian supersport ace Luca Scassa on the Cardion Aprilia and Aussie all-rounder Damian Cudlin on the PBM machine. Neither troubled the scorers, as Aleix Espargaro resumed his domination of the CRT class after his blip at Misano.

So Spanish domination of not just the MotoGP class but all the classes continued. Rossi was the only non-Spanish rostrum finisher of the weekend and the front rows of all three grids were populated entirely by Spaniards. The only surprise was that this was the first time it had ever happened. Even with four races to go, the only question left in most people's minds now was when Marquez would win the title, not if.

SENSORGATE

Race Direction had to wait until the Thursday of the Malaysian race before getting all the interested parties together to discuss what paddock wags were calling Sensorgate. The result was one penalty point on Marc Marquez's licence and a swingeing 25-point deduction from Honda's Constructors' Championship total.

Added to the two points he'd acquired at Silverstone, that put Marc within one point of having to start a

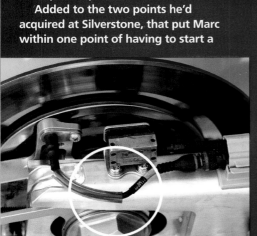

race from the back of the grid. It was a warning about his disconcerting habit of running in very close to the opposition on the brakes, and often having to take avoiding action – something Lorenzo had mentioned frequently in the aftermath of Jerez. Some construed it as a top-up for what was seen as his lenient treatment after the Silverstone crash under yellow flags.

Honda's punishment was for endangering riders' safety, not something the company usually considered as masters of detail enjoyed.

Race Direction hit them for both hardware and software oversights. Their crime was to run the rear-wheel speed sensor's cable along the top of the swinging arm with no protection or back-up. For starters, the cable should have been better protected or the system duplicated – as on the other factory bikes. And second, the software should have defaulted to a safe setting when the sensor was disconnected rather than allowing Pedrosa to be highsided. The faults, we were assured, had been rectified.

GRAN PREMIO IVECO DE ARAGÓN
MOTORLAND ARAGON
ROUND 14
September 29

SPEED TRAP
CORNER NUMBER
GEAR SELECTION/SPEED
SECTOR 1
SECTOR 2
SECTOR 3

RACE RESULTS

CIRCUIT LENGTH 3.155 miles
NO. OF LAPS 23
RACE DISTANCE 72.572 miles
WEATHER Dry, 23°C
TRACK TEMPERATURE 30°C
WINNER Marc Marquez
FASTEST LAP 1m 48.565s, 104.577mph, Dani Pedrosa (Record)
PREVIOUS LAP RECORD 1m 49.046s, 104.142mph, Casey Stoner, 2011

QUALIFYING

	Rider	Nation	Motorcycle	Team	Time	Pole +
1	Marquez	SPA	Honda	Repsol Honda Team	1m 47.804s	
2	Lorenzo	SPA	Yamaha	Yamaha Factory Racing	1m 47.814s	0.010s
3	Pedrosa	SPA	Honda	Repsol Honda Team	1m 47.957s	0.153s
4	Rossi	ITA	Yamaha	Yamaha Factory Racing	1m 47.962s	0.158s
5	Bradl	GER	Honda	LCR Honda MotoGP	1m 48.128s	0.324s
6	Bautista	SPA	Honda	GO&FUN Honda Gresini	1m 48.302s	0.498s
7	Crutchlow	GBR	Yamaha	Monster Yamaha Tech 3	1m 48.653s	0.849s
8	Smith	GBR	Yamaha	Monster Yamaha Tech 3	1m 48.854s	1.050s
9	Dovizioso	ITA	Ducati	Ducati Team	1m 49.219s	1.415s
10	Espargaro	SPA	ART	Power Electronics Aspar	1m 49.348s	1.544s
11	Hayden	USA	Ducati	Ducati Team	1m 49.428s	1.624s
12	Iannone	ITA	Ducati	Energy T.I. Pramac Racing	1m 50.094s	2.290s
13	Hernandez	COL	Ducati	Ignite Pramac Racing	1m 50.685s	Q1
14	Aoyama	JPN	FTR	Avintia Blusens	1m 50.995s	Q1
15	Petrucci	ITA	Ioda-Suter	Came IodaRacing Project	1m 51.030s	Q1
16	De Puniet	FRA	ART	Power Electronics Aspar	1m 51.297s	Q1
17	Edwards	USA	FTR Kawasaki	NGM Mobile Forward Racing	1m 51.327s	Q1
18	Corti	ITA	FTR Kawasaki	NGM Mobile Forward Racing	1m 51.519s	Q1
19	Barbera	SPA	FTR	Avintia Blusens	1m 51.552s	Q1
20	Laverty	GBR	ART	Paul Bird Motorsport	1m 51.639s	Q1
21	Staring	AUS	FTR Honda	GO&FUN Honda Gresini	1m 52.102s	Q1
22	Scassa	ITA	ART	Cardion AB Motoracing	1m 52.305s	Q1
23	Pesek	CZE	Ioda-Suter	Came IodaRacing Project	1m 52.989s	Q1
24	Cudlin	AUS	PBM	Paul Bird Motorsport	1m 53.521s	Q1

FINISHERS

1 MARC MARQUEZ Had to work hard twice over – first to reel in Lorenzo and then to catch his team-mate. Unfortunately, a mistake led to very slight contact with Pedrosa's bike which severed a cable and led to Dani's crash. Race Direction would make a judgement at the next race.

2 JORGE LORENZO Tried to implement his now standard plan of building a lead from the start but was caught by the Hondas. Got a second chance when the Repsol bikes came together and Pedrosa crashed, but the gap of 1.7s was not enough to prevent Marquez catching him.

3 VALENTINO ROSSI Used the harder front tyre, unlike the two who finished in front of him, which he reckoned was the reason he wasn't as quick. Still delighted to be back on the rostrum after fighting off a late challenge from Bautista.

4 ALVARO BAUTISTA Part of the race-long fight for third. Got involved with Bradl in the closing laps so couldn't attack Rossi. His best race for a while.

5 STEFAN BRADL Had to concede fourth to Bautista after a last-lap scrap, but always part of the four-man fight for the final rostrum position. Still ten points ahead of the Spaniard in the battle of the satellite Hondas.

6 CAL CRUTCHLOW Very unhappy with his engine. Despite fitting a new unit for Sunday he was slower than the Hondas and factory Yamahas. Convinced he would've had a much better result if he had some speed, but it was all he could do to hang on to the three in front of him.

7 BRADLEY SMITH His best finish since Germany and a major step forward. Despite a bad Friday he didn't just ride with the factory Ducatis, he passed Dovizioso and then rode away from them.

8 ANDREA DOVIZIOSO Knew he'd be in trouble at a track that doesn't suit the Ducati, and indeed Dovi couldn't achieve his ambition of staying with Smith.

9 NICKY HAYDEN One can never accuse Nicky of not trying. Ran off the track three times, including one excursion into the gravel trap at Turn 8 that cost him 12 seconds – the gap to his team-mate.

10 ANDREA IANNONE Happy to be able to stay with the factory Ducatis in the early laps, even getting between them, but once the grip level dropped he had to let them go or risk falling again. The positives were his bike management and a top-ten finish.

11 ALEIX ESPARGARO Top CRT again after the interruption last time out. Mixed it up with Iannone and Hayden for most of the race but lost out to the factory machines on the straights.

12 YONNY HERNANDEZ First ride on the Pramac Ducati as full-time replacement for Spies and his best result of the season so far. Happy with lap times that were only a few seconds off other Ducati riders but more concerned with learning about tyre life, traction control and 'other important things' before the upcoming triple-header.

13 RANDY DE PUNIET Relieved to enjoy a race and have what he called the first 'normal Sunday' in a while after the usual set-up problems. The bike moved a lot in corners, probably because of the soft tyre, but he was happy. Second-best CRT behind his team-mate.

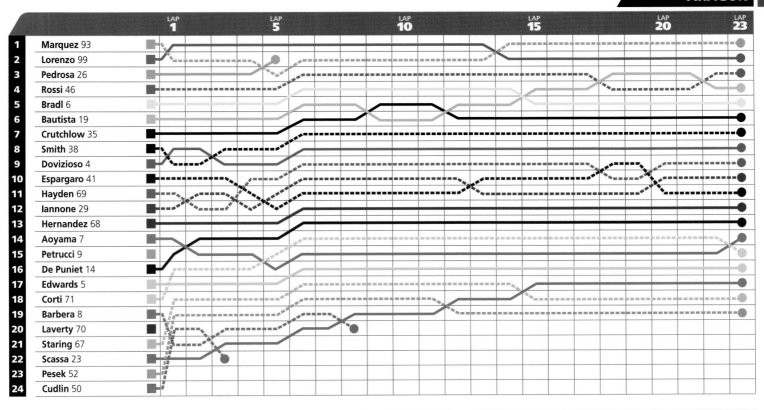

		LAP 1	LAP 5	LAP 10	LAP 15	LAP 20	LAP 23
1	Marquez 93						
2	Lorenzo 99						
3	Pedrosa 26						
4	Rossi 46						
5	Bradl 6						
6	Bautista 19						
7	Crutchlow 35						
8	Smith 38						
9	Dovizioso 4						
10	Espargaro 41						
11	Hayden 69						
12	Iannone 29						
13	Hernandez 68						
14	Aoyama 7						
15	Petrucci 9						
16	De Puniet 14						
17	Edwards 5						
18	Corti 71						
19	Barbera 8						
20	Laverty 70						
21	Staring 67						
22	Scassa 23						
23	Pesek 52						
24	Cudlin 50						

RACE

	Rider	Motorcycle	Race Time	Time +	Fastest Lap	Avg. Speed	B
1	Marquez	Honda	42m 03.459s		1m 48.788s	103.520mph	S/M
2	Lorenzo	Yamaha	42m 04.815s	1.356s	1m 48.860s	103.458mph	S/M
3	Rossi	Yamaha	42m 16.386s	12.927s	1m 48.976s	102.961mph	H/M
4	Bautista	Honda	42m 17.246s	13.787s	1m 49.455s	102.961mph	H/M
5	Bradl	Honda	42m 17.432s	13.973s	1m 49.259s	102.961mph	H/M
6	Crutchlow	Yamaha	42m 18.121s	14.662s	1m 49.227s	102.899mph	H/M
7	Smith	Yamaha	42m 34.679s	31.220s	1m 50.237s	102.216mph	H/M
8	Dovizioso	Ducati	42m 44.130s	40.671s	1m 50.214s	101.843mph	H/M
9	Hayden	Ducati	42m 56.872s	53.413s	1m 50.654s	101.346mph	H/M
10	Iannone	Ducati	42m 58.526s	55.067s	1m 50.824s	101.284mph	H/M
11	Espargaro	ART	43m 01.460s	58.001s	1m 50.919s	101.159mph	H/S
12	Hernandez	Ducati	43m 08.972s	1m 05.513s	1m 51.126s	100.911mph	H/M
13	De Puniet	ART	43m 10.048s	1m 06.589s	1m 51.526s	100.849mph	S/S
14	Aoyama	FTR	43m 12.133s	1m 08.674s	1m 52.114s	100.786mph	H/S
15	Corti	FTR Kawasaki	43m 12.589s	1m 09.130s	1m 51.652s	100.724mph	H/S
16	Edwards	FTR Kawasaki	43m 15.500s	1m 12.041s	1m 51.659s	100.600mph	H/S
17	Scassa	ART	43m 48.611s	1m 45.152s	1m 52.545s	99.357mph	H/S
18	Staring	FTR Honda	43m 48.687s	1m 45.228s	1m 53.127s	99.357mph	H/S
19	Pesek	Ioda-Suter	43m 49.042s	1m 45.583s	1m 53.544s	99.357mph	H/S
NF	Barbera	FTR	15m 26.508s	15 Laps	1m 52.496s	98.052mph	H/S
NF	Pedrosa	Honda	9m 08.055s	18 Laps	1m 48.565s	103.583mph	H/M
NF	Cudlin	PBM	6m 00.254s	20 Laps	1m 55.593s	94.573mph	S/S
NF	Petrucci	Ioda-Suter		0 Lap			H/S
NF	Laverty	ART		0 Lap			H/S

CHAMPIONSHIP

	Rider	Nation	Team	Points
1	Marquez	SPA	Repsol Honda Team	278
2	Lorenzo	SPA	Yamaha Factory Racing	239
3	Pedrosa	SPA	Repsol Honda Team	219
4	Rossi	ITA	Yamaha Factory Racing	185
5	Crutchlow	GBR	Monster Yamaha Tech 3	156
6	Bradl	GER	LCR Honda MotoGP	135
7	Bautista	SPA	GO&FUN Honda Gresini	125
8	Dovizioso	ITA	Ducati Team	112
9	Hayden	USA	Ducati Team	102
10	Smith	GBR	Monster Yamaha Tech 3	80
11	Espargaro	SPA	Power Electronics Aspar	76
12	Pirro	ITA	Ignite Pramac Racing	50
13	Iannone	ITA	Energy T.I. Pramac Racing	47
14	Edwards	USA	NGM Mobile Forward Racing	31
15	Barbera	SPA	Avintia Blusens	27
16	De Puniet	FRA	Power Electronics Aspar	23
17	Petrucci	ITA	Came IodaRacing Project	23
18	Hernandez	COL	Paul Bird Motorsport	11
19	Spies	USA	Ignite Pramac Racing	9
20	Corti	ITA	NGM Mobile Forward Racing	8
21	Aoyama	JPN	Avintia Blusens	8
22	De Angelis	RSM	Ignite Pramac Racing	5
23	Abraham	CZE	Cardion AB Motoracing	5
24	Laverty	GBR	Paul Bird Motorsport	3
25	Staring	AUS	GO&FUN Honda Gresini	2
26	Del Amor	SPA	Avintia Blusens	1

14 HIROSHI AOYAMA Looking more like his old self. Hiro and Corti passed and repassed each other at least three times on the last lap, with the Japanese winning that fight to finish third CRT.

15 CLAUDIO CORTI Not helped by the transponder falling off its mounting and jamming his rear brake pedal. Despite front-brake trouble early on, causing him to run wide, fought with the three men in front throughout the race; happy with the weekend.

16 COLIN EDWARDS New electronics both helped and hindered. Found himself running wide regularly on a couple of corners, including the final one – not an Edwards trait at all, but he was confident he knew the fixes.

17 LUCA SCASSA Took over the Cardion AB team's ART Aprilia after Abraham decided on shoulder surgery. Finished his first Grand Prix in front of two other CRT machines despite losing time because of the first-lap Laverty–Petrucci incident.

18 BRYAN STARING Lost focus after an early mistake.

19 LUKAS PESEK Another confidence-free weekend but at least he finished, for the first time in five races.

NON-FINISHERS

HECTOR BARBERA Started from pit lane on his second bike after a sensor failure on the sighting lap. Unsurprisingly, he had to retire from the race.

DANI PEDROSA Crashed after having his traction control disabled when his team-mate severed the unprotected cable on his swinging arm.

DAMIAN CUDLIN Drafted into the team to replace Hernandez, taking over the PBM-chassised machine from Laverty, but dropped out early with gearbox problems.

DANILO PETRUCCI Crashed on the first lap.

MICHAEL LAVERTY Swapped to the ART Aprilia. Taken out on the first lap by Petrucci.

NON-STARTERS

KAREL ABRAHAM Waiting to have shoulder surgery, which will put him out for the rest of the season. Replaced by Scassa.

BEN SPIES Had already announced that he'd be out for the rest of the year. Yonny Hernandez moved from the PBM team to replace him for the rest of the season.

BRIDGESTONE

CENTRE
LEFT RIGHT
FRONT SOFT (**S**) / HARD (**H**)

CENTRE
LEFT RIGHT
REAR SOFT (**S**) / MEDIUM (**M**) / HARD (**H**)

MILD ◯◯◯◯● SEVERE

SHELL ADVANCE MALAYSIAN MOTORCYCLE GRAND PRIX

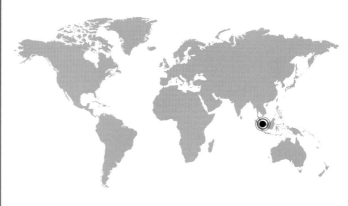

THE THIRD MAN

Pedrosa reminded everyone that there were still three aliens out there while Lorenzo went on the offensive, literally and metaphorically

Just when it seemed there were only two contenders in this championship, the perennial nearly man handed them both a comprehensive beating. That man is, of course, Dani Pedrosa and his win was all the more remarkable for the fact that the crash in Aragon had hurt him and severely hampered his preparation. He'd landed hard on his knees, been unable to walk for three days, and had only become fully mobile just before flying to Malaysia. Nevertheless, it was a classic Dani win: he waited a few laps before passing the inevitable early leader Jorge Lorenzo, then pulled away instantly. That left Lorenzo and Marc Marquez to carry on the fight that had started at the Thursday press conference.

Race Direction's deliberations on the events of Aragon resulted in a one-point penalty on Marquez's licence and a storm of sarcasm from Lorenzo. He praised the show Marc had put on at Jerez, at Silverstone, and when passing Rossi on the outside of the track at Laguna Seca. As the show is more important than safety, he went on, Marquez should have been given an extra championship point, not suffered a penalty. Pedrosa refused to get involved; Marquez looked decidedly uncomfortable but said the decision must be respected before pointing out that he wouldn't change.

That warmed things up nicely for the biggest crowd ever for a race in Malaysia. If there'd been any doubt about why the factories are so keen to race in this part of the world, Sepang's grandstands set matters right. As we now expected, Lorenzo did his best to bolt from the start but he never managed to open a gap. Like Aragon, Sepang is a track that most definitely favours the Honda, but there again so is Silverstone…

There was no escape. Dani went past at the end of

ABOVE Rossi and Crutchlow seemed surprised to see each other in parc fermé after qualifying so maybe it was no surprise neither made the rostrum

RIGHT Record crowds watched the Malaysian GP and of course saw Jorge Lorenzo lead into the first corner

OPPOSITE Bradley Smith underlined his steady improvement in his rookie season with a good finish right behind his team-mate Cal Crutchlow

the back straight, just as we would expect a Honda rider to do, and Marc tried to follow him. Jorge was not, as they say, having it. In a startling role reversal, Lorenzo did anything and everything to keep Marc behind him. It is a statement of the obvious to say that at this stage in the championship every point is vital and Jorge had no option but to employ tactics that he usually eschews. Accordingly he stuffed the Yamaha into spaces it didn't want to go and generally did a good impression of Marc Marquez at his loosest. Not that Marquez complained afterwards; he called it fun.

In truth, these were desperate measures from Jorge, whose bike was slower than in practice, probably due to the heat. He knew he couldn't compete so the only question for the second half of the race was whether Marc would catch Dani. He tried, he really tried, but when he realised he was making absolutely no impression on Pedrosa's lead – in fact it was increasing – Marquez settled for 20 points, saying afterwards that his main objective for the weekend had been to beat Lorenzo.

For his part, Dani couldn't help but look back to Aragon and opine that it should have been two wins in a row. It was difficult to argue with that view, and also not to sympathise.

There was a lot of sympathy, too, for Stefan Bradl, victim of a freak accident. He was in the process of sliding harmlessly to a halt after a gentle crash at the first corner when his foot caught in a tear in the trackside Astroturf, ripped open moments earlier by his sliding bike. The result was a broken ankle and the end of his fight with Crutchlow and Bautista for fifth place

ABOVE Luca Scassa was confirmed as full-time replacement for Abraham and got within a couple of seconds of the points

BELOW Hiro Aoyama, almost recovered from his injuries, had his best result of the year on his favourite track

OPPOSITE Lorenzo did his usual trick of leading from the start but this time he couldn't break away from the Hondas

in the championship. Nicky Hayden was another who suffered, but the fracture was to his bike rather than his person. He was chasing Bradley Smith when the Ducati came to a smoky halt right in front of the main grandstand as its nearly new motor failed. Rossi was again fourth and trying to work out whether the gap to Jorge was good or bad. Either way, it was very strange to hear Valentino attempting to be upbeat over a gap of more than ten seconds to the winner. Maybe it was the gap of three-and-a-half seconds to his team-mate in third place that he found pleasing.

As we've become accustomed to when the subject is Dani Pedrosa's championship chances, the phrase 'What if' was used a lot after the race. 'You can't look back,' said Pedrosa, right after indulging in a little bit of wistful speculation. And can you blame him? Repeatedly denied a tilt at the title by injury, Dani started the season fully fit but has been scuppered by two incidents. The crash in Germany has to go down as his own fault, but the cutting of a cable, probably by his team-mate's clutch lever, was a preposterous piece of bad luck. It is difficult to escape the feeling that Dani has run out of chances. He long ago overtook Randy Mamola for the unwanted distinction of the most successful rider never to win the title and it is now difficult, if not almost impossible, to see that changing.

The gap at the top of the championship was now back up to 43 points with three races left. That's why Lorenzo had to use any weapon at his disposal and why both he and Pedrosa, despite both still having mathematical chances of the title, were now talking as if the fight was over.

FAR EAST, MAN

The Sepang crowd demonstrated just why the factories are so anxious to race in this part of the world, and the number of wild cards from the home nation as well as Thailand and Indonesia showed the strength of domestic racing. Honda have been sending men like Tady Okada and Makoto Tamada to work with Malaysian teams for several seasons; now the effort has been switched to

discovering new talent with the Shell Advance Asia Talent Cup. The series will follow the proven path marked out by the Telefonica Movistar Cup held in Spain in the late 1990s which uncovered the talents of Dani Pedrosa and Toni Elias, among others.

Two test days at the Sepang International Circuit the week after the GP selected 22 teenage riders from all over Asia who will ride

identical Honda NSF250R racers, as used in Moto3, at tracks in Qatar, Indonesia, China, Japan, Malaysia and India. The field will consist of seven Japanese racers, six Malaysians, three each from Indonesia and Thailand, plus one each from China, the Philippines and Singapore. Anyone who immediately stands out may find themselves competing in the Spanish Championship or Red Bull Rookies.

The series will use the Sepang Circuit as its headquarters and will be overseen by Alberto Puig, long-time mentor of Dani Pedrosa and the man who organised the Telefonica series. The one surprising aspect of the Cup is that Japanese riders are now seen as needing this sort of help to make it on to the world stage. However, there is only one in all three classes who regularly challenged for a rostrum so maybe this sort of support is necessary. As for Puig, his split from Pedrosa looks like an indication of where Honda think his time would be better spent. And it's not on another attempt to get Dani to the title.

'IT'S A PITY ABOUT ARAGON BECAUSE WE HAD THE PACE AND THE SAME CHANCE TO WIN AS HERE'
DANI PEDROSA

SHELL ADVANCE MALAYSIAN MOTORCYCLE GRAND PRIX
SEPANG INTERNATIONAL CIRCUIT

ROUND 15
October 13

RACE RESULTS

CIRCUIT LENGTH 3.447 miles
NO. OF LAPS 20
RACE DISTANCE 68.94 miles
WEATHER Dry, 31°C
TRACK TEMPERATURE 44°C
WINNER Dani Pedrosa
FASTEST LAP 2m 01.415s, 102.216mph, Marc Marquez (Record)
PREVIOUS LAP RECORD 2m 02.108s, 101.635mph, Casey Stoner, 2007

- S SPEED TRAP
- 1 CORNER NUMBER
- 1 GEAR SELECTION/SPEED
- SECTOR 1
- SECTOR 2
- SECTOR 3

QUALIFYING

	Rider	Nation	Motorcycle	Team	Time	Pole +
1	Marquez	SPA	Honda	Repsol Honda Team	2m 00.011s	
2	Rossi	ITA	Yamaha	Yamaha Factory Racing	2m 00.336s	0.325s
3	Crutchlow	GBR	Yamaha	Monster Yamaha Tech 3	2m 00.359s	0.348s
4	Lorenzo	SPA	Yamaha	Yamaha Factory Racing	2m 00.578s	0.567s
5	Pedrosa	SPA	Honda	Repsol Honda Team	2m 00.692s	0.681s
6	Bautista	SPA	Honda	GO&FUN Honda Gresini	2m 00.974s	0.963s
7	Smith	GBR	Yamaha	Monster Yamaha Tech 3	2m 01.306s	1.295s
8	Dovizioso	ITA	Ducati	Ducati Team	2m 01.635s	1.624s
9	Espargaro	SPA	ART	Power Electronics Aspar	2m 02.151s	2.140s
10	Iannone	ITA	Ducati	Energy T.I. Pramac Racing	2m 02.536s	2.525s
11	Hayden	USA	Ducati	Ducati Team	2m 02.900s	2.889s
12	Bradl	GER	Honda	LCR Honda MotoGP		
13	Edwards	USA	FTR Kawasaki	NGM Mobile Forward Racing	2m 02.858s	Q1
14	Corti	ITA	FTR Kawasaki	NGM Mobile Forward Racing	2m 03.175s	Q1
15	Barbera	SPA	FTR	Avintia Blusens	2m 03.212s	Q1
16	Aoyama	JPN	FTR	Avintia Blusens	2m 03.418s	Q1
17	Hernandez	COL	Ducati	Ignite Pramac Racing	2m 03.651s	Q1
18	De Puniet	FRA	ART	Power Electronics Aspar	2m 03.805s	Q1
19	Laverty	GBR	ART	Paul Bird Motorsport	2m 04.198s	Q1
20	Petrucci	ITA	Ioda-Suter	Came IodaRacing Project	2m 04.310s	Q1
21	Scassa	ITA	ART	Cardion AB Motoracing	2m 05.199s	Q1
22	Staring	AUS	FTR Honda	GO&FUN Honda Gresini	2m 06.038s	Q1
23	Pesek	CZE	Ioda-Suter	Came IodaRacing Project	2m 06.203s	Q1
24	Cudlin	AUS	PBM	Paul Bird Motorsport	2m 06.273s	Q1

FINISHERS

1 DANI PEDROSA As good a win as anyone had all year. Started very well from the second row, followed early leader Lorenzo for four laps, but once he led was never threatened. Doubly impressive as he'd been unable to train after the Aragon crash. Kept alive his chances, albeit mathematical, of the championship.

2 MARC MARQUEZ Once he'd managed to dispose of an extremely feisty Lorenzo, he soon realised that trying to reel in Pedrosa wasn't a good idea. Beating Jorge meant it would now be possible to win the title at Phillip Island.

3 JORGE LORENZO Threw his weight about on and off the track but couldn't make his usual early charge work. Never opened up a gap and was passed on lap five, after which he fought to no avail.

4 VALENTINO ROSSI On the front row for the second time in three races, but again couldn't make any impression on the top three. Started fast and when pushed from second back to fourth was fortunate to avoid Bautista running on. Other than that, it was a lonely race.

5 ALVARO BAUTISTA Another good race. Had a small problem with his front brake that caused him to run on at the end of the front straight, narrowly missing Rossi. Took a little while to regain his confidence but came back to fight with, and pass, Crutchlow.

6 CAL CRUTCHLOW In contrast to the previous GP reckoned that too much power compromised his race. Spun the tyre too much, which may have been down to race-day temperatures being five degrees higher than the rest of the weekend.

7 BRADLEY SMITH A lonely race but another significant step. A great start put him with the leading group and he could still see Crutchlow and Bautista at the flag. Improved every session and managed the tricky conditions well.

8 ANDREA DOVIZIOSO Started well and was trying to stay with Smith when he lost the front and had an off-track excursion on lap three. That lost Dovi nearly ten seconds and condemned him to a lonely race.

9 ALEIX ESPARGARO First CRT and again able to stay with the prototype Ducatis while he had grip. Now leading the CRT classification by over 50 points and hoping to retain his title at the next race.

10 YONNY HERNANDEZ A little confused about set-up during practice but grabbed three places in the first two laps and then held on to tenth for the rest of the race. Delighted with his best result of the season.

11 HIROSHI AOYAMA His best result of the season on a favourite circuit despite troubles in practice and qualifying. Much happier after warm-up and despite vibration when the bike was at the limit.

12 RANDY DE PUNIET Like other CRT riders using the softer tyre, he suffered a serious drop in grip around mid-race. Survived one major moment with the front that prevented him challenging Aoyama.

13 CLAUDIO CORTI Dropped six positions early on when he lost the front trying to take Hernandez. Also lost feel on the brakes and found the heat exacerbated chatter – otherwise, said Corti, he would have been racing Aoyama.

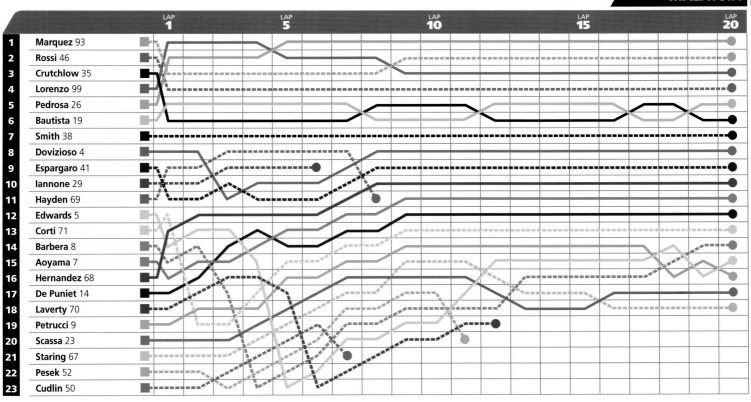

		LAP 1	LAP 5	LAP 10	LAP 15	LAP 20
1	Marquez 93					
2	Rossi 46					
3	Crutchlow 35					
4	Lorenzo 99					
5	Pedrosa 26					
6	Bautista 19					
7	Smith 38					
8	Dovizioso 4					
9	Espargaro 41					
10	Iannone 29					
11	Hayden 69					
12	Edwards 5					
13	Corti 71					
14	Barbera 8					
15	Aoyama 7					
16	Hernandez 68					
17	De Puniet 14					
18	Laverty 70					
19	Petrucci 9					
20	Scassa 23					
21	Staring 67					
22	Pesek 52					
23	Cudlin 50					

RACE

	Rider	Motorcycle	Race Time	Time +	Fastest Lap	Avg. Speed	*B*
1	Pedrosa	Honda	40m 45.191s		2m 01.438s	101.470mph	M/M
2	Marquez	Honda	40m 47.948s	2.757s	2m 01.415s	101.346mph	M/M
3	Lorenzo	Yamaha	40m 51.860s	6.669s	2m 01.632s	101.221mph	M/M
4	Rossi	Yamaha	40m 55.542s	10.351s	2m 01.498s	101.035mph	M/M
5	Bautista	Honda	41m 07.340s	22.149s	2m 01.551s	100.538mph	M/M
6	Crutchlow	Yamaha	41m 07.492s	22.301s	2m 01.793s	100.538mph	M/M
7	Smith	Yamaha	41m 16.055s	30.864s	2m 02.544s	100.227mph	M/M
8	Dovizioso	Ducati	41m 30.302s	45.111s	2m 03.080s	99.668mph	M/M
9	Espargaro	ART	41m 44.455s	59.264s	2m 03.621s	99.047mph	M/S
10	Hernandez	Ducati	41m 46.608s	1m 01.417s	2m 04.282s	98.984mph	H/M
11	Aoyama	FTR	41m 48.856s	1m 03.665s	2m 04.235s	98.922mph	M/S
12	De Puniet	ART	41m 59.447s	1m 14.256s	2m 04.419s	98.487mph	M/S
13	Corti	FTR Kawasaki	42m 06.794s	1m 21.603s	2m 05.047s	98.177mph	M/S
14	Barbera	FTR	42m 13.167s	1m 27.976s	2m 04.104s	97.928mph	H/S
15	Edwards	FTR Kawasaki	42m 14.633s	1m 29.442s	2m 04.192s	97.866mph	M/S
16	Petrucci	Ioda-Suter	42m 14.742s	1m 29.551s	2m 05.719s	97.866mph	H/M
17	Scassa	ART	42m 33.121s	1m 47.930s	2m 06.479s	97.182mph	H/M
18	Staring	FTR Honda	42m 38.118s	1m 52.927s	2m 06.465s	96.996mph	M/S
NF	Laverty	ART	25m 45.684s	8 Laps	2m 05.214s	96.313mph	M/S
NF	Pesek	Ioda-Suter	23m 44.392s	9 Laps	2m 06.750s	95.815mph	H/S
NF	Hayden	Ducati	16m 44.030s	12 Laps	2m 02.782s	98.860mph	M/M
NF	Cudlin	PBM	15m 11.023s	13 Laps	2m 06.546s	95.318mph	M/S
NF	Iannone	Ducati	12m 26.255s	14 Laps	2m 02.786s	99.730mph	M/M

CHAMPIONSHIP

	Rider	Nation	Team	Points
1	Marquez	SPA	Repsol Honda Team	298
2	Lorenzo	SPA	Yamaha Factory Racing	255
3	Pedrosa	SPA	Repsol Honda Team	244
4	Rossi	ITA	Yamaha Factory Racing	198
5	Crutchlow	GBR	Monster Yamaha Tech 3	166
6	Bautista	SPA	GO&FUN Honda Gresini	136
7	Bradl	GER	LCR Honda MotoGP	135
8	Dovizioso	ITA	Ducati Team	120
9	Hayden	USA	Ducati Team	102
10	Smith	GBR	Monster Yamaha Tech 3	89
11	Espargaro	SPA	Power Electronics Aspar	83
12	Pirro	ITA	Ignite Pramac Racing	50
13	Iannone	ITA	Energy T.I. Pramac Racing	47
14	Edwards	USA	NGM Mobile Forward Racing	32
15	Barbera	SPA	Avintia Blusens	29
16	De Puniet	FRA	Power Electronics Aspar	27
17	Petrucci	ITA	Came IodaRacing Project	23
18	Hernandez	COL	Paul Bird Motorsport	17
19	Aoyama	JPN	Avintia Blusens	13
20	Corti	ITA	NGM Mobile Forward Racing	11
21	Spies	USA	Ignite Pramac Racing	9
22	De Angelis	RSM	Ignite Pramac Racing	5
23	Abraham	CZE	Cardion AB Motoracing	5
24	Laverty	GBR	Paul Bird Motorsport	3
25	Staring	AUS	GO&FUN Honda Gresini	2
26	Del Amor	SPA	Avintia Blusens	1

14 HECTOR BARBERA Jumped the start and therefore had to take a ride-through penalty, so did well to score two points.

15 COLIN EDWARDS Jumped the start and took the ride-through penalty for the first time in 182 races. Then rode back up to Barbera and Petrucci, taking the final point-scoring position off the Italian on the last corner.

16 DANILO PETRUCCI A broken exhaust burnt the sole of his right foot and a faulty valve meant his drinks system flooded his crash helmet under braking.

17 LUCA SCASSA Went with the harder tyres, which may have been a mistake in the hotter conditions. Relieved to get through his first race at Sepang without crashing.

18 BRYAN STARING Another weekend in which the Aussie rider simply didn't generate any confidence in his bike.

NON-FINISHERS

MICHAEL LAVERTY Crashed out of a points-scoring position after a ride-through penalty for a jump start, which was triggered by Barbera moving early in front of him.

LUKAS PESEK Used his strength making up for a mistake and retired rather than risk a crash.

NICKY HAYDEN Having his best race for a while, pulling away from his team-mate and closing in on Smith, when he suffered engine failure.

DAMIAN CUDLIN Forced to retire when a new and untested exhaust ruptured.

ANDREA IANNONE Started well and was splitting the factory Ducatis when a tank slapper broke the steering damper mounting, forcing him to retire.

NON-STARTERS

STEFAN BRADL Broke his ankle is freakish circumstances in practice. Slid off, apparently harmlessly, but then caught his foot in a tear in the Astroturf made by his bike as it slid in front of him. Operated on in Kuala Lumpur and determined to try to race next weekend.

KAREL ABRAHAM Out for the season after shoulder surgery, but the team announced he would be back in 2014 on a customer Honda.

BEN SPIES Out for the season after shoulder surgery.

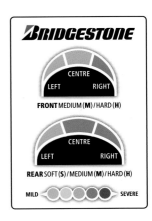

BRIDGESTONE

FRONT MEDIUM (**M**) / HARD (**H**)

REAR SOFT (**S**) / MEDIUM (**M**) / HARD (**H**)

MILD ⬤⬤⬤⬤⬤ SEVERE

TISSOT AUSTRALIAN GRAND PRIX

BLUNDERS DOWN UNDER

Tyre meltdown provided high drama, with Lorenzo starring and Honda the villains

Just when it seemed the championship was done and dusted, the best track on the calendar threw up shocks and incident on every front: embarrassment for both Bridgestone and Dunlop, the spec-tyre suppliers; a black-flag disqualification for championship leader Marc Marquez; and another thoroughly deserved victory for Jorge Lorenzo which reduced his deficit at the top of the table to just 18 points.

It was all down to the new surface, which everyone was very happy about on Friday. Bradley Smith reckoned it was nearly perfect – grippy, smooth and a major improvement on the bumpy, worn-out tarmac which had attracted criticism last year. Moto2 supplier Dunlop knew they had problems. They had data from the domestic superbike championship and had sent out rubber they thought suitable. Information from nearer the race date meant the hardest tyres in the catalogue were flown out for the GP, and even they weren't up to the job; the Moto2 race distance was cut almost in half.

Over in the MotoGP section of the paddock realisation was growing that even the emergency default extra-hard rear tyre wasn't going to go race distance. In fact it wasn't going to last half race distance, surely a consequence of there being no test on the new surface even though the track has always been the toughest on tyres. Race Direction now had a serious problem: how to give fans at the track and at home a race that lived up to its name and was worthy of 25 World Championship points. First, they awarded themselves the powers to do whatever was necessary. Then, after Bridgestone decided that their hard tyre, which would be mandatory for the race, could do no more than 14 laps they decided that a bike change

LEFT Aussie legends Stoner, Doohan and Gardner rode together before the main event and a relaxed Casey Stoner even put his picture up in the MotoGP Legends gallery

'WE HAD EVERYTHING WELL PLANNED AND I FOLLOWED THE INSTRUCTIONS ON MY PIT BOARD'
MARC MARQUEZ

would be necessary. It was a brave decision because the Phillip Island pit lane is the smallest on the calendar. Race distance was reduced to 26 laps with the bike change mandatory after no more than 12 laps, with a 14-lap maximum run. Pit lane was increased at both ends by extending the speed limit back up the entry road and by a white line on the exit, which it was forbidden to cross.

This brilliant compromise – nobody had any better ideas – sparked some frenzied bike-change practice during Sunday morning's warm-up. Unfortunately, the 20-minute session also produced some more worrying tyre data. Far from mellowing, the surface seemed to be getting more aggressive and race distance had to be shortened again. The total would now be 19 laps with the bike change mandatory by the end of the 10th lap on safety grounds. Simple enough, one would have thought.

It looked as if race day would go to the usual plan, albeit with the sideshow of some high-speed acrobatic bike changes. And it looked that way as Lorenzo led off pole pursued by the Hondas. Pedrosa was the first in, at the end of lap nine, Lorenzo and Marquez kept going and at the end of the 10th time round Jorge peeled off, as expected. Marquez didn't. Oblivious to what had happened, Marc's bike change included a 360-degree spin and a near-collision with Lorenzo as he emerged from the pits. It looked like another risky move from the youngster but Jorge was forgiving after the race – until he actually watched the incident on TV – but it became irrelevant because Marquez got the black flag: disqualification.

ABOVE Marc Marquez's bike change featured a flying dismount and a full twist; his mechanic – brave man – did well to field the bike

LEFT Classic Phillip Island action: the three Spaniards appear over Lukey Heights in the first half of the race

Someone had messed up, but the team weren't about to say who. Spanish TV had a camera in the pit which clearly showed Cristian Gabbarini of HRC making a throat-cutting gesture as soon as Marc went past, while mechanics waiting for their rider's arrival were clearly shocked as well. Who decided that it was a good idea to run that extra lap? Did Marquez receive the wrong signal on his pit board? There was a half-hearted attempt to argue that the instructions from Race Direction were ambiguous, which only led to

further incredulity. Team principal Livio Suppo eventually had to take the blame on behalf of the team.

As confusion reigned in the pits Lorenzo led the way home, only ever headed by Marquez during his stop, with Pedrosa second, although Dani had to survive a penalty for crossing the neutral line when he exited the pits. As it only involved conceding one position, to his team-mate as it happened, this wasn't a problem. Hiro Aoyama was the other one to fall foul of the white line.

Gabbarini's instant realisation contrasted with the other image that sticks in the mind, Lorenzo in pit lane with his arms round his mechanics, clearly laughing heartily. He'd rolled to a stop, flipped his visor up, listened intently and then started the celebrations. As expected when one of the aliens goes missing, Valentino Rossi completed the rostrum. He came out on top of a race-long dice with Crutchlow and Bautista with the aid of a highly efficient bike change.

Marquez, to his great credit, didn't complain. There was an entirely understandable flash of temper in his pit garage when he was told the reason for the black flag but after the event he stuck loyally to the party line: win as a team, lose as a team. The state of his rear tyre, with chunks missing, showed graphically why the 10-lap limit had been enforced.

The drama of the bike changes, Marquez's collision with Lorenzo and the Honda team's error conspired to obscure the fundamental question of why a spec-tyre supplier messed up so badly. Why hadn't there been a test? And the answer, of course, is money, or rather the lack of it. Not surprisingly, there will be a test before the 2014 race.

BRIDGESTONE'S VIEW

Here's what Bridgestone's Shinji Aoki, Motorsport Tyre Development Department Manager had to say:

'Due to the much improved track surface this year, the rear slick tyre allocation we supplied experienced extreme temperatures which affected their durability. The very high levels of traction offered by the tarmac resulted in some tyres having their tread torn off and cracked – a situation we definitely did not anticipate. When it became apparent that doing the full race distance on a single rear tyre was not feasible, we engaged in discussions with Dorna, the FIM and IRTA, who worked together to find a solution. Considering the allocation we had to work with, I am pleased at the outcome as the crowd, as well as fans around the world, got to witness a safe and exciting race. The teams and riders showed great flexibility and professionalism in adapting their programme for a flag-to-flag race and for this they should be congratulated.

'The decision to make a 26-lap race came after our advice that the maximum stint on a rear slick tyre must be 14 laps, following our tyre analysis on Saturday. With our mind on the safety of the riders, we asked the riders to do long runs on the harder option rear slicks in Sunday's warm-up session to see if running conditions were different, which could have a result on tyre longevity. Analysis of the tyres from warm-up showed that on Sunday, 10 laps was a safer distance on a single rear tyre so, for a one-stop race, 19 laps was deemed the best race distance. It seems that the improved set-up of the bikes in Sunday warm-up yielded better performance for the riders and hence increased the stress on tyres even further compared to Saturday.

'We knew that the track had been resurfaced resulting in the track being more severe and despite having special extra-hard rear slicks delivered to the circuit to address this change the improvement in the condition of the track surface caused us problems. Although we have to investigate our used tyres and look at data from the teams to reach a conclusion on all the contributing factors, the overall problem was sustained periods of very high tyre temperatures that, before this weekend, were unprecedented. Our initial findings suggest it wasn't just the vastly increased grip of the tarmac itself that caused the problem. The lack of bumps in the corners meant the tyres maintained more constant contact with the tarmac and this drove tyre temperatures even higher. We expected an increase in tyre temperatures this weekend and prepared for this, but the extreme temperatures that occurred were far beyond our expectations.

'The extra-hard rear slicks used in FP4 offered no benefit compared to the hard compound slick that was originally allocated. The extra-hard rear slick suffered from the same heat problems and also offered less grip than the hard rear, so it was withdrawn as a race option. Generally, harder rubber compounds offer better heat resistance, yet this wasn't always the case last weekend. Our hard compound rear slick fared better than our medium compound rear, but the extra-hard rear slick didn't cope as well as the hard option. This seems to be another peculiarity with the new Phillip Island track surface and this is something our engineers are currently investigating.'

BELOW Marc Marquez has seen the black flag, knows the race is over, and signals to the field that he is pulling in

TISSOT AUSTRALIAN GRAND PRIX
PHILLIP ISLAND

ROUND 16
October 20

OFFICIAL TIMEKEEPER

RACE RESULTS

CIRCUIT LENGTH 2.764 miles
NO. OF LAPS 19
RACE DISTANCE 52.516 miles
WEATHER Dry, 28°C
TRACK TEMPERATURE 34°C
WINNER Jorge Lorenzo
FASTEST LAP 1m 28.108s,
112.903mph, Marc Marquez (Record)
PREVIOUS LAP RECORD 1m 30.059s,
110.482mph, Nicky Hayden, 2008

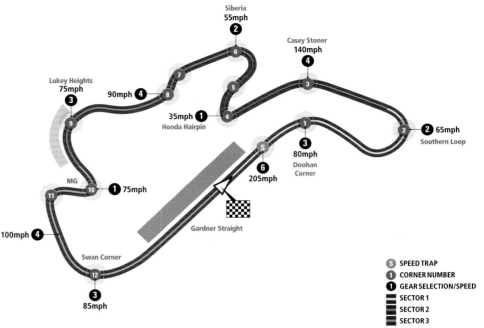

Siberia 55mph
Casey Stoner 140mph
Lukey Heights 75mph
90mph
Honda Hairpin 35mph
Southern Loop 65mph
Doohan Corner 80mph
205mph
MG
75mph
100mph
Gardner Straight
Swan Corner
85mph

S SPEED TRAP
1 CORNER NUMBER
1 GEAR SELECTION/SPEED
SECTOR 1
SECTOR 2
SECTOR 3

QUALIFYING

	Rider	Nation	Motorcycle	Team	Time	Pole +
1	Lorenzo	SPA	Yamaha	Yamaha Factory Racing	1m 27.899s	
2	Marquez	SPA	Honda	Repsol Honda Team	1m 28.120s	0.221s
3	Rossi	ITA	Yamaha	Yamaha Factory Racing	1m 28.647s	0.748s
4	Bautista	SPA	Honda	GO&FUN Honda Gresini	1m 28.713s	0.814s
5	Pedrosa	SPA	Honda	Repsol Honda Team	1m 28.748s	0.849s
6	Crutchlow	GBR	Yamaha	Monster Yamaha Tech 3	1m 28.809s	0.910s
7	Smith	GBR	Yamaha	Monster Yamaha Tech 3	1m 28.941s	1.042s
8	Hayden	USA	Ducati	Ducati Team	1m 29.295s	1.396s
9	Dovizioso	ITA	Ducati	Ducati Team	1m 29.660s	1.761s
10	Iannone	ITA	Ducati	Energy T.I. Pramac Racing	1m 29.756s	1.857s
11	Edwards	USA	FTR Kawasaki	NGM Mobile Forward Racing	1m 30.264s	2.365s
12	De Puniet	FRA	ART	Power Electronics Aspar	1m 30.735s	2.836s
13	Espargaro	SPA	ART	Power Electronics Aspar	1m 30.081s	Q1
14	Corti	ITA	FTR Kawasaki	NGM Mobile Forward Racing	1m 30.530s	Q1
15	Hernandez	COL	Ducati	Ignite Pramac Racing	1m 30.641s	Q1
16	Aoyama	JPN	FTR	Avintia Blusens	1m 30.733s	Q1
17	Petrucci	ITA	Ioda-Suter	Came IodaRacing Project	1m 30.894s	Q1
18	Laverty	GBR	ART	Paul Bird Motorsport	1m 30.979s	Q1
19	Barbera	SPA	FTR	Avintia Blusens	1m 31.061s	Q1
20	Scassa	ITA	ART	Cardion AB Motoracing	1m 31.093s	Q1
21	Staring	AUS	FTR Honda	GO&FUN Honda Gresini	1m 31.775s	Q1
22	Pesek	CZE	Ioda-Suter	Came IodaRacing Project	1m 32.474s	Q1
23	Cudlin	AUS	PBM	Paul Bird Motorsport	1m 33.007s	Q1

FINISHERS

1 JORGE LORENZO His 50th GP win put him right back in championship contention. Expressed some sympathy with Marquez before criticising him over the near-collision. In the midst of the drama it was easy to overlook the fact that Jorge led every lap (allowing for stops).

2 DANI PEDROSA Justified his pit-exit transgression by saying the line was difficult to see, and defended the Repsol team, claiming all the rule changes were 'confusing'. Dropped back a place after the penalty so was not further penalised after the event.

3 VALENTINO ROSSI Overtook Bautista and Crutchlow in the pits during the bike change and, once he understood his dice with Cal was for the podium, risked more than he thought sensible in the final laps on a circuit he loves.

4 CAL CRUTCHLOW Lapped faster than he'd expected but again let down by his start, which he described as 'not acceptable'. Only a tenth of a second off his first rostrum finish since Germany and looking more like his old, combative self.

5 ALVARO BAUTISTA Another cracking effort. Fought for third with Rossi and Crutchlow despite having to run the hard tyre which he knew would not suit his bike. Nevertheless, only two-tenths off a rostrum finish.

6 BRADLEY SMITH His best result since Germany, but probably Brad's best race so far. A great start put him battling for fourth in the early laps but he then did some damage to his tyre, so tried to give the second bike's rubber an easier time.

7 NICKY HAYDEN Dicing with Iannone and Dovi in the first half of the race, saw them go in so pushed hard on his in-lap and the out-lap to put two seconds over them. Got up to Smith but had trouble with the last corner and couldn't attack.

8 ANDREA IANNONE Extremely pleased to split the factory Ducatis – his ambition for the season was to be competitive with the works bikes. Found the mandatory stop messed with his concentration, but called the race 'fun'.

9 ANDREA DOVIZIOSO Described the race as 'more enjoyable than usual', which says something given that he was beaten by the satellite bike of Iannone.

10 RANDY DE PUNIET Celebrated his 250th GP with a trouble-free weekend and a great race to be top CRT and in the top ten for the first time in the season. A reminder of just how quick he can be in his role as Suzuki's test rider.

11 ALEIX ESPARGARO Had to beat Edwards to retain his CRT title, which he did. Failed to be top CRT finisher for only the third time so far this year, blaming chatter on the second bike.

12 COLIN EDWARDS Top CRT in qualifying and another solid race to good points despite being significantly slower on his second bike.

13 YONNY HERNANDEZ Broke a bone in his hand on Saturday and found the bike change challenging; nevertheless his best lap in the race was near his qualifying time and scored points for the third race in a row.

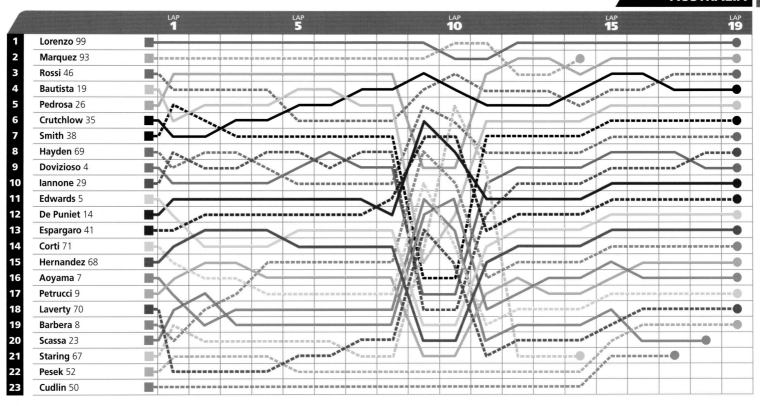

		LAP 1		LAP 5			LAP 10			LAP 15		LAP 19
1	Lorenzo 99											
2	Marquez 93											
3	Rossi 46											
4	Bautista 19											
5	Pedrosa 26											
6	Crutchlow 35											
7	Smith 38											
8	Hayden 69											
9	Dovizioso 4											
10	Iannone 29											
11	Edwards 5											
12	De Puniet 14											
13	Espargaro 41											
14	Corti 71											
15	Hernandez 68											
16	Aoyama 7											
17	Petrucci 9											
18	Laverty 70											
19	Barbera 8											
20	Scassa 23											
21	Staring 67											
22	Pesek 52											
23	Cudlin 50											

RACE

	Rider	Motorcycle	Race Time	Time +	Fastest Lap	Avg. Speed	
1	Lorenzo	Yamaha	29m 07.155s		1m 28.315s	108.181mph	XS/H
2	Pedrosa	Honda	29m 14.091s	6.936s	1m 28.323s	107.746mph	S/H
3	Rossi	Yamaha	29m 19.499s	12.344s	1m 28.868s	107.435mph	XS/H
4	Crutchlow	Yamaha	29m 19.615s	12.460s	1m 28.658s	107.435mph	S/H
5	Bautista	Honda	29m 19.668s	12.513s	1m 28.942s	107.373mph	S/H
6	Smith	Yamaha	29m 35.418s	28.263s	1m 29.328s	106.441mph	S/H
7	Hayden	Ducati	29m 40.108s	32.953s	1m 29.664s	106.192mph	S/H
8	Iannone	Ducati	29m 42.217s	35.062s	1m 30.030s	106.068mph	S/H
9	Dovizioso	Ducati	29m 42.259s	35.104s	1m 29.956s	106.068mph	S/H
10	De Puniet	ART	29m 44.581s	37.426s	1m 30.132s	105.882mph	XS/M
11	Espargaro	ART	29m 53.254s	46.099s	1m 30.152s	105.385mph	S/M
12	Edwards	FTR Kawasaki	29m 55.304s	48.149s	1m 30.206s	105.260mph	S/M
13	Hernandez	Ducati	29m 57.066s	49.911s	1m 30.825s	105.136mph	S/M
14	Barbera	FTR	29m 57.153s	49.998s	1m 30.817s	105.136mph	XS/M
15	Petrucci	Ioda-Suter	30m 05.873s	58.718s	1m 31.501s	104.639mph	XS/M
16	Scassa	ART	30m 05.946s	58.791s	1m 31.443s	104.639mph	XS/M
17	Corti	FTR Kawasaki	30m 15.260s	1m 08.105s	1m 31.560s	104.142mph	S/M
18	Laverty	ART	30m 34.385s	1m 27.230s	1m 31.620s	103.023mph	XS/M
19	Pesek	Ioda-Suter	30m 38.248s	1m 31.093s	1m 32.107s	102.837mph	XS/M
20	Aoyama	FTR	29m 33.585s	1 Lap	1m 31.510s	100.973mph	XS/M
21	Cudlin	PBM	30m 52.751s	2 Laps	1m 33.581s	91.279mph	XS/M
DQ	Staring	FTR Honda			1m 32.002s		XS/M
DQ	Marquez	Honda			1m 28.108s		S/H

CHAMPIONSHIP

	Rider	Nation	Team	Points
1	Marquez	SPA	Repsol Honda Team	298
2	Lorenzo	SPA	Yamaha Factory Racing	280
3	Pedrosa	SPA	Repsol Honda Team	264
4	Rossi	ITA	Yamaha Factory Racing	214
5	Crutchlow	GBR	Monster Yamaha Tech 3	179
6	Bautista	SPA	GO&FUN Honda Gresini	147
7	Bradl	GER	LCR Honda MotoGP	135
8	Dovizioso	ITA	Ducati Team	127
9	Hayden	USA	Ducati Team	111
10	Smith	GBR	Monster Yamaha Tech 3	99
11	Espargaro	SPA	Power Electronics Aspar	88
12	Iannone	ITA	Energy T.I. Pramac Racing	55
13	Pirro	ITA	Ignite Pramac Racing	50
14	Edwards	USA	NGM Mobile Forward Racing	36
15	De Puniet	FRA	Power Electronics Aspar	33
16	Barbera	SPA	Avintia Blusens	31
17	Petrucci	ITA	Came IodaRacing Project	24
18	Hernandez	COL	Paul Bird Motorsport	20
19	Aoyama	JPN	Avintia Blusens	13
20	Corti	ITA	NGM Mobile Forward Racing	11
21	Spies	USA	Ignite Pramac Racing	9
22	De Angelis	RSM	Ignite Pramac Racing	5
23	Abraham	CZE	Cardion AB Motoracing	5
24	Laverty	GBR	Paul Bird Motorsport	3
25	Staring	AUS	GO&FUN Honda Gresini	2
26	Del Amor	SPA	Avintia Blusens	1

14 HECTOR BARBERA Quick work in the pits made up for poor qualifying and enabled a points-scoring race.

15 DANILO PETRUCCI Celebrated the Ioda team's 100th GP with a point and was 1.5s quicker than in 2012. Still complaining about lack of development.

16 LUCA SCASSA Much happier on a track he knows. If Luca hadn't missed his pit board he would have attacked Petrucci on the last lap.

17 CLAUDIO CORTI Had tyre problems with both bikes in the race, which confused him as he'd had no such issues in practice.

18 MICHAEL LAVERTY Had brake problems, like his team-mate, not helped by being pushed off track on the first lap.

19 LUKAS PESEK Very happy to have a good weekend in which he could, for once, complete the race and overtake a few people.

20 HIROSHI AOYAMA No grip on the first bike, no brakes on the second, plus a ride-through penalty for crossing the pit-exit line.

21 DAMIAN CUDLIN Originally disqualified when he pitted late to sort out a brake problem but he continued anyway and was reinstated.

DISQUALIFIED

BRYAN STARING Disqualified for staying out for too many laps before changing bikes.

MARC MARQUEZ Disqualified after staying out too long before pitting to change bikes. His seemingly impregnable 43-point championship lead shrunk to a comparatively fragile-looking 18 points.

NON-STARTERS

STEFAN BRADL Rode in the first session but quickly realised that the ankle he broke in Sepang was too painful to try racing this weekend.

KAREL ABRAHAM Out for the season after shoulder surgery, but the team announced he'd be back in 2014 on a customer Honda. Replaced by Scassa.

BEN SPIES Out for the season after shoulder surgery. Replaced by Hernandez.

BRIDGESTONE

FRONT EXTRA-SOFT (**XS**) / SOFT (**S**)

REAR MEDIUM (**M**) / HARD (**H**)

MILD — SEVERE

AIRASIA GRAND PRIX OF JAPAN

HURRICANE JORGE

Lorenzo won again to take the championship down to the wire

The dramas of the Australian round the previous weekend had several knock-on effects. From Malaysia onwards it had seemed more than probable that Marquez would clinch the title in Japan at Honda's home track – until he received that black flag. Now he faced the prospect of a tense end to the year. Marc even started reminding us that this was his first season in the top class and winning the title had not been in the plan. This despite the fact he could have become champion here if Jorge Lorenzo and Dani Pedrosa had both suffered misfortune (although in Dani's case it must be said that his chances of taking the title were purely mathematical).

For most of the weekend it looked as if nobody was going to being doing anything anyway. The after-effects of Typhoon Francisco blanketed the Twin Ring circuit in cloud and rain, but while there was undoubtedly a lot of water around, the reason nothing went on track on Friday or Saturday morning was the medical helicopter. Japanese domestic aviation laws forbid helicopters flying in such conditions and the problem was simple – the helicopter was stranded at Mito City, site of the nearest hospital capable of dealing with the sort of demands a Grand Prix can put on medical services. The chopper did arrive on Saturday morning only to be grounded again, because this time it was Mito that was fogged in.

For the second race in a row Race Direction had to make up the rules as they went along. Qualifying became a single hour-and-a-quarter session on Saturday, with Sunday morning warm-up extended from 20 to 50 minutes and described as Free Practice. Qualifying was wet, Free Practice dry, resulting in one or two unfamiliar faces heading the grid, notably Nicky

ABOVE Yamaha test rider Katsuyuki Nakasuga and the full factory test team turned up to test some parts for 2014

RIGHT Regulations allow bigger than usual brake discs at Motegi, but neither Crutchlow nor Rossi could take advantage

OPPOSITE Alvaro Bautista crashed in practice but despite losing valuable track time finished the race in fourth

Hayden on the front row in third, reminding everyone that he was still quick although the Ducati was far from sorted. If anyone could work out why a bike that's apparently too stiff in the dry works so well in the wet, when conventional wisdom has it that soft settings are required, there's a job waiting for them in Bologna.

The bloke who is definitely going there was already having an effect, although on his old employer's business rather than his new one's. The announcement that Aprilia's Gigi Dall'Igna was to become general manager of Ducati Corse was made at the start of the three flyaway races and the market had now had time to react. Both the Cardion and Aspar teams seemed likely to defect from Aprilia to the new customer Honda, leaving the Ioda and Paul Bird teams as the only ones likely to run the ART in 2014. The other effect was that Vito Guareschi, long-time team-manager and formerly a Ducati test rider, announced that he would be leaving the factory to manage Valentino Rossi's new Moto3 team. The smart money was on Davide Tardozzi, Ducati's World Superbike team-manager in the glory days, coming back to the fold.

Reality bit back in the race. Hayden's start was awful, thanks to a clutch glitch, and he finished ninth on a track that has never done the red bikes any favours. Andrea Dovizioso also took advantage of the wet qualifying to get his best grid position since he was on the front row at Mugello, but he too ghosted backwards to end up tenth.

The other bike that wasn't supposed to go well at Motegi was the Yamaha. Indeed, the four Hondas finished line astern in second, third, fourth and fifth.

'TO TAKE THIS WIN AT THE HOME OF HONDA MAKES ME VERY HAPPY'

JORGE LORENZO

ABOVE Smith was starting to make good starts a habit; he was as high as fifth early on from 13th on the grid

BELOW Aussies Cudlin and Staring raced each other at the back of the field

In front of them was the Yamaha of Jorge Lorenzo. It was another of those remarkable rides that didn't look too spectacular on TV but was a model of precision to back up a brave tyre choice. Jorge was one of only four riders to use the softer option; unusually it was possible to race on the harder choice. The others to go for the soft tyre were Dovizioso and the Yamahas of Bradley Smith and wild card Katsuyuki Nakasuga.

Lorenzo used the sticky Bridgestone to effect his usual lightning start and grab a lead of over a second after two laps. This time there was no runaway. Marquez and Pedrosa closed in after Rossi went to second then twice outbraked himself at the end of the back straight. He wasn't the only one with brake problems. This is the only circuit at which the larger carbon rotors are used. Cal Crutchlow was one rider who had problems with the big brakes overheating early on, as he followed his team-mate Bradley Smith. Aleix Espargaro was another victim, his crash allowing Colin Edwards to be best CRT for the second time in five races.

Marquez did attack Lorenzo but a big crash in morning warm-up – sorry, Free Practice – was warning enough. Yet again luck was on Marc's side as he walked away from another big get-off. Aching ribs plus Lorenzo's now habitual near-perfect race persuaded Marc to ease off. The damage was limited to five points because, again as usual, Pedrosa couldn't find grip once the tyres began to wear. Nevertheless, the satellite Hondas weren't within range and they in turn were out of sight of the other Yamahas. Their results were perhaps the best indication of just what a brilliant race this was from Jorge Lorenzo. Rossi, Crutchlow and Smith finished in line astern from 25 to 30 seconds behind him.

It was a race that deserved to notch up Yamaha's 200th win in the top class. So instead of celebrating the championship win at their home circuit Honda had to host their rival's celebrations. One statistic illustrates what Jorge did on a track that more than any other should repay the Hondas' ability to get into and blast out of the short corners, few of which play to the M1's superior ability to carry corner speed. It was only the second time this year that Jorge set the fastest lap of a race.

RIGHT Lorenzo turned in yet another stellar performance that deserves the adjective perfect

DOUBLE TOP

Jorge Lorenzo's victory at Motegi was Yamaha's 200th in the top class. The first came at the final race of the 1972 season when British privateer Chas Mortimer took an oversize Yamaha 350 twin to the win on the Montjuich circuit in central Barcelona. With the title already won by the great Giacomo Agostini, the factory MV Agusta team didn't bother attending. Next year Yamaha's first four-cylinder 500 arrived and the lost genius Jarno Saarinen won the first two races of the season. In '74 Ago saw the two-stroke writing on the wall and joined Yamaha, winning the first of his six GPs for the company before becoming the first two-stroke champion in 1975.

The rest of the century belonged to the Americans: Kenny Roberts, Eddie Lawson and Wayne Rainey all took three championships on Yamahas in the 1970s, '80s and '90s, respectively. After an accident ended Rainey's career in 1993 Honda dominated and Yamaha wins were few and far between both on 500cc two-strokes and after the MotoGP formula arrived in 2002. Max Biaggi's two wins in the first year of MotoGP look better and better with perspective, but Yamaha had to wait until the arrival of Valentino Rossi in 2004 for the next win and the first four-stroke title. He retained it in 2005, regained it in '08 and retained it again in '09. Add in this season's win and Valentino scored 47 of his 80 top-class wins on a Yamaha. All of Lorenzo's 29 wins (to date) have come since he joined Yamaha in 2008. Together, they have taken 49 of the last 50 Yamaha victories.

AIRASIA GRAND PRIX OF JAPAN
TWIN-RING MOTEGI
ROUND **17**
October 27

RACE RESULTS

CIRCUIT LENGTH 2.983 miles
NO. OF LAPS 24
RACE DISTANCE 71.597 miles
WEATHER Dry, 20°C
TRACK TEMPERATURE 31°C
WINNER Jorge Lorenzo
FASTEST LAP 1m 45.736s, 101.532mph, Jorge Lorenzo
LAP RECORD 1m 45.589s, 101.656mph, Dani Pedrosa, 2012

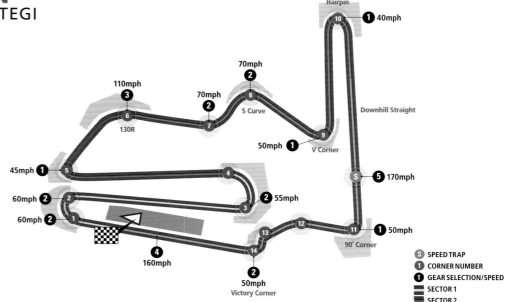

Circuit map with marked corners:
- Hairpin — 10 — 40mph
- 70mph — 2
- 110mph — 3
- 70mph — 2
- 8
- S Curve
- Downhill Straight
- 6
- 130R
- 7
- 9
- 50mph — 1
- V Corner
- 45mph — 1 — 5
- 4
- S — 5 — 170mph
- 60mph — 2 — 2
- 2 — 55mph
- 3
- 60mph — 2 — 1
- 13 — 12
- 11 — 1 — 50mph
- 90° Corner
- 4 — 160mph
- 14
- 2
- 50mph
- Victory Corner

- **S** SPEED TRAP
- **1** CORNER NUMBER
- **1** GEAR SELECTION/SPEED
- SECTOR 1
- SECTOR 2
- SECTOR 3

QUALIFYING

	Rider	Nation	Motorcycle	Team	Time	Pole +
1	Lorenzo	SPA	Yamaha	Yamaha Factory Racing	1m 53.471s	
2	Marquez	SPA	Honda	Repsol Honda Team	1m 54.129s	0.658s
3	Hayden	USA	Ducati	Ducati Team	1m 54.539s	1.068s
4	Pedrosa	SPA	Honda	Repsol Honda Team	1m 54.542s	1.071s
5	Rossi	ITA	Yamaha	Yamaha Factory Racing	1m 54.732s	1.261s
6	Dovizioso	ITA	Ducati	Ducati Team	1m 55.036s	1.565s
7	Bautista	SPA	Honda	GO&FUN Honda Gresini	1m 55.135s	1.664s
8	Bradl	GER	Honda	LCR Honda MotoGP	1m 55.610s	2.139s
9	Espargaro	SPA	ART	Power Electronics Aspar	1m 55.719s	2.248s
10	Hernandez	COL	Ducati	Ignite Pramac Racing	1m 55.998s	2.527s
11	Crutchlow	GBR	Yamaha	Monster Yamaha Tech 3	1m 56.058s	2.587s
12	Nakasuga	JPN	Yamaha	Yamaha YSP Racing Team	1m 56.125s	2.654s
13	Smith	GBR	Yamaha	Monster Yamaha Tech 3	1m 57.114s	3.643s
14	Edwards	USA	FTR Kawasaki	NGM Mobile Forward Racing	1m 57.297s	3.826s
15	Iannone	ITA	Ducati	Energy T.I. Pramac Racing	1m 57.347s	3.876s
16	Petrucci	ITA	Ioda-Suter	Came IodaRacing Project	1m 57.540s	4.069s
17	De Puniet	FRA	ART	Power Electronics Aspar	1m 57.715s	4.244s
18	Aoyama	JPN	FTR	Avintia Blusens	1m 57.994s	4.523s
19	Laverty	GBR	ART	Paul Bird Motorsport	1m 58.540s	5.069s
20	Scassa	ITA	ART	Cardion AB Motoracing	1m 58.802s	5.331s
21	Corti	ITA	FTR Kawasaki	NGM Mobile Forward Racing	1m 59.617s	6.146s
22	Barbera	SPA	FTR	Avintia Blusens	1m 59.646s	6.175s
23	Cudlin	AUS	PBM	Paul Bird Motorsport	2m 00.982s	7.511s
24	Staring	AUS	FTR Honda	GO&FUN Honda Gresini	2m 02.712s	9.241s
25	Pesek	CZE	Ioda-Suter	Came IodaRacing Project	2m 02.932s	9.461s

FINISHERS

1 JORGE LORENZO Led every lap to take Yamaha's 200th win in GP racing at Honda's home circuit, and reduce Marquez's lead to 13 points to take the title fight down to the final round. Yet another stellar ride, and on a circuit which is more suited to the Hondas. Used the soft tyre to build a lead and hung on at the end.

2 MARC MARQUEZ After a Sunday morning crash in warm-up and two big moments while trying to close on Lorenzo he decided that losing only five points to his championship rival was a pretty good deal.

3 DANI PEDROSA Apart from lap one he was in third for the whole race, which he described as 'boring'. Couldn't get the power to the ground and the situation became worse towards the end of the race.

4 ALVARO BAUTISTA Equalled his best results of the year after two crashes, one on Sunday morning. Hadn't used the front tyre at all before the race and was ninth on the first lap before a stirring ride up the field. He couldn't help but wonder if he should have been on the rostrum.

5 STEFAN BRADL Just two weeks after breaking his ankle in Malaysia Stefan started from the third row and picked up 11 points. Said the ankle was at 85 per cent.

6 VALENTINO ROSSI Looked like he was going to back his team-mate when he got away second, but outbraked himself at the end of the straight on the second lap and then did it again next time round.

7 CAL CRUTCHLOW Used the harder tyre and also had trouble with the brakes, which compromised his early laps, but came good in the second half of the race and sealed his championship position as top non-factory rider of the year.

8 BRADLEY SMITH Put the soft tyre to good use off the start to lead his team-mate and follow Bradl. Pleased with his progress on a full tank and with the shrinking gap to the leading satellite bikes.

9 NICKY HAYDEN The wet weather helped Nicky to his only front-row start of the year, but things reverted to normal in the dry race. Clutch problems undid all the good work off the start and then he struck edge-grip problems, though got quicker towards the end of the race.

10 ANDREA DOVIZIOSO Even unhappier than usual on a track where he's previously had success. Distracted by backmarkers on the last lap and ran on at the end of the back straight, letting his team-mate through.

11 KATSUYUKI NAKASUGA Yamaha's test rider was a wild-card entry. He and his usual test team did what they wanted to, testing new parts for the 2014 M1 at race pace. Disappointed with his finishing position but pleased with a job well done.

12 COLIN EDWARDS Top CRT for the second time in five races. After his jump start in Australia he'd promised the team he would win the class in Japan, and did. Followed Espargaro until the Spaniard crashed, knew that de Puniet was chasing and controlled the gap.

13 RANDY DE PUNIET Looked like he could challenge Edwards for top CRT honours but from about lap seven lost rear grip. Seven laps from the flag Randy decided to settle for three points.

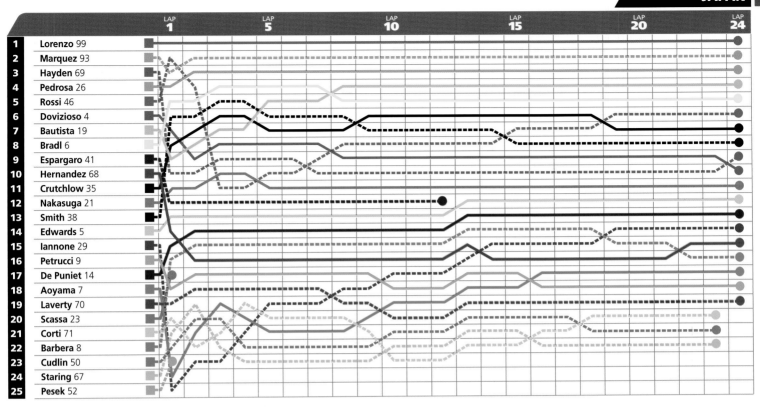

		LAP 1	LAP 5	LAP 10	LAP 15	LAP 20	LAP 24
1	Lorenzo 99						
2	Marquez 93						
3	Hayden 69						
4	Pedrosa 26						
5	Rossi 46						
6	Dovizioso 4						
7	Bautista 19						
8	Bradl 6						
9	Espargaro 41						
10	Hernandez 68						
11	Crutchlow 35						
12	Nakasuga 21						
13	Smith 38						
14	Edwards 5						
15	Iannone 29						
16	Petrucci 9						
17	De Puniet 14						
18	Aoyama 7						
19	Laverty 70						
20	Scassa 23						
21	Corti 71						
22	Barbera 8						
23	Cudlin 50						
24	Staring 67						
25	Pesek 52						

RACE

	Rider	Motorcycle	Race Time	Time +	Fastest Lap	Avg. Speed	
1	Lorenzo	Yamaha	42m 34.291s		1m 45.736s	100.849mph	M/XS
2	Marquez	Honda	42m 37.479s	3.188s	1m 45.828s	100.724mph	M/S
3	Pedrosa	Honda	42m 38.883s	4.592s	1m 45.792s	100.724mph	M/S
4	Bautista	Honda	42m 54.046s	19.755s	1m 46.469s	100.103mph	M/S
5	Bradl	Honda	42m 57.101s	22.810s	1m 46.637s	99.979mph	M/S
6	Rossi	Yamaha	42m 58.928s	24.637s	1m 46.526s	99.916mph	M/S
7	Crutchlow	Yamaha	43m 01.787s	27.496s	1m 46.831s	99.792mph	M/S
8	Smith	Yamaha	43m 05.260s	30.969s	1m 47.019s	99.668mph	M/XS
9	Hayden	Ducati	43m 11.301s	37.010s	1m 47.336s	99.419mph	M/S
10	Dovizioso	Ducati	43m 17.235s	42.944s	1m 47.317s	99.233mph	M/S
11	Nakasuga	Yamaha	43m 27.636s	53.345s	1m 47.950s	98.798mph	M/XS
12	Edwards	FTR Kawasaki	43m 37.504s	1m 03.213s	1m 48.049s	98.425mph	M/SS
13	De Puniet	ART	43m 41.131s	1m 06.840s	1m 48.244s	98.301mph	M/SS
14	Iannone	Ducati	43m 42.509s	1m 08.218s	1m 47.900s	98.239mph	M/XS
15	Hernandez	Ducati	43m 52.531s	1m 18.240s	1m 48.812s	97.866mph	M/S
16	Barbera	FTR	43m 53.399s	1m 19.108s	1m 48.351s	97.866mph	M/SS
17	Aoyama	FTR	43m 55.465s	1m 21.174s	1m 48.421s	97.742mph	M/SS
18	Petrucci	Ioda-Suter	44m 04.837s	1m 30.546s	1m 49.347s	97.431mph	M/SS
19	Laverty	ART	44m 57.649s	2m 23.358s	1m 49.161s	95.505mph	S/SS
20	Corti	FTR Kawasaki	42m 53.344s	1 Lap	1m 48.877s	95.940mph	M/SS
21	Cudlin	PBM	43m 10.959s	1 Lap	1m 50.996s	95.318mph	M/SS
22	Staring	FTR Honda	43m 13.290s	1 Lap	1m 51.626s	95.194mph	M/XS
NF	Espargaro	ART	21m 49.913s	12 Laps	1m 47.908s	98.363mph	M/SS
NF	Scassa	ART	1m 59.749s	23 Laps	2 Laps	89.664mph	M/SS
NF	Pesek	Ioda-Suter	2m 04.018s	23 Laps	2 Laps	86.557mph	S/SS

CHAMPIONSHIP

	Rider	Nation	Team	Points
1	Marquez	SPA	Repsol Honda Team	318
2	Lorenzo	SPA	Yamaha Factory Racing	305
3	Pedrosa	SPA	Repsol Honda Team	280
4	Rossi	ITA	Yamaha Factory Racing	224
5	Crutchlow	GBR	Monster Yamaha Tech 3	188
6	Bautista	SPA	GO&FUN Honda Gresini	160
7	Bradl	GER	LCR Honda MotoGP	146
8	Dovizioso	ITA	Ducati Team	133
9	Hayden	USA	Ducati Team	118
10	Smith	GBR	Monster Yamaha Tech 3	107
11	Espargaro	SPA	Power Electronics Aspar	88
12	Iannone	ITA	Energy T.I. Pramac Racing	57
13	Pirro	ITA	Ignite Pramac Racing	50
14	Edwards	USA	NGM Mobile Forward Racing	40
15	De Puniet	FRA	Power Electronics Aspar	36
16	Barbera	SPA	Avintia Blusens	31
17	Petrucci	ITA	Came IodaRacing Project	24
18	Hernandez	COL	Paul Bird Motorsport	21
19	Aoyama	JPN	Avintia Blusens	13
20	Corti	ITA	NGM Mobile Forward Racing	11
21	Spies	USA	Ignite Pramac Racing	9
22	Nakasuga	JPN	Yamaha YSP Racing Team	5
23	De Angelis	RSM	Ignite Pramac Racing	5
24	Abraham	CZE	Cardion AB Motoracing	5
25	Laverty	GBR	Paul Bird Motorsport	3
26	Staring	AUS	GO&FUN Honda Gresini	2
27	Del Amor	SPA	Avintia Blusens	1

14 ANDREA IANNONE Went off track on the third lap when he nearly tailgated Nakasuga but rejoined and rode back into the points.

15 YONNY HERNANDEZ Severely handicapped by the hand injury he'd picked up in Australia, especially on race day after it stopped raining.

16 HECTOR BARBERA Fastest CRT until something broke on the bike and set off a vibration that steadily got worse. Angry, as he was convinced he could win the class.

17 HIROSHI AOYAMA Another rider with brake problems. Ran off track on the first lap and spent the rest of the race fiddling with the brake adjuster. Thought about retiring, but couldn't do so at his home race.

18 DANILO PETRUCCI Right up with Edwards in the wet but nearly two seconds a lap slower on race day. His race lap times were very consistent, though, suggesting he was getting the maximum out of the Suter.

19 MICHAEL LAVERTY Started the race with only 18 laps of Motegi under his belt and finished it by running out of petrol and pushing the bike over the line.

20 CLAUDIO CORTI Went off track twice, the first time avoiding Laverty and then again trying to make up time.

21 DAMIAN CUDLIN Like his team-mate, did not have the track time he needed before the race thanks to the weather, and then received a reprimand for holding up the leader.

22 BRYAN STARING Another miserable weekend for the Australian.

NON-FINISHERS

ALEIX ESPARGARO Got away with the front men but immediately noticed problems with his brakes and started running wide. Tried to stay with his team-mate and, inevitably, crashed, fortunately without injury.

LUCA SCASSA Forced to retire due to a bike defect, probably sustained in his warm-up crash.

LUKAS PESEK More problems with electronics. The bike was so nervous when he got on the gas that Lukas was forced to retire.

NON-STARTERS

KAREL ABRAHAM Out due to the shoulder injury sustained at Indianapolis. Replaced by Scassa.

BEN SPIES Announced his retirement from racing just before race weekend.

BRIDGESTONE

FRONT SOFT (**S**) / MEDIUM (**M**)

REAR SUPER-SOFT (**SS**) / EXTRA-SOFT (**XS**) / SOFT (**S**)

MILD ⬤ SEVERE

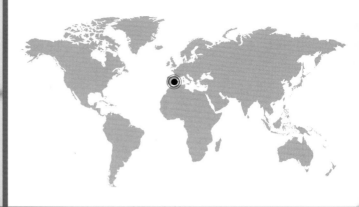

YOUNG AT HEART

Marc Marquez became World Champion as a rookie, but not before Jorge Lorenzo put on one last act of glorious defiance

The last time we had to wait until the final round to crown the champ was 2006, Nicky Hayden's year. That was tense, and so was 2013. Marc Marquez arrived on home soil needing only to finish fourth to break yet another record, that of being the youngest ever World Champion in the top class. Jorge Lorenzo, now the only rider who could prevent Marquez making yet another piece of history, knew the odds were against him but wore the satisfied air of a man who had done all he could. He was coming off consecutive victories and could only hope Marquez would be unable to resist racing him and just maybe repeat his only mistake so far this season, when he crashed out in Italy. Sure, he'd crashed a lot, admitted Marc, but apart from that Mugello incident it had only been in practice as he deliberately sought the limits. If any good fortune was involved, and there assuredly is in any champion's season, it was that he had avoided major injury.

The Spanish public didn't think it was all over. The event was a sell-out and the faithful hordes were rewarded with unseasonably fine weather all weekend. Any thoughts they had about Marquez playing for the points were swiftly put back in their box in practice and qualifying: he was on pole by a third of a second on a track where small time differences are more difficult than usual to overcome. It would equate to over half a second on most other circuits.

Lorenzo had managed to be quicker in the two sessions, albeit the ones that don't matter so much, FP4 and warm-up. The question now was how he would approach the race and what the pair could expect in the way of help from their team-mates. Rossi said he'd help if he could, by getting in front of Marquez; Dani Pedrosa

was of the opinion that the best way to assist his team (he didn't mention Marquez by name) was to win the race.

Race day started with a suitably frenzied climax to the Moto3 season that featured three riders, all of them Spanish of course, with a chance of the title and a Moto2 win for local hero Nico Terol. Over 100,000 fans were coming nicely to the boil as Lorenzo and Marquez lined up first and second on the grid; not long ago the stands would have been tinged yellow with Valentino Rossi shirts, hats and flags; now the supporters of Marquez had turned them red.

Sure enough, Lorenzo blazed into the lead followed by Pedrosa, with Marquez just behind. But Jorge didn't pull away – instead, he tried to slow the pace of the race to allow other riders to get among the top three, specifically the other Yamaha men. Dani breezed past at the end of the front straight on the second and third laps only for Lorenzo to push back to the front at the second corner both times. And so it went on, with Lorenzo finding a way back past as quickly as possible. This was no time for delicacy; paint was exchanged more than once. On lap ten Pedrosa again used Honda power to come out of Turn 1 in front, this time with what looked like enough of a margin to keep Lorenzo behind him at the slow left-hander. Jorge ran up the inside, shoving Dani wide. Both men lost momentum and Dani had to save the bike off the front. That let Marquez through to the lead and dropped Pedrosa back to fifth. Crucially the man in third was now Alvaro Bautista who had made it clear he wasn't going to get in the way of the men fighting for the title, but he was fast enough to keep Rossi behind him.

Lorenzo was quickly back in front of Marquez, who

LEFT Lap one, turn one and Lorenzo leads the way in front of a full house

OPPOSITE Turn two, lap ten and Lorenzo barges back past Pedrosa hard enough for Dani to lose the front

ABOVE Espargaro finished top CRT for the 14th time in 18 races

ABOVE Lorenzo's game plan was to slow the race down and hope the other Yamahas could help him; they couldn't

BELOW Nicky Hayden ended five years with the Bologna factory by finishing as top Ducati

OPPOSITE The grandstands are now red for Marquez, not yellow for Rossi

managed to resist getting involved. A look over his shoulder told Jorge that Rossi was too far back to help him and as Cal Crutchlow – who'd looked the man most likely to come to his aid – had crashed, he had one option left: go for the win, notching up his eighth victory of the year, the most by any rider in any of the three classes. Pedrosa recovered to take second and set the fastest lap as his team-mate cruised home in third to become the youngest ever World Champion in the top class and the first rookie champion since Kenny Roberts Snr in 1978. Marquez also became only the fourth man ever to become champion in all three classes after Mike Hailwood, Phil Read and Rossi.

There was also a slew of other records great and small he took off more of the sport's greats: all the youngest-ever marks off Freddie Spencer, all the rookie records off Roberts, and he now holds more circuit best laps than anyone else. Yet despite comprehensively rewriting the record books it has to be noted that he eventually won the title by the trifling margin of just four points.

Jorge Lorenzo ended the season with a hat-trick of victories and eight wins to Marquez's six. There is no doubt that the Honda grew into a – very slightly – better all-round motorcycle than the Yamaha, but the contrast between the forensic precision of Lorenzo's style as he extracted the maximum from the M1 and the permanently on-the-edge way in which Marquez arm-wrestled the RCV was wonderful to behold. Now we need to know if Marquez will, like Spencer, burn brightly but fade quickly or shine for a decade like Rossi. If 2014 is to be a repeat of the Marquez versus Lorenzo match of this season, it would be wise to buy your tickets early.

A MESSY DIVORCE

The World Championship showdown was all but overshadowed by the shocking news that Valentino Rossi had decided to dispense with the services of his race engineer, Jerry Burgess. The two had worked together since Valentino came into the 500cc class in 2000.

News had leaked out on an Italian website with connections to Rossi's inner circle and Valentino had no option but to confirm the decision. Next day Yamaha called a conference, at Jerry's instigation. He didn't want to answer the same set of questions three hundred times, he said. Burgess and Rossi sat at a table, the Aussie looking composed, the Italian like he'd rather be somewhere else. The rest of the manly Aussie pit crew slipped in the back door and stood stony-faced at the side of the room, exiting just as stealthily at the end of the formal proceedings.

Both men made statements and answered a few questions before there was a long, dignified round of applause for Jerry from the biggest audience seen at a press conference for some time. Valentino confirmed he'd had a change

of mind for a while but the leak had forced him to tell people earlier than he'd wanted to. Jerry confirmed it had come as a shock to him, but was very keen to say that if that was what was needed to get Vale back to the front then it was a good thing. JB said he read lots of sporting biographies and he'd noted that a lot of sportsmen change their caddie or coach in the final years of their career to try and squeeze out another

couple of years. Asked afterwards if any of those veterans had benefited from the change he replied succinctly: 'None.'

After name-checking Wayne Rainey and Erv Kanemoto as his toughest opposition, Jerry reckoned that his next appearance at a GP will be Indianapolis 2014 so he can see a few American friends.

It felt like the end of an era. For more than one reason.

'AT THE START I WAS VERY NERVOUS, I KNOW I SAID I WASN'T BUT I REALLY WAS'
MARC MARQUEZ

OFFICIAL TIMEKEEPER

GRAN PREMIO GENERALI DE LA COMUNITAT VALENCIANA
CIRCUITO RICARDO TORMO

ROUND 18
November 10

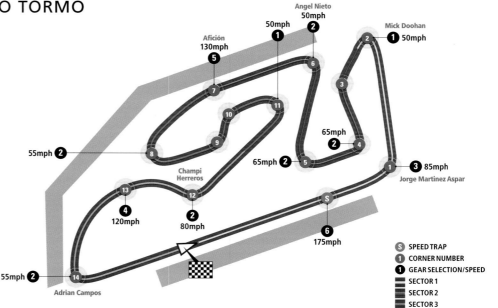

RACE RESULTS

CIRCUIT LENGTH 2.489 miles

NO. OF LAPS 30

RACE DISTANCE 74.658 miles

WEATHER Dry, 23°C

TRACK TEMPERATURE 26°C

WINNER Jorge Lorenzo

FASTEST LAP 1m 31.628s, 97.742mph, Dani Pedrosa (Record)

PREVIOUS LAP RECORD 1m 32.582s, 96.767mph, Casey Stoner, 2008

Circuit diagram labels: Afición 130mph (5), Angel Nieto 50mph (1)(2), Mick Doohan 50mph (1), Jorge Martinez Aspar 85mph (3), Champi Herreros, Adrian Campos, 55mph (2), 65mph, 80mph, 120mph, 175mph

Legend: **S** SPEED TRAP · **1** CORNER NUMBER · **1** GEAR SELECTION/SPEED · SECTOR 1 · SECTOR 2 · SECTOR 3

QUALIFYING

	Rider	Nation	Motorcycle	Team	Time	Pole +
1	**Marquez**	SPA	Honda	Repsol Honda Team	1m 30.237s	
2	**Lorenzo**	SPA	Yamaha	Yamaha Factory Racing	1m 30.577s	0.340s
3	**Pedrosa**	SPA	Honda	Repsol Honda Team	1m 30.663s	0.426s
4	**Rossi**	ITA	Yamaha	Yamaha Factory Racing	1m 30.920s	0.683s
5	**Crutchlow**	GBR	Yamaha	Monster Yamaha Tech 3	1m 31.113s	0.876s
6	**Smith**	GBR	Yamaha	Monster Yamaha Tech 3	1m 31.201s	0.964s
7	**Bautista**	SPA	Honda	GO&FUN Honda Gresini	1m 31.594s	1.357s
8	**Bradl**	GER	Honda	LCR Honda MotoGP	1m 31.638s	1.401s
9	**Dovizioso**	ITA	Ducati	Ducati Team	1m 31.718s	1.481s
10	**Hayden**	USA	Ducati	Ducati Team	1m 31.870s	1.633s
11	**Iannone**	ITA	Ducati	Energy T.I. Pramac Racing	1m 31.963s	1.726s
12	**Petrucci**	ITA	Ioda-Suter	Came IodaRacing Project	1m 33.116s	2.879s
13	**Barbera**	SPA	FTR	Avintia Blusens	1m 32.773s	Q1
14	**Espargaro**	SPA	ART	Power Electronics Aspar	1m 32.807s	Q1
15	**Corti**	ITA	FTR Kawasaki	NGM Mobile Forward Racing	1m 32.961s	Q1
16	**Hernandez**	COL	Ducati	Ignite Pramac Racing	1m 32.966s	Q1
17	**Pirro**	ITA	Ducati	Ducati Test Team	1m 32.966s	Q1
18	**Edwards**	USA	FTR Kawasaki	NGM Mobile Forward Racing	1m 33.203s	Q1
19	**Aoyama**	JPN	FTR	Avintia Blusens	1m 33.328s	Q1
20	**De Puniet**	FRA	ART	Power Electronics Aspar	1m 33.869s	Q1
21	**Laverty**	GBR	ART	Paul Bird Motorsport	1m 34.018s	Q1
22	**Scassa**	ITA	ART	Cardion AB Motoracing	1m 34.113s	Q1
23	**Staring**	AUS	FTR Honda	GO&FUN Honda Gresini	1m 34.805s	Q1
24	**Cudlin**	AUS	PBM	Paul Bird Motorsport	1m 34.903s	Q1
25	**Pesek**	CZE	Ioda-Suter	Came IodaRacing Project	1m 34.993s	Q1
26	**Bauer**	AUT	S&B Suter	Remus Racing Team	1m 35.277s	Q1

FINISHERS

1 JORGE LORENZO Changed his usual race plan and attempted to hold up the Hondas and allow the second group to catch them. When Crutchlow crashed out and Rossi couldn't help, Jorge put his head down and won his eighth race of the year, the most by any rider in any class.

2 DANI PEDROSA Involved in fairing-bashing with Lorenzo in the opening laps as the Yamaha rider tried to back the factory Hondas up. The coming-together at Turn 1 on lap ten was enough to send Dani off track and down to fifth. Got back past Marquez but the winner had disappeared.

3 MARC MARQUEZ World Champion, but by only four points. Confessed to being nervous before the start and unsure what tactics to use in the race. Took advantage of Lorenzo and Pedrosa's coming-together to lead, but only for a lap. Settled for the rostrum and a place in the history books.

4 VALENTINO ROSSI The race was a microcosm of his season: fourth place but unable to lay a glove on the top three. Vale's weekend was dominated by the news of his split from race engineer Jerry Burgess, who had been with him since he joined the top class in 2000.

5 ALVARO BAUTISTA Got a really good start and was with the leading bunch until

his soft tyre started to go off. Made sure he didn't get in the way of the two men fighting for the title.

6 STEFAN BRADL Despite front-end problems all weekend delighted to finish the race — for the simple reason it was the first time he'd ever finished a race at the Ricardo Tormo Circuit.

7 BRADLEY SMITH A fitting end to an impressive rookie year. Finishing well ahead of the Ducatis, less than 30 seconds down on the winner and ending the season in the top ten.

8 NICKY HAYDEN Finished his five years with the factory as top Ducati.

Again suffered from a clutch-related bad start, just as in Japan. Got up to eighth, halved the gap to Smith, then got flicked through the screen coming off the final corner and lost the time he'd gained.

9 ANDREA DOVIZIOSO Hated the whole weekend. No feel on a track he doesn't like, and for once he couldn't race his team-mate.

10 MICHELE PIRRO Racing for the first time in two months, as a wild card. A crash in qualifying led to him using up his tyre getting past the CRTs.

11 ALEIX ESPARGARO Top CRT for the 14th time in 18 races — just the way he

wanted to sign off from the Aspar team, especially after the crash last time out.

12 HECTOR BARBERA Fast enough to give Espargaro a fight for top CRT in front of his fans (Hector is a local). Happy to finish second CRT in the race but unhappy not to have achieved the same result in the championship.

13 CLAUDIO CORTI Got stuck in traffic early on, then waited until late in the race to pass Petrucci. Disappointed because his race pace could have seen him competing for top CRT.

14 DANILO PETRUCCI Top CRT in qualifying and as fast as any of them

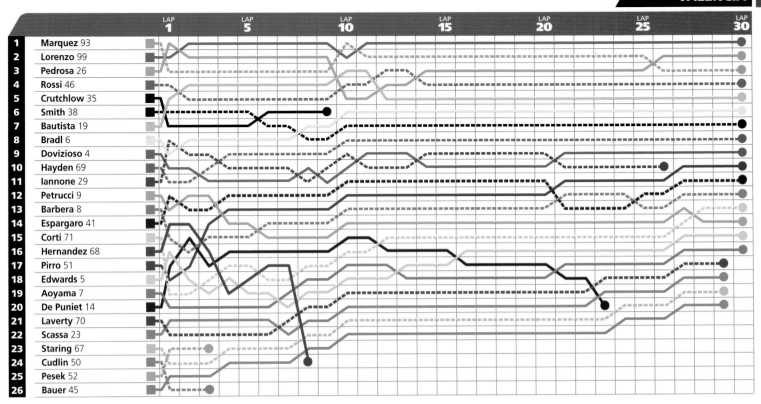

		LAP 1	LAP 5	LAP 10	LAP 15	LAP 20	LAP 25	LAP 30
1	Marquez 93							
2	Lorenzo 99							
3	Pedrosa 26							
4	Rossi 46							
5	Crutchlow 35							
6	Smith 38							
7	Bautista 19							
8	Bradl 6							
9	Dovizioso 4							
10	Hayden 69							
11	Iannone 29							
12	Petrucci 9							
13	Barbera 8							
14	Espargaro 41							
15	Corti 71							
16	Hernandez 68							
17	Pirro 51							
18	Edwards 5							
19	Aoyama 7							
20	De Puniet 14							
21	Laverty 70							
22	Scassa 23							
23	Staring 67							
24	Cudlin 50							
25	Pesek 52							
26	Bauer 45							

RACE

	Rider	Motorcycle	Race Time	Time +	Fastest Lap	Avg. Speed	B
1	Lorenzo	Yamaha	46m 10.302s		1m 31.701s	96.996mph	S/H
2	Pedrosa	Honda	46m 14.236s	3.934s	1m 31.628s	96.872mph	S/H
3	Marquez	Honda	46m 17.659s	7.357s	1m 31.787s	96.747mph	S/H
4	Rossi	Yamaha	46m 20.881s	10.579s	1m 31.987s	96.623mph	S/H
5	Bautista	Honda	46m 25.267s	14.965s	1m 32.157s	96.437mph	S/M
6	Bradl	Honda	46m 34.701s	24.399s	1m 32.319s	96.126mph	S/H
7	Smith	Yamaha	46m 39.345s	29.043s	1m 32.596s	96.002mph	S/H
8	Hayden	Ducati	46m 50.195s	39.893s	1m 32.764s	95.629mph	S/H
9	Dovizioso	Ducati	47m 03.498s	53.196s	1m 33.112s	95.132mph	S/H
10	Pirro	Ducati	47m 13.285s	1m 02.983s	1m 33.459s	94.821mph	S/M
11	Espargaro	ART	47m 14.499s	1m 04.197s	1m 33.323s	94.759mph	XS/S
12	Barbera	FTR	47m 17.128s	1m 06.826s	1m 33.551s	94.697mph	S/S
13	Corti	FTR Kawasaki	47m 21.783s	1m 11.481s	1m 34.021s	94.573mph	S/M
14	Petrucci	Ioda-Suter	47m 23.945s	1m 13.643s	1m 34.153s	94.448mph	S/S
15	Edwards	FTR Kawasaki	47m 34.551s	1m 24.249s	1m 33.869s	94.138mph	S/M
16	Aoyama	FTR	47m 43.312s	1m 33.010s	1m 34.514s	93.827mph	S/S
17	Laverty	ART	46m 21.726s	1 Lap	1m 34.772s	93.392mph	XS/S
18	Scassa	ART	46m 21.917s	1 Lap	1m 34.799s	93.330mph	S/S
19	Staring	FTR Honda	46m 22.033s	1 Lap	1m 34.815s	93.330mph	S/S
20	Bauer	S&B Suter	47m 09.329s	1 Lap	1m 35.514s	91.777mph	S/S
NF	Iannone	Ducati	40m 44.674s	4 Laps	1m 33.045s	95.256mph	S/M
NF	De Puniet	ART	36m 39.690s	7 Laps	1m 34.181s	93.641mph	S/S
NF	Crutchlow	Yamaha	14m 00.197s	21 Laps	1m 32.369s	95.940mph	S/H
NF	Hernandez	Ducati	12m 59.556s	22 Laps	1m 34.182s	91.901mph	S/M
NF	Pesek	Ioda-Suter	4m 55.433s	27 Laps	1m 35.366s	90.969mph	S/S
NF	Cudlin	PBM	4m 58.255s	27 Laps	1m 35.886s	90.099mph	S/S

CHAMPIONSHIP

	Rider	Nation	Team	Points
1	Marquez	SPA	Repsol Honda Team	334
2	Lorenzo	SPA	Yamaha Factory Racing	330
3	Pedrosa	SPA	Repsol Honda Team	300
4	Rossi	ITA	Yamaha Factory Racing	237
5	Crutchlow	GBR	Monster Yamaha Tech 3	188
6	Bautista	SPA	GO&FUN Honda Gresini	171
7	Bradl	GER	LCR Honda MotoGP	156
8	Dovizioso	ITA	Ducati Team	140
9	Hayden	USA	Ducati Team	126
10	Smith	GBR	Monster Yamaha Tech 3	116
11	Espargaro	SPA	Power Electronics Aspar	93
12	Iannone	ITA	Energy T.I. Pramac Racing	57
13	Pirro	ITA	Ignite Pramac Racing	56
14	Edwards	USA	NGM Mobile Forward Racing	41
15	De Puniet	FRA	Power Electronics Aspar	36
16	Barbera	SPA	Avintia Blusens	35
17	Petrucci	ITA	Came IodaRacing Project	26
18	Hernandez	COL	Paul Bird Motorsport	21
19	Corti	ITA	NGM Mobile Forward Racing	14
20	Aoyama	JPN	Avintia Blusens	13
21	Spies	USA	Ignite Pramac Racing	9
22	Nakasuga	JPN	Yamaha YSP Racing Team	5
23	De Angelis	RSM	Ignite Pramac Racing	5
24	Abraham	CZE	Cardion AB Motoracing	5
25	Laverty	GBR	Paul Bird Motorsport	3
26	Staring	AUS	GO&FUN Honda Gresini	2
27	Del Amor	SPA	Avintia Blusens	1

mid-race, despite lacking grip at the start. Lost out to Corti when rear-tyre wear led to the suspension pumping.

15 COLIN EDWARDS Has never liked the Valencia track and this race gave Colin no reason to change his mind.

16 HIROSHI AOYAMA Another who had to wait for the grip to come to him – by which time a points-scoring finish was out of the question, despite an improvement in lap times. Announced he will be riding for Aspar's team in 2014 on a customer Honda.

17 MICHAEL LAVERTY Hampered by severe rear-grip problems, but consistent times in the race showed he was making the most of the bike's potential.

18 LUCA SCASSA Never bettered the time he set on Friday. Disappointed not to score a point during his MotoGP adventure.

19 BRYAN STARING Hoping for a decent race to end his MotoGP journey, but it didn't happen.

20 MARTIN BAUER His second wild-card ride and the Austrian veteran wasn't disgraced. Discovered how much the bike has to be adjusted to suit the tyres and lamented the lack of time and testing.

NON-FINISHERS

ANDREA IANNONE Another man whose season was summed up by this race: a front-end crash. Had a few words to say about Ducati and his hopes for next season.

RANDY PE PUNIET Afflicted by multiple set-up problems at a track he likes. A combination of worn tyres and engine-braking woes forced his retirement.

CAL CRUTCHLOW Doing his damnedest to get across to the lead group when he slid off after clipping a kerb. Not the way Cal wanted to end his Yamaha days, but typically he was on the gas and going for it.

YONNY HERNANDEZ Retired after a slide tweaked his injured right hand – specifically the broken little finger.

LUKAS PESEK Ended a dismal and literally pointless year with a third-lap crash.

DAMIAN CUDLIN Pushed too hard on a full tank and slid off without injury.

NON-STARTERS

KAREL ABRAHAM Recovering from shoulder surgery. Replaced by Scassa.

BEN SPIES Had announced his retirement before the previous race.

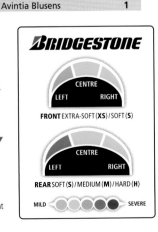

BRIDGESTONE

CENTRE
LEFT   RIGHT

FRONT EXTRA-SOFT (**XS**) / SOFT (**S**)

CENTRE
LEFT   RIGHT

REAR SOFT (**S**) / MEDIUM (**M**) / HARD (**H**)

MILD   SEVERE

WORLD CHAMPIONSHIP CLASSIFICATION

MotoGP

	Rider	Nation	Motorcycle	QAT	AME	SPA	FRA	ITA	CAT	NED	GER	USA	INP	CZE	GBR	RSM	ARA	MAL	AUS	JPN	VAL	Points
1	Marquez	SPA	Honda	16	25	20	16	–	16	20	25	25	25	25	20	20	25	20	–	20	16	334
2	Lorenzo	SPA	Yamaha	25	16	16	9	25	25	11	–	10	16	16	25	25	20	16	25	25	25	330
3	Pedrosa	SPA	Honda	13	20	25	25	20	20	13	–	11	20	20	16	16	–	25	20	16	20	300
4	Rossi	ITA	Yamaha	20	10	13	4	–	13	25	16	16	13	13	13	13	16	13	16	10	13	237
5	Crutchlow	GBR	Yamaha	11	13	11	20	16	–	16	20	9	11	–	9	10	10	10	13	9	–	188
6	Bautista	SPA	Honda	10	8	10	10	–	–	9	11	13	10	11	11	9	13	11	11	13	11	171
7	Bradl	GER	Honda	–	11	–	6	13	11	10	13	20	9	10	10	11	11	–	–	11	10	156
8	Dovizioso	ITA	Ducati	9	9	8	13	11	9	6	9	7	6	9	–	8	8	8	7	6	7	140
9	Hayden	USA	Ducati	8	7	9	11	10	–	5	7	8	7	8	8	7	7	–	9	7	8	126
10	Smith	GBR	Yamaha	–	4	6	7	7	10	7	10	–	8	–	7	5	9	9	10	8	9	116
11	Espargaro	SPA	ART	5	5	7	3	8	8	8	8	–	4	6	6	3	5	7	5	–	5	93
12	Iannone	ITA	Ducati	7	6	–	5	3	–	3	–	–	5	7	5	–	6	–	8	2	–	57
13	Pirro	ITA	Ducati	–	–	5	8	9	6	2	6	–	–	4	4	6	–	–	–	–	6	56
14	Edwards	USA	FTR Kawasaki	–	–	1	–	2	7	–	3	4	3	5	2	4	–	1	4	4	1	41
15	De Puniet	FRA	ART	4	2	–	–	5	–	4	4	–	–	1	–	–	3	4	6	3	–	36
16	Barbera	SPA	FTR	3	–	4	–	6	–	5	6	–	–	3	–	–	2	2	–	4	35
17	Petrucci	ITA	Ioda-Suter	–	–	2	2	4	5	–	2	3	–	3	1	1	–	–	1	–	2	26
18	Hernandez	COL	Ducati	2	1	–	–	–	–	3	–	–	1	–	–	–	4	6	3	1	–	21
19	Corti	ITA	FTR Kawasaki	–	–	–	–	–	4	–	1	–	2	–	–	–	1	3	–	–	3	14
20	Aoyama	JPN	FTR	1	–	–	–	–	–	–	–	–	1	2	–	2	2	5	–	–	–	13
21	Spies	USA	Ducati	6	3	–	–	–	–	–	–	–	–	–	–	–	–	–	–	–	–	9
22	Nakasuga	JPN	Yamaha	–	–	–	–	–	–	–	–	–	–	–	–	–	–	–	–	5	–	5
23	De Angelis	RSM	Ducati	–	–	–	–	–	–	–	–	5	–	–	–	–	–	–	–	–	–	5
24	Abraham	CZE	ART	–	–	–	1	1	–	1	–	2	–	–	–	–	–	–	–	–	–	5
25	Laverty	GBR	PBM	–	–	3	–	–	–	–	–	–	–	–	–	–	–	–	–	–	–	3
26	Staring	AUS	FTR Honda	–	–	–	–	2	–	–	–	–	–	–	–	–	–	–	–	–	–	2
27	Del Amor	SPA	FTR	–	–	–	–	–	1	–	–	–	–	–	–	–	–	–	–	–	–	1

CONSTRUCTOR

	Motorcycle	QAT	AME	SPA	FRA	ITA	CAT	NED	GER	USA	INP	CZE	GBR	RSM	ARA	MAL	AUS	JPN	VAL	Points
1	Honda	16	25	25	25	20	20	20	25	25	25	25	20	20	13	25	20	20	25	389
2	Yamaha	25	16	16	20	25	25	25	20	16	16	16	25	25	20	16	25	25	20	381
3	Ducati	9	9	9	13	11	9	6	9	8	7	9	8	8	8	8	9	7	9	155
4	ART	5	5	7	3	8	8	8	8	2	4	6	6	3	5	7	6	3	7	99
5	FTR Kawasaki	–	–	1	–	2	7	–	3	4	3	5	2	4	1	3	4	4	11	46
6	FTR	3	–	4	–	6	1	–	5	6	1	2	3	2	2	5	2	–	3	46
7	FTR Honda	–	–	–	–	2	–	–	–	–	–	–	–	–	–	–	–	–	2	2

TEAM

	Motorcycle	QAT	AME	SPA	FRA	ITA	CAT	NED	GER	USA	INP	CZE	GBR	RSM	ARA	MAL	AUS	JPN	VAL	Points
1	Repsol Honda Team	29	45	45	41	20	36	33	25	36	45	45	36	36	25	45	20	36	36	634
2	Yamaha Factory Racing	45	26	29	13	25	38	36	16	26	29	29	38	38	36	29	41	35	38	567
3	Monster Yamaha Tech 3	11	17	17	27	23	10	23	30	9	19	–	16	15	19	19	23	17	9	304
4	Ducati Team	17	16	17	24	21	9	11	16	15	13	17	8	15	15	8	16	13	15	266
5	GO&FUN Honda Gresini	10	8	10	10	–	2	9	11	13	10	11	11	9	13	11	11	13	11	173
6	LCR Honda MotoGP	–	11	–	6	13	11	10	13	20	9	10	10	11	11	–	–	11	10	156
7	Power Electronics Aspar	9	7	7	3	13	8	12	12	–	4	7	6	3	8	11	11	3	5	129
8	Pramac Racing Team	13	9	–	13	3	6	5	6	5	5	11	9	6	10	6	11	3	–	121
9	NGM Mobile Forward Racing	–	–	1	–	2	11	–	4	4	5	5	2	4	1	4	4	4	4	55
10	Avintia Blusens	4	–	4	–	6	1	–	5	6	1	2	3	2	2	7	2	–	4	49
11	Came IodaRacing Project	–	–	2	2	4	5	–	2	3	–	3	1	1	–	–	1	–	2	26
12	Paul Bird Motorsport	2	1	3	–	–	3	–	–	1	–	–	–	–	–	–	–	–	–	10
13	Cardion AB Motoracing	–	–	–	1	1	–	1	–	2	–	–	–	–	–	–	–	–	5

Moto2™
CHAMPIONSHIP

ESPARGARO'S COMEBACK

Scott Redding had one hand on the 2013 Moto2™ world title, but eventually the crown went to Pol Espargaro

The battle for the 2013 Moto2 title was a straight duel. Six different riders may have won races (one more than in 2012) but there were only two men in the hunt for the championship: Pol Espargaro and Scott Redding.

The Spanish and the British pair's duel swayed this way and that as the advantage moved from one rider to the other and then back again. Second behind Marc Marquez in 2012, Espargaro started as title favourite, dominated the first race and fooled himself into thinking the championship was his for the taking. 'We were so fast in pre-season testing and then I won the race in Qatar, so it seemed like it was all going to be easy,' he said.

How wrong can you be? Espargaro crashed at two of the next three races while Redding was on a roll, scoring back-to-back wins at Le Mans and Mugello. Suddenly, the Spaniard seemed out of the hunt. Going into round six at Barcelona he was 47 points down on Redding. Then big brother came to the rescue. 'Aleix made the difference – he motivated the team and he motivated me,' said Pol, who won that race and the next at Assen.

Redding wasn't done yet, though, beating his rival twice in the next four races and then scoring his best victory yet at Silverstone, where Espargaro struggled home in eighth. Six races remained and the Spanish rider was still 38 points down.

A change in riding style was crucial to Espargaro's eventual success. 'My team-mate Tito [Rabat] is so smooth with the throttle, which was perfect for the tyres, so I tried to learn from him.' The turning point came at Misano, where Espargaro finally gelled with

RIGHT Scott Redding's first win of the season, and his first ever Moto2 win, came at Le Mans

BELOW The first race of the year set the pattern: Redding and Espargaro battle at Qatar

a new Dunlop rear slick. From there, Redding's points lead dwindled and the pressure finally told at Phillip Island where he crashed and broke a wrist. A week later, at Motegi, his great rival won his sixth victory to secure the crown.

Although the title fight was a two-way contest, Rabat came close to making it a three-way thing. It had taken the young Spaniard nine years and more than a hundred GPs to achieve his first victory – to rapturous applause at Jerez – and then he scored further successes at Indianapolis and Sepang. Rabat looked great on his Kalex, his more exact riding style working very nearly as well as the more aggressive techniques used by Espargaro and Redding.

Rabat wasn't the only slow-burner finally to make good in 2013. Finn Mika Kallio – riding his third Moto2

1 – QATARI GP	2 – AMERICAS GP	3 – SPANISH GP	4 – FRENCH GP	5 – ITALIAN GP
Pol Espargaro (HP Tuenti Kalex) was firm favourite for the first Moto2 win of the year after dominating winter testing and taking pole at Losail, despite a crash at the start of qualifying. But the Spaniard had to fight Scott Redding (Marc VDS Kalex) every inch of the way for victory. At the flag Espargaro was just eight-tenths in front. The pair dominated the final stages after taking over from early leader Takaaki Nakagami (Italtrans Kalex) who scored his first GP podium in third. The Japanese rider's stunning speed in the early laps wasn't matched by his pace on used tyres, an issue that would bother him throughout the season. Dominique Aegerter (Technomag Suter) was next, winning a frenzied 11-man skirmish for fourth place ahead of Mika Kallio (Marc VDS Kalex), Julian Simon (Italtrans Kalex), Simone Corsi (NGM Speed Up), Alex de Angelis (NGM Speed Up) and Esteve Rabat (HP Tuenti Kalex).	Former 125 world champ Nico Terol (Mapfre Suter) walked away with the Moto2 race to score his first victory in the class. He left behind a frantic three-way contest for second. Rabat won the battle, coming through brilliantly from ninth place on lap one to grab the runner-up spot at the final corner, where Kallio made a mistake. Aegerter crossed the line just behind Kallio after making contact with the Finn a few corners from the finish and almost falling. Redding started from pole for the first time in Moto2 but it was Nakagami who led from the grid, though only for a lap. As the race went on he ran into serious tyre problems and eventually pulled into the pits. Redding had taken the lead from the Japanese and stayed ahead until Terol assumed control. He finished fifth, also struggling with tyre wear. Qatar winner Espargaro crashed out.	Rabat didn't do a thing wrong at Jerez: pole position, start-to-finish win, new lap record and the World Championship lead. It had been a while coming – this was his first GP win in seven years of trying. 'I've had a good feeling all weekend,' he said. 'I got a good start and pushed, pushed, pushed to make the gap.' The Spaniard's success came at the front of an unusually processional Moto2 race, Rabat comfortably ahead of Redding who was well ahead of a battle for third between Rabat's team-mate Espargaro and Nakagami. Espargaro only caught the Japanese in the final laps when the pair swapped places several times, Nakagami once again running out of grip, which allowed title-favourite Espargaro to prevail. Terol, so dominant in Texas, was never in the hunt and finished fifth, almost four seconds down on Nakagami and just ahead of Xavier Simeon (Desguaces La Torre Maptaq Kalex) who was starting to show his speed after an off-season switch to a Kalex chassis.	Redding finally came of age as a Moto2 rider, winning his first victory in the intermediate class to take the championship lead for the first time. The race started in gloomy conditions with the track still not fully dry in places following earlier rain. Espargaro, Rabat and Nakagami were up front after the start, but as they fought among themselves Rabat slid off on a damp patch at Musée Corner, followed immediately by Espargaro. Nakagami lost the lead soon afterwards when he too crashed. Redding meanwhile had made a disastrous start from pole to end the first lap in eighth. He fought back brilliantly to take the lead from local Johann Zarco (Came Suter), who had the French crowd roaring their approval. The positions behind Redding were fought over by his team-mate Kallio, Simeon, Aegerter and Zarco, who finished in that order. The foursome crossed the line separated by less than a second.	A huge crash on Saturday morning couldn't stop Redding from scoring a second pole and a second consecutive victory to move well ahead in the standings, with 43 points over second-placed Terol. His crew had worked flat out to build him a new bike after he destroyed his number-one machine, and Redding then took pole and chased early leader Terol, who made the mistake of letting the Briton past, hoping for a tow around high-speed Mugello. Once ahead, Redding put the hammer down to escape from the pack, leaving Terol to fend off Zarco, who took third place at his team's home race. Espargaro was a distant fourth after charging through a group of nine other riders fighting for the position. Almost ten seconds down on Redding, he beat Kallio by a hundredth of a second, with Jordi Torres in a best-yet sixth, then Corsi, de Angelis and Tom Luthi (Interwetten Suter). Fourth to ninth was covered by just 1.1 seconds.

season, like Rabat – came through to win his first intermediate-class victory at Brno. Three more podiums put him fourth overall, giving the top four positions in the championship to two teams and just one chassis maker: Espargaro and Rabat at Sito Pons's Tuenti HP40 squad and Redding and Kallio at Marc VDS, all of them aboard the rider-friendly Kalex, which took over from the Suter as the machine of choice.

There were two other race winners – Nico Terol and Jordi Torres of Jorge Martinez's Aspar outfit, riding Suters – meaning that only three teams and two different chassis constructors won Moto2 races during 2013.

The other three stand-out riders of the year also used either the Swiss or the German frames: Dominique Aegerter and Tom Luthi on Suters and Takaaki Nakagami

ABOVE RIGHT Takaaki Nakagami looked like he might be a contender, taking four second places on the bounce

ABOVE Nakagami leads Tom Luthi, who came good late in the season after recovering from a pre-season testing injury

LEFT Genial Jordi Torres was a surprise winner in Germany

6 – CATALAN GP	7 – DUTCH TT	8 – GERMAN GP	9 – INDIANAPOLIS GP	10 – CZECH REPUBLIC GP

Espargaro reignited his challenge for the title with his first win since Qatar. The local – born just eight kilometres from the circuit – dominated the event following a vital pep talk from older brother Aleix. After scoring his first pole since Qatar, Espargaro beat Rabat by a fraction of a second after the team-mates had made the race their own.

Espargaro led, let Rabat past, then three laps later retook the advantage and held it to the end. There were certainly no team orders; Rabat was trying everything to get ahead and only failed by less than a tenth of a second. If the race had gone on any longer it could have been very different – at the finish Espargaro's rear tyre was badly split.

More than five seconds further back Luthi was third, his first podium since coming back from pre-season injury at Jerez. He comfortably got the better of Redding who finished ahead of Nakagami and Randy

Espargaro continued his impressive return to form with a crucial victory over title leader Redding. The Briton led for most of the way, shadowed by Espargaro, who moved ahead, only to be bettered again with a few laps to go. The Spaniard had it all under control, though, going past Redding at the start of the final lap to reduce his championship deficit to 30 points.

A thrilling four-way battle for the final place on the podium went to Aegerter who had run with the leaders in the early stages and briefly got the better of both of them. This was the Swiss youngster's first podium of the season and he'd had to fight hard for it, bettering Redding's hard-charging team-mate Kallio by less than two-tenths of a second, with Rabat and Zarco right behind, the four of them covered by just half a second.

Belgian Simeon had another strong ride to seventh, well clear of Luthi.

Simeon scored his first GP pole position at the Sachsenring, making him the first Belgian to start a GP race from pole since Didier de Radiguès qualified fastest for the 1989 Belgian 250 GP at Spa-Francorchamps.

The win went elsewhere. Half-way through his second full Grand Prix season Torres scored his first victory, after following compatriot Espargaro for much of the race. Corsi also played his part in the lead battle, with any of the leading three in with a chance of success to the very end.

Torres's winning move was the classic Sachsenring overtaking manoeuvre: building speed through the treacherous high-speed Turn 11 to set up a pass into Turn 12, the penultimate corner, at two-thirds distance. Espargaro had no answer, explaining afterwards that his tyres were well past their best, which is why he fell victim to Corsi on the final lap.

Espargaro was at least happy to have further reduced his points disadvantage to championship leader Redding, who could only

Tyre worries seemed to affect Rabat less than everyone else. The Spaniard started well from fourth on the grid only for Nakagami to take the lead, which he increased to 2.5 seconds at half-distance. But the Japanese wasn't as good on used tyres, so his advantage was gradually whittled away as Rabat came good. This wouldn't be the last time Nakagami suffered such a morale-draining defeat after building a strong lead.

Rabat won by just under a second, while pole-sitter Redding took the final place on the podium after pulling one of the finest moves of the season – in any class – to fight his way past Espargaro in the final stages. 'It was a hard move,' the Briton admitted. 'But sometimes you've got to be hard.'

Espargaro had to be happy with fourth, just a fraction ahead of a hard-charging Aegerter. Behind the Swiss came a three-way contest for sixth place, which was won by Corsi

Kallio won his first Moto2 victory at the end of a frantic battle in MotoGP's intermediate class. The Finn – who took his last GP win on a 250 in 2008 – beat Nakagami, Luthi, Espargaro and Zarco over the line, the five of them separated by just 1.1 seconds.

It was a hectic race, with Kallio, Nakagami, Luthi and Terol all leading at one point. Finally, the winner regained the lead from Luthi during the last few laps. 'I was confident I could do it,' said Kallio. 'I pushed all the time and my last lap was really special.'

Terol eventually finished sixth, just behind the lead group and almost a second ahead of Rabat. Redding had his worst result of the season so far, coming home in eighth place after failing to get a good set-up for Dunlop's new rear slick.

RIGHT Esteve 'Tito' Rabat won three races and takes Scott Redding's place at the Marc VDS team in 2014

BELOW Nico Terol was another three-time winner, but could only finish seventh in the championship

BELOW RIGHT Scott Redding's win at Silverstone in front of a delirious home crowd was his best ride of the year

on a Kalex. Aegerter was the only rider to score points in all 17 rounds, including Japan where he suffered a dislocated shoulder in the chaotic first lap, popped the shoulder back in and rode to eighth in the restart. Luthi recovered well from pre-season injury to score six podiums. Nakagami took four consecutive runner-up finishes mid-season, after he too came back from injury.

The fact that just three teams won races in 2013 confirms that the Honda CBR600-powered series has changed during its first four years. Moto2 is no longer the harum-scarum class that it was during its inaugural 2010 season, when victories were flung far and wide between a variety of riders and no fewer than nine different teams. As the richer teams have pinpointed exactly what's needed to find the tiny advantage required to win in Moto2, the action has become more technical than manic.

11 – BRITISH GP

The title advantage seemed to sway back in favour of Redding at Silverstone, where the Briton scored a vital home Moto2 win, dominating the race to beat perennial runner-up Nakagami and Luthi. Victory was made all the more significant by the fact that this time it was Redding's title rival Espargaro's turn to struggle, the Spaniard finishing in eighth place, a morale-busting result that left him trailing by 38 points. He was so distraught after the race that he again had to be comforted by older brother Aleix.

Redding had to fight all the way for his third win of the year. Nakagami put a great pass on him on lap ten, only for Redding to retake the lead a few laps later. That was the break the Briton needed because while Nakagami and Luthi fought over second, he was able to get away to build a one-second advantage. Rabat was a close fourth after setting a new lap

12 – SAN MARINO GP

The pendulum swung yet again in the title duel. Two weeks after points leader Redding won at Silverstone, where Espargaro had floundered in eighth, Redding had tyre issues at Misano and could finish no better than sixth while Espargaro took the victory.

Nakagami once again led for most of the way, building what looked like a good enough advantage to take his first GP win. But it was not to be. As tyre performance went down, Nakagami's pace began to falter and in the end he had no answer for a hard-charging Espargaro who took the lead for the first time with a lap and a half to go. The Japanese was in tears following his fourth successive runner-up finish, in part because he had so wanted to dedicate his win to Shoya Tomizawa, who lost his life during the 2010 Misano Moto2 race.

Rabat took third, ahead of a four-man battle for fourth won

13 – ARAGON GP

Terol scored a runaway win, just as he had done in Texas, well ahead of Rabat, while the interest focused on the battle for third place between title rivals Espargaro and Redding.

Series leader Redding started from 13th on the grid after running into set-up problems during practice, but he miraculously fought his way into second in the first few laps. At first he battled with Rabat, who eventually made second place his own, then Espargaro.

The Spaniard and the Briton gave no quarter, touching at one stage and swapping places on several occasions. Finally Espargaro's lighter weight made the difference, as he swept past Redding on Aragon's long main straight. The pair crossed the line separated by just two-tenths, with Redding's team-mate Kallio a similar margin behind. Redding's lead was now down to 20 points.

14 – MALAYSIAN GP

Rabat kept alive his outside hopes for the world title with his second pole of the year and then a runaway victory ahead of Espargaro, who was at least happy to have taken another chunk out of the championship lead of Redding, who could only manage seventh in the tropical heat.

It might have been different for Redding if the race hadn't been stopped on the first lap after a huge five-bike pile-up. The Brit had made a stunning start, from the fourth row to fourth place in two corners, but the restart was very different; he was 12th on lap one.

After grabbing the lead from Espargaro, Rabat was never challenged in the shortened race. His eventual winning margin was 1.5 seconds over his team-mate, who spent much of the race disputing second place with Luthi. Kallio won an intense duel for fourth with Aegerter. Redding struggled with rear grip

15 – AUSTRALIAN GP

Redding went to Phillip Island nursing a nine-point lead, knowing full well that he had to stop the rot and beat Espargaro. But it was not to be. During practice his Kalex threw itself into a vicious tank-slapper which snapped Redding's left wrist before hurling him to the ground.

That left Espargaro to score his second successive victory at the track – a start-to-finish affair in a half-distance race, shortened due to concerns over tyre life. The Spaniard was nevertheless chased all the way, crossing the line six-tenths ahead of Luthi, with Torres just one-tenth further back. 'This is the best day of my life,' said the Spaniard. 'I've spent so much time thinking about the championship and finally we are nearly there. But it would've been better to win with Scott here.'

NGM Speed Up team-mates Simone Corsi and Alex de Angelis were fourth and fifth

ABOVE Pol Espargaro celebrates his title with the Sito Pons-run Tuenti team

RIGHT The two main men of the 2013 Moto2 championship will meet again in MotoGP in 2014

CHAMPIONSHIP STANDINGS

	Rider	Nat	Team	Motorcycle	Points
1	Pol Espargaro	SPA	Tuenti HP 40	Kalex	265
2	Scott Redding	GBR	Marc VDS Racing Team	Kalex	225
3	Esteve Rabat	SPA	Tuenti HP 40	Kalex	215
4	Mika Kallio	FIN	Marc VDS Racing Team	Kalex	187
5	Dominique Aegerter	SWI	Technomag carXpert	Suter	157
6	Thomas Luthi	SWI	Interwetten Paddock Moto2	Suter	155
7	Nicolas Terol	SPA	Aspar Team Moto2	Suter	150
8	Takaaki Nakagami	JPN	Italtrans Racing Team	Kalex	148
9	Johann Zarco	FRA	Came Ioda Racing Project	Suter	139
10	Jordi Torres	SPA	Aspar Team Moto2	Suter	126
11	Simone Corsi	ITA	NGM Mobile Racing	Speed Up	105
12	Xavier Simeon	BEL	Maptaq SAG Zelos Team	Kalex	88
13	Julian Simon	SPA	Italtrans Racing Team	Kalex	79
14	Alex de Angelis	RSM	NGM Mobile Forward Racing	Speed Up	76
15	Anthony West	AUS	QMMF Racing Team	Speed Up	61
16	Mattia Pasini	ITA	NGM Mobile Racing	Speed Up	55
17	Marcel Schrotter	GER	Maptaq SAG Zelos Team	Kalex	33
18	Toni Elias	SPA	Blusens Avintia	Kalex	21
19	Randy Krummenacher	SWI	Technomag carXpert	Suter	20
20	Sandro Cortese	GER	Dynavolt Intact GP	Kalex	19
21	Mike di Meglio	FRA	Jir Moto2	Motobi	18
22	Danny Kent	GBR	Tech 3	Tech 3	15
23	Ricard Cardus	SPA	NGM Mobile Forward Racing	Speed Up	7
24	Axel Pons	SPA	Tuenti HP 40	Kalex	5
25	Louis Rossi	FRA	Tech 3	Tech 3	4
26	Gino Rea	GBR	Gino Rea Montaze Broz Racing	Speed Up	4
27	Alex Mariñelarena	SPA	Blusens Avintia	Kalex	2
28	Doni Tata Pradita	INA	Federal Oil Gresini Moto2	Suter	1

16 – JAPANESE GP

Espargaro won the world title at Motegi in the best possible way, with a comfortable win.

The race had been red-flagged and restarted after a horrible pile-up triggered by Rabat, who highsided out of the first double right, taking out Alex Mariñelarena (Blusens Kalex) and the unfortunate Redding, who was riding following an operation in Australia to pin his fractured left wrist.

Redding's team-mate Kallio led the shortened restart, but not for long, and that was the way it stayed, with the Finn unable to get close enough to Espargaro to attack. In what was a rather processional race, Luthi ran third from the second lap to the finish.

The hero was Aegerter, who had his own crash on the first lap of the first start. He dislocated a shoulder in the fall, popped the shoulder back in by himself, got his bike fixed and rode to eighth in the restart!

17 – VALENCIAN GP

Two weeks after wrapping up the title at Motegi, Espargaro wanted to show everyone what he could do when he didn't need to ride for points. He qualified on pole by almost three-tenths, led from the start, built up a 1.5s lead in the first seven laps and then crashed out. At least he didn't need the points…

Espargaro's tumble put Terol ahead, chased by Corsi, who succumbed to Torres with just six laps to go. While Terol built up an impressive four-second lead and Torres made sure of second place, Corsi then found himself losing ground to Zarco. He did everything in his power to hold on to the final podium position, losing out in the final sprint to the chequered flag by just one thousandth of a second.

Rabat finished in fifth place, which confirmed him in third place overall, ten points behind Redding, who finished 15th and in considerable pain from his Phillip Island and Motegi prangs.

LAST-GASP SHOWDOWN

The Moto3™ class served up the closest action in 2013 and an enthralling three-way title fight at the final round

The hype at Valencia may have centred on the MotoGP title duel, but it was Moto3 that served up the most thrilling climax of the season. After 16 races, the three championship contenders went into the last round separated by just five points. Thus no clever mathematics were required to work out who would win the title – whoever won the race would be champion. No surprise there, since Moto3's average winning margin during 2013 was a mere quarter of a second.

Seven months earlier, the eventual title hopefuls – Maverick Viñales, Luis Salom and Alex Rins – all had high hopes of doing well in Moto3's second series. Inaugural Moto3 World Champion Sandro Cortese had moved up to Moto2, leaving 2012 runner-up Salom as 2013 title favourite. Promoted to the factory Red Bull KTM team, it seemed Salom would have everything he needed to take the title.

His biggest threat was expected to come from Viñales, who had won five races during 2012 despite riding an under-powered Honda NSF250R. The tough man of the class, Viñales now had a KTM, though without a crew of factory engineers in his pit. Honda riders were nowhere in 2013 – the Japanese brand didn't score a single Moto3 podium. Rins, also on a KTM, had been Rookie of the Year in 2012, but few expected him to challenge for the title.

Salom won the first race, Rins the second and Viñales the third, then Salom appeared to gain the upper hand with a hat-trick of wins at Mugello, Catalunya and Assen. All that changed at Indy where Salom crashed in practice, breaking an ankle. After that his results became more haphazard.

After his two early victories, Viñales didn't have the speed to win races and gradually slipped behind Salom

ABOVE Teenagers at work; Isaac Viñales and John McPhee try to occupy the same piece of tarmac

RIGHT Alex Rins on the way to his first Grand Prix win at Round two in Texas

ABOVE RIGHT The second half of Luis Salom's season was compromised by the ankle injury he sustained at Indianapolis

and Rins, who belied his lack of experience by scoring a further five victories between Germany and Australia. Going into the penultimate race in Japan, Viñales seemed out of the hunt. Everything changed at Motegi, however. First, Salom got taken out on the first lap, handing a clear championship advantage to Rins, who then squandered his big chance by tumbling in the closing stages, leaving Marc Marquez's younger brother Alex to score his first GP win.

At the final round in Valencia Salom was still favourite: he had won more races than anyone else and he still had the factory advantage. But this time it was his turn to make a mistake. He slid off, leaving Viñales and Rins to sort it out between them. At the do-or-die final corner, leader Viñales came up with a brave and ice-cool strategy. He knew that

1 – QATARI GP

Factory KTM rider Luis Salom (Red Bull KTM) took the first race of the Moto3 season, winning a hugely entertaining five-man, all-KTM battle that lasted pretty much throughout the 18 laps.

The 21-year-old from Majorca – the same Mediterranean island that bred Jorge Lorenzo – swapped the lead with Maverick Viñales (Calvo KTM) and Estrella Galicia KTM team-mates Alex Rins and Alex Marquez, with Jonas Folger (Mapfre Kalex KTM) trying his best to get the better of the Spanish riders.

Salom strove to make good his escape, but he couldn't drop Viñales. At the finish his winning advantage was four-tenths, with Viñales hanging on to second by less than a hundredth from Rins, with Marquez and Folger a fraction further behind. The top five were covered by just eight-tenths of a second, a portent of the great racing to come; the all-Spanish podium gave a clear indication of how the season would pan out.

2 – AMERICAS GP

Round two turned into a five-lap dash when the original race was stopped and scrubbed after Dutchman Jasper Iwema (RW Racing Kalex KTM) fell and knocked himself out. The shortened race was much like Qatar, with Salom, Viñales, Rins, Marquez and Folger providing the fun up front. Marquez was in over his head, however, and crashed out on the third lap.

On lap five Rins led, then Salom, then Rins, then Salom, but his final manoeuvre past his compatriot into the last corner was over-optimistic. He led for a moment, then ran wide and both Rins and Viñales came past on the run to the line. Rins was delighted to score his first GP win, which would set him up as a serious title challenger.

Folger was a close fourth and well clear of Miguel Oliveira (Mahindra), who beat hard-charging Aussie Jack Miller (Caretta FTR Honda) at the final turn.

3 – SPANISH GP

Viñales won his first race on a KTM and his first since Mugello the previous July, topping the third all-KTM podium in as many races. The Spaniard's victory and the continuing KTM domination proved beyond doubt that he had done the right thing in defecting from the Honda team at the end of 2012.

Once again it was Salom, Viñales, Rins and Folger leading the way up front, until Rins crashed out. Later the race became a straight duel between the surviving two Spaniards, with Viñales just ahead. Any plans that Salom might have had for a final assault were thwarted when Alan Techer (CIP TSR Honda) fell and was knocked out, bringing out the red flags.

By then Folger had dropped back to a lonely third. South African Brad Binder (Ambrogio Suter Honda) was the top Honda, in fourth place. Viñales's success moved him past Rins and Salom into the points lead.

4 – FRENCH GP

Viñales took his second consecutive victory to extend his World Championship lead, winning a tense race-long encounter with Rins on a track that was still damp in places from early rainfall. In fact Viñales had it all worked out – he got his head down in the final two laps, increasing his pace to put himself 1.2 seconds ahead of his countryman at the flag.

Salom and Folger made it the usual foursome up front until Rins grabbed second from Folger, putting the German down a slip road, which cost him any chance of a podium. During the later stages Salom chased Rins, despite pain from a fall in practice, to finish just over a tenth of a second behind his compatriot.

Folger came in fourth, 14 seconds behind Salom and no less than 23 seconds ahead of Marquez, such was the leading group's pace.

5 – ITALIAN GP

This was a typical Mugello slipstreaming battle, with the first six riders ducking and diving all the way to the flag, where they were separated by just 1.4 seconds. Pole-position man Folger led from the start with Viñales, Rins, Marquez, Salom and Oliveira hunting him through the epic Italian track's fast sweepers.

Slowly but surely Folger was relegated to the back of the group as Viñales, Marquez and Oliveira took their turns up front. But a rider only needs to lead on the one lap that matters and it was Salom who dominated the final laps to beat Rins by a tenth. Viñales was a close third to complete a familiar-looking podium and Oliveira was fourth, just a few tenths off Mahindra's first podium. Marquez was fifth, less than a second down on the winner. Folger had lost the tow by the end and finished alone but still well ahead of the first Honda rider, seventh-placed Niccolò Antonelli (Go & Fun Honda).

Rins would attack so, at the last moment, he opened the door just enough for Rins to take the bait and dive past on the brakes. Inevitably, Rins ran wide at the apex while Viñales was able to get on the throttle sooner, taking him past his rival as they dashed towards the chequered flag. So Viñales won the title from Rins by less than two-tenths of a second, one of the closest finishes in championship history. All the more remarkable was the fact that this was Viñales's first win in 13 races. The teenager ended the year with three victories to Salom's seven, and six wins for Rins.

Also of historical note at Valencia was lady rider Ana Carrasco's eighth-place result, just one position off the best-ever GP seventh-place finish by a female achieved by Taru Rinne in 1989 and by Tomoko Igata in 1995.

ABOVE LEFT Jack Miller rode brilliantly but not even he could get a Honda on the rostrum

ABOVE Miguel Oliveira made history when he put the Indian Mahindra on the rostrum in Malaysia

LEFT Alex Rins crashes out of the Japanese GP, letting his team-mate Alex Marquez past for the win

6 – CATALAN GP	7 – DUTCH TT	8 – GERMAN GP	9 – INDIANAPOLIS GP	10 – CZECH REPUBLIC GP

On home tarmac it was once again the Spanish trio – mirroring the country's similar podium domination in MotoGP – who dominated proceedings. Rins was strongest in the early stages, chased closely by up to seven riders. Midway through the race both Salom and Viñales attempted to break away from the pack but neither could manage it.

Instead Salom won the hard way, fending off his pursuers all the way to the chequered flag, eventually bettering Rins by two-tenths, while Viñales was another four-tenths down and well clear of Marquez in fourth. Mahindra team-mates Efren Vazquez and Oliveira were a few seconds further back in fifth and sixth for the Indian factory's best team result so far. Miller was top Honda rider again, in seventh.

Salom's second consecutive

Salom completed a hat-trick of victories in another edge-of-the-seat race to extend his points lead and confirm his pre-season status as championship favourite.

The Spaniard rode another perfectly judged race to get the better of a five-way battle for victory in the closing stages. Yet again, he saved his best for last, letting the others do most of the work while he waited and then took the lead for the first time with two laps to go. Viñales fought back to get ahead briefly once more, but Salom retook the advantage with a masterly move three corners from the flag. He crossed the line just over a tenth in front.

Rins – who appeared to have made the break at half-distance, but couldn't maintain his pace – was third, just ahead of Oliveira (who had earlier given Mahindra their first Moto3 pole) and Marquez. Just 0.4 seconds

For the fifth race in succession the podium featured the same three Spaniards and for the umpteenth race in a row it was a battle royal up front, although this time it was just the three of them instead of the usual half dozen or so.

Rins once again set the pace, with Salom and Viñales close behind. For the first few laps they also had to contend with Miller, making the most of the Sachsenring's twisting layout to stick with the KTMs, but even the Aussie couldn't compensate for the horsepower handicap for long.

Salom used his usual tactic, taking the lead in the late stages, but this time Rins was ready and he snatched victory at the penultimate corner. Viñales crossed the line in third, a mere 0.248 seconds covering the leading trio. Oliveira won a three-way battle for fourth place with Marquez and Vazquez.

The title contest was blown wide open when Salom crashed on Saturday afternoon, breaking an ankle. The championship leader made the grid, all strapped up and pumped full of painkillers, to race to a heroic fifth-place finish, which maintained his points lead.

With Salom out of the running for victory, the sharp end of the race nevertheless had a very familiar feel, with Rins leading most of the way from Viñales and Marquez. In the final stages it was the Estrella team-mates who displayed the most speed, the pair swapping the lead until the penultimate lap when Rins got back in front and stayed there, albeit by less than two-tenths at the flag. Viñales was third, a further nine-tenths down.

Folger took fourth, less than a second ahead of Salom, with Red Bull KTM's Aussie rider Arthur Sissis scoring his best

Just one week after Indy, Salom was still getting around the Brno paddock on crutches – but that didn't stop him from coming out on top, despite having to fight every inch of the way. Another dogfight saw the first five men over the line covered by just 1.2 seconds.

The battle raged throughout, featuring the usual suspects: Viñales, Rins, Folger, Marquez and Salom. Viñales and Rins did most of the leading; Salom, as usual the canniest, waited until the final lap to make his winning move. By the time they got to the finish he was half a second ahead of Viñales. Folger took advantage of an in-team duel between Marquez and Rins to grab third at the final esses for his first podium since the Spanish GP.

Alexis Masbou (Ongetta-Rivacold FTR Honda) had manfully chased the leading group in the early stages, crossing the line three seconds behind

ABOVE Miguel Oliveira goes over the handlebars of his Mahindra on the first lap of the Australian GP

11 – BRITISH GP

Salom scored his sixth win of the year in another frantic encounter, the Red Bull rider heading an all-Spanish top four that were covered by just 0.849 seconds.

As usual, Salom left it until the second half to move to the front, fighting off team-mates Rins and Marquez in the dash to the finish line. Viñales led for most of the first half of the race, but didn't quite have the pace when it mattered and he ended up an anguished fourth, less than two-tenths behind Marquez. This was the first time all year that Viñales had finished off the podium and it left him trailing Salom by 26 points, with the on-form Rins sneaking up behind him.

Such was the pace of the leading group that fifth-place finisher Oliveira was almost 20 seconds further back, though only a fraction ahead of Folger and Miller.

12 – SAN MARINO GP

For once, there were only two riders in the victory hunt: Rins and Viñales. During the first few laps they'd had pole-starter Folger with them, but the pace proved too much for the German who suffered a massive highside that left him with a broken ankle.

Viñales led for most of the way, only to be denied on the last lap when Rins pounced for his fourth victory of the year. The pair's domination of this race moved them closer still to title leader Salom, who'd finished a distant fourth behind Marquez (who had established a new lap record trying in vain to catch the leaders).

Salom, who aggravated his Indy injuries with a fall in practice, had his work cut out to head home a frantic five-man group, with Miller, Malaysian Zulfahmi Khairuddin (Red Bull KTM), Oliveira and Antonelli right behind him at

13 – ARAGON GP

This was a carbon copy of Misano both in terms of the result and the way the race unfolded. Viñales and Rins escaped from the pack to sort out their differences and again, just like Misano, Viñales did most of the leading but had no answer to the stunning end-of-race speed of Rins. Rins attacked at the start of the last lap and by the flag he had dropped Viñales by four-tenths. This second consecutive victory moved him past Viñales in the championship chase and to within nine points of series leader Salom, who finished fourth, still hurting from his recent injuries.

Marquez was once again alone in third spot, well ahead of Salom, who fended off Oliveira by less than a tenth of a second. Philipp Oettl (Interwetten Kalex KTM) – son of 1980s and 1990s GP winner Peter Oettl – scored a career-

14 – MALAYSIAN GP

As usual, this was the best race of the day with half a dozen riders battling like crazy all the way to the flag, where the top six finishers were covered by just 1.1 seconds. And with only three races left after Sepang, the two main protagonists –Salom and Rins – knew full well that they weren't only fighting for the race win.

The two title fighters swapped the lead, Salom finally getting the better of his compatriot, to shore up his points advantage that had been dwindling at recent races. Rins was just 0.069 seconds down at the flag, with Oliveira putting an Indian machine (in fact made in Switzerland) on a GP podium for the first time in history. Viñales was fifth, with Miller the first Honda rider in sixth and closer than ever to the front, most probably because his Honda NSF250R engine suffered less in the steamy

15 – AUSTRALIAN GP

The low-powered Moto3 bikes were the only class deemed safe to race full distance – and what a race it was. There were seven riders crawling all over each other, positions changing at every corner and every time they rode down the start–finish straight. In the end the magnificent seven were covered by just 1.1 seconds. Rins took the lead on the last lap from Folger, who was then pushed wide and down to sixth. It was that close.

Like pretty much everyone else in the group, Viñales and Salom led several times, only to finish second and third. Viñales crossed the line three-thousandths of a second behind Rins and just over a tenth ahead of Salom. This sixth victory for Rins reduced Salom's title lead to just five points and this was the eighth and last time that the three Spaniards monopolised the podium.

ABOVE Typical Moto3 action: Rins and Folger drag to the flag in Valencia

RIGHT Maverick Viñales celebrates after his last-corner, last-race championship victory

Dorna's complex Moto3 technical rules – price caps and so on – had made real their hopes for a closely fought class, but there was a little too much sameness, with all 17 races won by Spaniards riding KTMs. Honda observed its policy of not getting involved as a factory throughout 2013 but will field an official team in 2014. Also new for 2014 will be random engine allocation, designed to prevent manufacturers from focusing attention on their factory riders.

Indian company Mahindra was the only other brand involved, with an engine and chassis built by Suter in Switzerland. Mahindra showed promise with its first Moto3 pole position – with Miguel Oliveira on board at Assen – and certainly has the budget to make further inroads into MotoGP's beginners' class.

16 – JAPANESE GP

The championship contest was turned on its head at Motegi when the riders holding first and second in the title chase crashed. Title leader Salom was the first to go, taken out by a high-siding Isaac Viñales (Ongetta FTR Honda) on the very first lap. Salom rejoined the race, only to crash out again as he fought to get into the points.

That effectively put Rins in the championship lead, until he foolishly crashed out of a close third place with just four laps to go. He did remount, but finished 24th with no points. The win went to first-timer Marquez, who bravely pounced on Viñales with two corners remaining.

Following Rins's *faux pas*, Salom still led the championship, but by just two points from Rins, with Viñales a further three behind. Thus it would be winner takes all at Valencia.

17 – VALENCIAN GP

The Valencia hype may have focused on MotoGP, but the biggest title battle was in the littlest race.

KTM's three contenders started the weekend perfectly by monopolising the front row – Rins, Salom and Viñales – and were at the front throughout, or at least until Salom crashed out just after halfway while still in the lead group, which also included Folger. That left Viñales and Rins hard at it – no quarter asked, none given.

The two Spaniards, and everyone else, knew it would all come down to the final corner, and indeed it did. On the last lap they changed position several times, Rins falling for a Viñales trick at the final turn, grabbing the lead and then running wide. So often beaten in earlier races, Viñales won the race that mattered most, taking the title by 0.186 seconds. Rins's error allowed Folger to grab second at the line, but he had the slight consolation of being second in the championship, with Salom pushed down in third.

CHAMPIONSHIP STANDINGS

	Rider	Nat	Team	Motorcycle	Points
1	Maverick Viñales	SPA	Team Calvo	KTM	323
2	Alex Rins	SPA	Estrella Galicia 0,0	KTM	311
3	Luis Salom	SPA	Red Bull KTM Ajo	KTM	302
4	Alex Marquez	SPA	Estrella Galicia 0,0	KTM	213
5	Jonas Folger	GER	Mapfre Aspar Team Moto3	Kalex KTM	183
6	Miguel Oliveira	POR	Mahindra Racing	Mahindra	150
7	Jack Miller	AUS	Caretta Technology – RTG	FTR Honda	110
8	Alexis Masbou	FRA	Ongetta-Rivacold	FTR Honda	94
9	Efren Vazquez	SPA	Mahindra Racing	Mahindra	82
10	Romano Fenati	ITA	San Carlo Team Italia	FTR Honda	73
11	Jakub Kornfeil	CZE	Redox RW Racing GP	Kalex KTM	68
12	Zulfahmi Khairuddin	MAL	Red Bull KTM Ajo	KTM	68
13	Brad Binder	RSA	Ambrogio Racing	Mahindra	66
14	Niklas Ajo	FIN	Avant Tecno	KTM	62
15	Arthur Sissis	AUS	Red Bull KTM Ajo	KTM	59
16	Niccolò Antonelli	ITA	GO&FUN Gresini Moto3	FTR Honda	47
17	Isaac Viñales	SPA	Ongetta-Centro Seta	FTR Honda	47
18	Philipp Oettl	GER	Interwetten Paddock Moto3	Kalex KTM	34
19	John McPhee	GBR	Caretta Technology – RTG	FTR Honda	24
20	Danny Webb	GBR	Ambrogio Racing	Suter Honda	15
21	Ana Carrasco	SPA	Team Calvo	KTM	9
22	Livio Loi	BEL	Marc VDS Racing Team	Kalex KTM	8
23	Alan Techer	FRA	CIP Moto3	TSR Honda	8
24	Jasper Iwema	NED	RW Racing GP	Kalex KTM	8
25	Eric Granado	BRA	Mapfre Aspar Team Moto3	Kalex KTM	7
26	Alessandro Tonucci	ITA	La Fonte Tascaracing	FTR Honda	6
27	Matteo Ferrari	ITA	Ongetta-Centro Seta	FTR Honda	2
28	Hyuga Watanabe	JPN	La Fonte Tascaracing	FTR Honda	1

RED BULL MotoGP ROOKIES

PETER CLIFFORD

a maelstrom raged around him. Only twice was he excluded by racing accidents, the first time in Race 1 at the Sachsenring where he saved a vicious slide only to collide with 14-year-old Italian Stefano Manzi as he regained the racing line. The second was in Race 2 at Silverstone, when he was taken out by 15-year-old Spaniard Diego Pérez on the last lap while in a position to claim the title with three races remaining.

His season-long rival, 15-year-old Jorge Martín, was also knocked off on that final lap just seconds later, but he was able to remount and score enough points to keep his title hopes mathematically alive. The following round was at Misano and though Hanika was robbed of a likely victory by mechanical failure, Martín had an uncharacteristically awful weekend and the Czech left Italy with the Cup in his hand.

Manzi should have won that Misano race but he was robbed on the run in to the line by fellow Italian Manuel Pagliani, the 17-year-old taking the win in an impressive first season. Manzi had looked a likely winner ever since the tail end of 2012, his first year, but the youngster concluded his second season third in the points table behind Martín, with four second places his best results in 2013, including the last race of the year, Race 2 at Aragon, a stunner that typified the Rookies Cup.

This final contest was decided by the last and best lap of the year as 15-year-old Italian Enea Bastianini got the better of Manzi and 15-year-old Spaniard Marcos Ramírez. Bastianini clinched his second win of the season, but no-one rode that final 5.078km (3.155 miles) better than Toprak Razgatlioglu. The 16-year-old Turk was half a second behind the leading trio going into the final lap, but he cut his way to the front in sensational style. Tucking in his lanky frame as much as possible he led his rivals on to the back straight, but the

Fourteen races at eight Grands Prix is a huge amount of action, especially in the Red Bull MotoGP Rookies Cup where passing and repassing at every corner is the norm. What can look like a schoolyard brawl was turned into an art form by 17-year-old Czech Karel Hanika who took home the Cup in this, its seventh season. His points score looked totally dominant, but the individual races were very different.

Finishing either first or second in every race where he saw the finish line, Hanika did an incredible job of staying out of trouble as

FUTURE PERFECT

LEFT The change to four-strokes didn't dampen the Rookies' enthusiasm: Eventual champion Hanika (Czech Republic) leads Mir (Spain) and Manzi (Italy)

INSETS Karel Hanika sealed the title with a double win at home on the Brno circuit. He was perhaps the most convincing winner in the seven-year history of the series

smaller men behind picked up his slipstream and he was powerless to prevent them passing him. He crossed the line fourth ahead of a Spanish trio, Diego Pérez, Joan Mir (aged 16) and Martín.

The race could have gone to any of ten riders but it was Rookies Cup winner Hanika who had looked strongest as he headed the pack mid-race. He remained unruffled as Manzi, Ramírez and co. took their chances to lead, but the opportunity to secure the 11th win of his two-season career and his 8th of 2013 ended on lap 12 of the 15-lap race with a technical failure.

That seemed to inspire everyone else. The first to pick up the gauntlet was Scott Deroue, but the 17-year-old Netherlander slid off a lap later. It was then five abreast at times, with Manzi and Ramírez both looking for their first Rookies Cup victories. On to the last lap and it was Manzi who led Bastianini across the line, with Ramírez a close third. Razgatlioglu had been nowhere near the front; he was 11th with four laps to go and had only just caught the lead pack going on to that last lap.

In the end it was third place for the fifth time for Ramírez and he ended the year fifth in the points behind Bastianini, closely mirroring his Spanish Championship season where he led the points table for much of the year but just couldn't clinch a race win. He finally lost that title by a couple of points at the last round where he was second behind the claiming champion.

Razgatlioglu needed that great finish to the season to remind himself that he was a potential winner. He had been at the front from the start of the year when he scored two thirds in Texas, but at times he could not get the bike to work for him. That was something that

struck a number of riders. The first season using the new Moto3-spec KTM RC 250 R led to some development issues that affected some more than others.

One of the worst hit was Bradley Ray. After the Briton, who was still only 15 at the time, won the opening round in Texas he fell into a bit of a hole and struggled to make the bike work in the way he wanted. Things got sorted towards the end of the season, but by then the title chase was over and he could still not match his early pace. Bradley ended the year 11th in the points table, just behind Razgatlioglu.

Doubtless the Briton's third Rookies Cup season in 2014, and the Turk's second, will be better. With more consistency either could take the Cup – but then so could Pagliani, who was sixth this year. Scott Deroue will not have that chance as he bows out after three seasons. The Dutch rider took a long while to get to like the four-stroke after being in the hunt for the Cup last year, but he won Race 2 at Silverstone and was also right there at the final rounds to claim seventh overall.

The level of talent in the Rookies Cup increases every year and there could potentially have been a number of worthy champions. Hanika, however, stood clear, probably the most convincing winner in the history of the series. He did not run away with races – each was a tough contest – but when he finished he was always either first or second, and of the four DNFs only one was even remotely his fault. The Czech rider could so easily have claimed ten wins in the season, as opposed to the seven that grace the record books, and he now moves on to the Moto3 World Championship as part of the factory Red Bull KTM Ajo Motorsport team, with a very good chance of making his mark there as well.

RIDERS FOR HEALTH
BARRY COLEMAN

riders

MOTORCYCLES SAVE LIVES

LEFT Bubacarr Jallow is a health worker based in the village of Mara Kissa in the Gambia. He is responsible for 13 villages containing around 13,000 people. His bike lets him see up to six times as many people, and spend up to twice as long with the families in his care

Riders for Health started in Somalia in November 1988, when Randy Mamola and I stood outside the Ministry of Health (they had one then) in Mogadishu staring at an almost-new motorcycle while a couple of European blokes told us lies about it. Well, not lies exactly, but maybe even worse than lies. They told us – as they had told their Somali colleagues – that the motorcycle had broken down (which it had) because motorcycles were completely useless in such a hot and dusty country.

For a moment Randy and I stared at the blokes. They were doctors, so they knew everything. Then we forgot about it, sort of. Until, elsewhere in the country, we began to see more and more motorcycles and other vehicles in just as totally and just as shockingly broken-down states.

The Mogadishu motorcycle had done 800 kilometres and there it was, dead. That wouldn't have mattered much in itself, except that you couldn't help but wonder how many human beings were also dead – just because whatever it was this motorcycle was supposed to be doing in the field of health was plainly not being done.

Almost exactly a year later, I was working with the World Health Organisation in the Gambia, trying to figure out what the hell was going on with all these dead and dying motorcycles (and thus, dead and dying people). The dead and dying bikes there were Hondas – funny little CT110s, ordered up by UNICEF. Because of the death rate, people naturally assumed that the problem lay with Honda – that Honda, whoever they were, didn't really know how to make motorcycles. If only they had Yamahas – they probably knew how to do it.

RIGHT Bubacarr was told by Meta Kujabi that her village of Mara Kissa had a big problem with waterborne diseases. So Bubacarr arranged to talk to the community about how to prevent disease

OPPOSITE In Zimbabwe an environmental health technician rides their bike to their next appointment. Motorcycles allow health workers to travel along narrow paths and tracks that would not be passable for four-wheeled vehicles

BELOW The health centre at Brikama in the Gambia now has an ambulance for emergencies, and thanks to Riders for Health it never breaks down or runs out of fuel when it is needed

Around that time, I started explaining about motorcycle racing. We have Hondas in motorcycle racing, I said. This Honda, this CT110, probably produces about six horsepower (don't ask) at the rear wheel. The Hondas they race in Grands Prix probably produce around 40 times that much power. And in spite of the fact that they are being ridden by psychopathic monomaniacs at the very limit of what is known about a two-wheeled vehicle on this planet, they do not break down.

I constantly told myself this, while I was figuring out, with the dedicated African men and women who later became our colleagues and dear friends, what to

do. Mick Doohan's bikes do not break down, I mystically chanted to myself as I wandered around in the heat and the dust, looking in the sheds behind hospitals and the records of non-governmental organisations; Wayne Rainey's bikes do not break down.

Of course, the answer is obvious, now that we know it and practise it. Actually, it was obvious all along, although turning the answer into a durable system in seven African countries was tricky at times: good rider training, good technicians, good equipment and good supply chain. Abracadabra – Riders for Health.

Now, five years ago we were able to use our

Over 20 years since Riders for Health started telling people that managed transport is a fundamental aspect of any health system, the world is sitting up and recognising it. In October 2013, Riders for Health's co-founder and CEO, Andrea Coleman, won the Barclays Women of the Year Award for bringing transport to the forefront of international development. Earlier in the year, at the Third Sector Excellence Awards, Riders' work in Lesotho was recognised for improving diagnosis and treatment of HIV in rural communities. And Riders' partnership with the Gambian government was awarded at the Aspen Institute's Global Leaders Council for enabling the delivery of maternal health care to the whole country, thanks to a reliable fleet of vehicles. It is only with support from the motorcycle racing community that Riders have been able to shine a light on this vital issue.

experience and skills to put in place in the Gambia a completely unique system for financing and managing all the motorcycles and other vehicles needed to reach the entire population with health care. We were able to do this because our Gambia team had looked after their previous fleet so well that it was possible to view the bikes and other vehicles as assets rather than liabilities. This made them valuable and thus a bank was able to support the whole scheme with appropriate finance.

Had Randy and I been part of some other sport, or even if we had run the entire motor vehicle industry, that would not have happened, because if anyone had told us that motorcycles were inappropriate in a hot and dusty country, we would have believed them. Look at the evidence, in 1988, in Somalia. Broken bikes everywhere. And look what would have happened. Nothing.

After the first five years, our fleet in the Gambia has clocked up well over 10 million kilometres. And during the first 10 million, we experienced no breakdowns at all. And we owe that to Mick and Wayne – and Honda and Yamaha, of course, because they make good machinery. So good, in fact, that during the course of 40 minutes of automotive hell, not even Mick and Wayne could break them. Well, not often.

That's what motorcycle racing has done for the health of the African continent. And now other governments have been to the Gambia to witness what happens when vehicles are managed along the Mick-and-Wayne model. And those countries now want to do what the Gambians do. Exactly the same thing. Why not? In Africa, it's the only known way, so far, to reach a country's entire population with health care.

So next time you see Vale grinning under all his hats at Day of Champions or Dani's elbows polishing the tarmac in super-slo-mo, ask not what your sport can do for you (because we already know that) but what you can do for your sport, given what it and it alone has done for the world.

Once again, with feeling: 10 million kilometres, no breakdowns. Thanks, Mick. Thanks, Wayne. We get it.

WHERE THE MONEY COMES FROM

Led by our fantastic events manager, Jeanette Wragg, and hundreds of dedicated volunteers all over the world, Riders for Health and MotoGP™ work together to offer fans exclusive MotoGP experiences at races throughout the season. Not only do they allow fans to experience behind the scenes of MotoGP and get closer to their heroes, but they also raise vital funds for Riders' lifesaving work in Africa.

In 2013, thanks to lots of hard work from MotoGP teams and riders, we put together more unique MotoGP packages than ever before. Visit our website www.riders.org/get-involved/experiences to find out more and keep up to date with our plans for 2014.

DAY OF CHAMPIONS

Riders' flagship fundraising event is held at Silverstone before the British MotoGP. Thousands of fans come out to support Riders on one of the best days out in British motorsport. The event, which includes a ride-in, access to the paddock and pit lane, stunt shows, live music and much more culminates in a huge auction where MotoGP riders take to the stage with personal signed racing memorabilia.

DAY OF STARS

Held before the US MotoGP at Laguna Seca, California, Day of Stars is an intimate event limited to just 50 people, hosted by Riders for Health co-founder Randy Mamola. Fans spend the day meeting MotoGP stars, touring the paddock, taking to the Laguna circuit and enjoying a motorcycle tour of the beautiful Carmel Valley.

OTHER MotoGP™ FUNDRAISING EVENTS

With support from local volunteers, Riders also hosted fundraising events offering exclusive access to the paddock and pit lane and auctions of signed racing memorabilia at the MotoGP races at Jerez, Catalunya, Sachsenring, Indianapolis, Brno and Valencia.

PADDOCK PASS AUCTIONS

MotoGP generously donate a pair of exclusive paddock passes for each race on the calendar to Riders for Health to auction on eBay. Forget watching the race at home on the sofa, the winning bidder and their guest spend the whole GP weekend at the heart of the action in the paddock. In 2013, MotoGP also donated grid passes for MotoGP at Valencia, which Riders auctioned on eBay.

DUCATI TWO-SEAT RIDE

This is a once-in-a-lifetime chance to complete a lap of one of the fastest circuits in the world on the same weekend as the stars of MotoGP. The British MotoGP at Silverstone is the only place on earth where you can ride the specially modified MotoGP bike. The ride is piloted by Grand Prix legend and Riders for Health co-founder, Randy Mamola.

VIP MotoGP™ COMPETITION

From September–October 2013, Riders ran an online competition to win an all-expenses-paid trip to the Valencia MotoGP to include paddock passes, grid passes, hospitality, invites to the End of Season Awards ceremony and the chance to meet Valentino Rossi. For just a £3 donation, fans from all over the world could enter the prize draw.

EXPERIENCE AFRICA

This nine-day off-road bike ride through Zambia, in southern Africa, allows participants to witness Riders for Health's inspiring work at first hand and see how motorcycles are saving lives. In 2011, MotoGP star Alvaro Bautista joined the first Experience Africa and described it as 'a once in a lifetime adventure'.

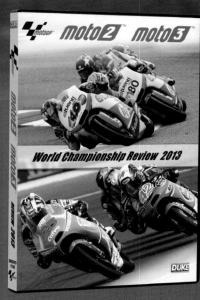
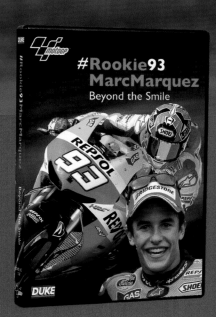